DAVID OWEN

BRITISH

FOREIGN

POLICY

AFTER

BREXIT

AN INDEPENDENT VOICE

\Bᵇ\
Biteback Publishing

First published in Great Britain in 2017 by
Biteback Publishing Ltd
Westminster Tower
3 Albert Embankment
London SE1 7SP
Copyright © David Owen and David Ludlow 2017

ISBN 978-1-78590-234-5

10 9 8 7 6 5 4 3 2 1

A CIP catalogue record for this book is available from the British Library.

Set in Minion Pro

Printed and bound in Great Britain by
CPI Group (UK) Ltd, Croydon CR0 4YY

MIX
Paper from
responsible sources
FSC® C020471

CONTENTS

INTRODUCTION

'AN INDEPENDENT BRITISH VOICE'. HENRY KISSINGER

In the midst of the UK referendum campaign in 2016, I visited Canada to discuss future trading arrangements and visited New York to call on the former US Secretary of State, Henry Kissinger, whom I have known since I was appointed Foreign Secretary in February 1977. He told me on 3 May that he was facing a deadline to decide before the end of the day whether to sign a letter with other prominent members of the American foreign policy establishment, arguing that Britain should not leave the EU. It soon became clear that he had no intention of signing and his reasoning was clear and simple: 'I do not want a world in which there is not an independent British voice.'

I wrote to him to seek his agreement before recording his view in this book, and he wrote back on 20 December: 'The quote is exactly correct. It is what I said and what I felt. You have my permission to use it.' It is to help establish that independent British voice in 2017 and beyond that this book is written. In doing so, I am fortunate to have as a co-author someone twenty-five years younger and with far more recent experience of working with the Foreign and Commonwealth Office (FCO), who voted to 'remain'.

We want to demonstrate that after leaving the EU, the UK can confidently play a full and constructive role in a shifting global environment, while shaping a new relationship of mutual benefit with our twenty-seven former partners in the EU, and ultimately building a more prosperous and secure country.

Neither of us are federalists and we explain what that term means in concrete terms in this book. In my case, the rejection of federalism dates back to what Hugh Gaitskell, the then Leader of the Opposition, said in 1962 when we were applying to join the Common Market. It also dates back to the strategy paper that, as Foreign Secretary, I wrote for the Cabinet in the summer of 1977. Nevertheless, my opposition to federalism did not affect a longstanding friendship with Michel Rocard, an ardent federalist, who served as Prime Minister under President Mitterrand. In January 2013, when I was in Paris to discuss my recent book *Europe Restructured*, Michael publicly called for he UK to leave the EU with friendship.[1] He put me in touch with Emmanuel Macron, then in the Elysée under President Hollande, and we exchanged letters and had a telephone conversation. I was left in no doubt after this that Macron broadly shared Michel's view about the need for a federalist future for France, and he demonstrated that in his successful Presidential election campaign by playing the 'Ode to Joy', the anthem of the European Union, alongside the French national anthem and flying the European flag alongside the tricolour. I, nevertheless, wanted him to become President. He is highly intelligent and dedicated to a reform of the Eurozone, which is in everyone's interests.

In this book we have not set out to present a comprehensive review of all aspects of the UK's international activities, but rather focus on those areas where we see the greatest challenges, where there are lessons to be learnt, and where there is potential for that independent British voice to bring new ideas to the table. Nor are we attempting to write a diplomatic history of the late twentieth and early twenty-first centuries. However, we have given weight to the historical background where we feel it appropriate, sharing the view of former chief FCO historian Gill Bennett when she writes: 'There is no doubt that in the realm of foreign making, history can be a constructive tool rather than a misleading guide.'[2]

David Ludlow and I worked together for two years from 1992 when I was the EU Co-Chairman of the International Conference on the former Yugoslavia. He returned to the FCO, subsequently working for Schroders (later acquired by Citigroup) in London and Dubai and then Standard Chartered Bank. He came back to London in 2014 to work for two years for the UK's export credit agency as Head of Business Development, which took him to many of the high-growth markets that are now a target for British businesses. We have written this book together in the time since he left that role at the end of 2016.

I also went into business after my tenure in the former Yugoslavia. From 1995 to 2006, I served as chairman of UK-based company GNE, which invested in a modern steel plant in Russia and petrol stations in the UK. From 2006 to 2015, I was chairman of Europe Steel, which traded steel and iron ore and was owned by the Russian company Mettaloinvest, as well as being a consultant for various companies. I was also chairman of Yukos International for three years and served as a non-executive director of Coats Viyella in London for six years, Abbott Laboratories in Chicago for fifteen years, and Hyperdynamics in Houston for seven years.

This book is not about the Article 50 process. The UK will, as a result of the 2017 election manifesto commitments of the Conservative Party, Labour Party and Democratic Unionist Party (DUP) from Northern Ireland, leave the EU at the end of March 2019, unless another general election takes place before that date. However, during any such election, the Conservative and Labour manifestos are unlikely to change in relation to the referendum decision to leave the EU. So whichever party were to win an early election, we as a nation are going to leave the EU. Only the much hyped new 'EU party' – which never emerged in 2017 – would be likely to fight a new election on a commitment to stay in the EU, and the chances of it being established were reduced following the Liberal Democrats' election performance.

Where the argument between the parties has a renewed strength is around what sort of access the UK should try to establish with the EU's single market. Here, the arguments of the ten DUP MPs, who do not want the return of a hard border with the Republic of Ireland, deserve serious consideration; likewise those of the twelve new Conservative

MPs from Scotland, who will want to demonstrate they best represent the interests of Scotland rather than the Scottish National Party (SNP), whose number of MPs has fallen sharply to thirty-five. Scottish Labour and Liberal Democrat MPs will also want to do the same.

Keir Starmer, the shadow Brexit Secretary, who skilfully handled his party's manifesto position, must in a hung parliament be given access to more confidential information, as before the talks are completed he could be responsible in government for negotiating on behalf of us all. Traditionally when international negotiations are underway, there are regular exchanges of information with the official opposition, and David Davis has a good record of openness. After both the 2016 referendum and the 2017 general election, Brexit has become an issue where the national interest must now predominate. Some who voted Remain are still not ready to accept the referendum result; that is their constitutional right and their views deserve respect. The unelected House of Lords, however, can no longer claim any right to block Brexit. Under the Salisbury Convention – agreed after the 1945 Labour landslide victory – manifesto commitments cannot be overturned by the Lords.

The really substantive issue, however, is: after leaving the EU in March 2019, how does the UK negotiate for the implementation of a lasting EU–UK trade agreement? I believe the UK should remain a Contracting Party to the EEA Agreement during this transition period. There is nothing in the Agreement's provisions that convincingly serves to establish that the UK will cease to be a Contracting Party on withdrawal from the Treaty of Lisbon and leaving the EU. The significance of this interpretation is that it is consistent with the purposes of the EEA and with the Vienna Conventions on disputes over international treaties,[3] and is difficult to overstate. Continuing as a Contracting Party would avoid any cliff edge which the EU Article 50 procedures might force upon us in ways potentially very damaging to UK interests.

The overall UK strategy should be to exit the Lisbon Treaty in March 2019 as a first step, continue as a Non-EU Contracting Party to the EEAA as a second step and negotiate trading agreements with the EU and with Norway, Iceland and Liechtenstein as the third step, while being ready to give a year's notice of leaving the EEAA when appropriate in relation to the trade negotiations before or during 2022. To pave the way for this in the summer of 2017, the UK should tell the EU and the Non EU Contracting Parties to the EEA Agreement that we consent to be bound by the Law on Succession of States 1978 (Article 2.1 (g)).[4] We should also indicate that while we do not accept the validity of an exit tax in any shape or form, we are ready to pay the cost of compensating UK citizens who have been employed by the EU and whose job prospects are affected by our leaving. Also for the duration of any 'implementation period' as a Non-EU Contracting Party to the EEA Agreement, we are ready, following precedent, to voluntarily pay a financial contribution.

Successful negotiations with the EU over the next four to five years will need clarity of purpose, to build on precedent and to follow the wording of Article 8 in the Treaty of Lisbon on good neighbourliness that is spelt out in practical terms throughout this book. They will also need a close degree of cross-party cooperation.

David Owen
June 2017

PART 1

STRATEGIC PERSPECTIVES

...The world is a tough, complicated, messy, mean place, and full of hardship and tragedy. And in order to advance both our security interests and those ideals and values that we care about, we've got to be hardheaded at the same time as we are bighearted, and pick and choose our spots, and recognise that there are going to be times where the best that we can do is to shine a spotlight on something that's terrible, but not believe that we can automatically solve it. There are going to be times where our security interests conflict with our concerns about human rights. There are going to be times where we can do something about innocent people being killed, but there are going to be times where we can't.

President Obama, *The Atlantic*, March 2016

CHAPTER 1

A FOUNDATION FOR
GLOBAL DIPLOMACY

As we leave the EU – to whose Common Foreign and Security Policy, and Common Security and Defence Policy we devoted so much diplomatic and military energy in the recent past – we must take the opportunity now, urgently, to redirect that energy into policies which allow us to move forward and face the future with confidence, delivering on the UK citizens' understandable aspiration for greater prosperity and security. The 2016 referendum decision was not just a decision to leave the EU and invoke Article 50 in the Treaty of Lisbon; it was a decision to mark a change in the UK's relationship with the world. As the historian Lord Hennessy of Nympsfield said in a House of Lords debate on 20 February 2017 on Article 50:

> It is a key element in what will be the fourth of our country's great geopolitical shifts since 1945. The first was the protracted withdrawal from Empire – from India in 1947 to Rhodesia/Zimbabwe in 1980. The second was joining the European Economic Community in 1973 – or 'Brentry' as the Economist rather neatly described it the other day. The third was the ending of the Cold War between 1989 and 1991.

The challenge presented by this fourth great shift is to move the emphasis from a European focus on world events, to a global focus through diplomacy, military support and free trade.

Brexit involved a choice. We could – and many wanted to – stay with the European focus on our economic and foreign policy that started in 1973. Or we could choose – for mixed motives and with differing priorities, as in any referendum – to restore a global orientation. Many who hoped to stay in the EU, warts and all, understandably feel rejected and bruised. Many important decisions are taken on the margin. This should be respected. We must learn to live with and respect each other's views. Practically no argument is won by a 100 per cent majority. Indeed, the referendum was decisive but the margin not great. The spirit of the country, however, is to get on with the task ahead. The overriding task facing the UK now is to make a success of Brexit, economically, socially, politically and in terms of national security.

There is a sense of adventure in taking to the high seas again, developing 'blue water diplomacy' and worldwide commerce. But there is a danger in overstretching our capacity. We have to be selective, and we will be helped in doing that by returning to being a nation that has greater control of its own destiny. There is a hard-headed calculation to be made concerning what sort of role we wish to play in the world, and how we can be best positioned to achieve our goals. As Prime Minister Theresa May said in her speech in the US in January 2017,[1] the UK sees itself as 'by instinct and history a great, global nation that recognises its responsibilities to the world'. We share this view.

Brexit means Britain is freer to work through global policies we wish to espouse; to gain some of the clarity or harder edge that cannot usually be found in an EU policy agreed amongst twenty-seven other countries. It would be foolish to give the impression that everything will suddenly change. EU policies may still be appropriate, and we in the UK have benefited from pooling knowledge on foreign and security policy with other EU member states. Post-Brexit the UK will not be developing policies on our own. We will be cooperating within NATO at a more intensive level and we will be stepping up our activity under the UN Charter and within the UN Security Council. This chapter focuses on the United Nations and the next on NATO.

For all its acknowledged shortcomings, the UN sits at the centre of many key aspects of multilateral diplomacy, including conflict resolution and peacekeeping, and provides a focal point for the rules-based international system. It is also where we continue to hold the much-envied position as one of the permanent five (P5),* veto-wielding, members of the UN Security Council.

In the search for unifying themes in foreign policy within the UN for the UK after Brexit, some urge the primacy of security; others the primacy of democracy, despite democracy not being mentioned in the UN Charter; while others believe there can be no lasting security or democracy without the underpinning of human rights.

In Europe, many take human rights for granted as having been in existence since the dawn of time. However, as the philosopher Isaiah Berlin made clear 'the notion of individual rights was absent from the legal conceptions of the Romans and the Greeks; this seems to hold equally of the Jewish, Chinese and all other ancient civilisations...'[2] We, in the UK, tend to look back to clause thirty-nine of the Magna Carta of 1215, which gave all 'free men' the right to justice and a fair trial. There is a general sense in the New World that the concept of human rights was the product of Europe and the Enlightenment. This came specifically to prominence in the Declaration of the Rights of Man, adopted in revolutionary Paris on 26 August 1789, which in its first article states that, 'Men are born and remain free and equal in rights.' This was followed on 15 December 1791 by a US Bill of Rights. A strong stance in support of human rights as a continuing guide to British foreign policy in 2017 cannot be a mere add-on. While much has been achieved by the UK's efforts in the UN, a lot remains to be done, for example, in the area of women's rights, where there are still many serious abuses, particularly where rights conflict with religious practices. This is a matter in which the UK has shown a readiness to take a lead, such as with its work on the Preventing Sexual Violence in Conflict Initiative. It also has to be recognised that any human

---

* The US, UK, France, China and the Russian Federation.

rights-based policy creates conflicts of interest and a lot of compro-
mises, some of them embarrassing. But far better that a dialogue and
debate takes place than sweep issues under the carpet.

Even while the Second World War was still raging the UK, as one of
the 'Big Four', met at the Dumbarton Oaks Conference in 1944 to plan
for a post-war world. The US insisted on a reference to a Universal
Declaration of Human Rights, against – let it not be forgotten – Soviet
and British objections. On 25 April 1945, in San Francisco, the founding conference of the UN started and soon the US Secretary of State,
Edward Stettinius, made clear that the US expected a Human Rights
Commission to be established 'to promptly undertake to prepare an
International Bill of Rights'. The eventual full UN Commission on
Human Rights met in January 1947 at Lake Success in New York State
with Eleanor Roosevelt in the chair. It was because of her unyielding
belief in human rights that they became so firmly ensconced in the
UN under President Truman and shaped the UN's identity in the first
few years. But a large section of US opinion has long been sceptical, to
say the least, of foreign embroilment, and the work of the UN in particular. We must continue to work to demonstrate that putting trust
in the UN is justified, which includes a continued drive for reform in
the organisation.

Human rights were centre-stage in the UK's foreign policy from
1977, which coincided with President Carter's period in office. Under
Carter, the US was at last sufficiently self-confident to build on the
remarkable achievements of President Johnson's civil rights legislation, which was brought about in the aftermath of the assassination
of President Kennedy. In 1977, Carter's presidency began an open reinforcement and espousal of human rights worldwide but particularly
in southern Africa, where the US began to champion freedom and
attack racial discrimination. The Anglo-American plan for Rhodesia
led to the Lancaster House Agreement in late 1979 after the successful
Commonwealth Conference in Lusaka. Negotiations on South West
Africa, later Namibia, took place in 1977–78 under the auspices of
the Western Contact Group, made up of representatives from the US,

UK, France, Germany and Canada. The foreign ministers of those countries met with President Botha and his government in Pretoria. The commitment made at that time to hold UN-supervised elections paved the way twelve years later for Namibia to become independent. This period also saw the rise of Charter 77 in Eastern Europe after the signature of the Helsinki Final Act in 1975.

When President Reagan succeeded Carter, he appointed Ernest Lefever, a conservative Democrat who had opposed Carter's human rights policy as head of the Human Rights Bureau. What looked like a clever way of wrong-footing the Democrats backfired and, after four days of hearings, Lefever's nomination was rejected by the Republican-controlled Foreign Relations Committee.[3] Elliot Abrams, a 33-year-old Assistant Secretary for International Organization Affairs, wrote: 'the government should not abandon human rights. We will never maintain wide support for our foreign policy unless we can relate it to American ideals and to the defence of freedom.' The Reagan White House listened and a 'Republican' human rights policy was constructed.[4] President Trump, in ordering a military strike against Syria for its use of chemical weapons in April 2017, shows that he too sees a human rights element in his foreign policy, and we look to his administration to build on this.

An ethical foreign policy was tried by the Labour government from 1997 when Robin Cook was Foreign Secretary, but it was contested from No. 10 and finally died on the streets of Baghdad after the invasion in 2003. Limping along since that period in British foreign policy has been morality wrapped up in a mantra of, 'It is the right thing to do', when it came to further interventions. This was an expression frequently used by Prime Ministers Blair and Cameron, and more recently, surprisingly, taken up in 2017 by President Putin. The problems come when 'the right thing to do' has little to no basis either in UN Security Council resolutions or in international law, but is rather just an expression of national interest.

Why not, some therefore argue, simply label our foreign policy based on 'British interests', since they seem to have determined British foreign policy over the centuries? The answer is not that it may appear selfish and introverted, and to parrot 'America First'; nor that it recalls a period when the British Empire meant that we ruled and influenced much of the globe and enforced our interests. There is a more basic reason for not using the term 'British interests' too readily: for who wants policies from their government that are not in their interest? It is now a term used to cast doubt on a policy where too little regard is felt to have been given to the potential consequences; too little attention to the cautious question, 'Is this in our interests?', or statement, 'This is not a British interest'. We shall come back to this subject when looking at the issues surrounding recent military interventions in which the UK has been involved.

If we had to choose a single word to describe where the UK foreign policy is heading, it would be global. But whereas some might have previously stressed human rights as being at the heart of a global policy, the more nuanced 'shared values' is becoming a much-used term in many countries. We need to be clear what those concepts mean in concrete terms and how they will influence our actions. 'Rights' is a far stronger word than 'values', which vary between countries. We as a nation should remain bound to respect human rights as laid down in the UN Charter. In view of serious criticisms of past British foreign policy, we need to emphasise that we want to implement a foreign policy rooted in respect for the UN Charter and the body of international conventions, treaties and related international law. That said, we should not pull back from espousing our core values, such as our commitment to an open, liberal democracy, freedom of the press, free trade and the rule of law.

We must acknowledge that the effectiveness of a UN without US support will be much diminished. Indeed, a real challenge for our diplomacy will be how we deal with US attitudes towards the UN. In 2017, at the start of US President Trump's four-year term in office, his stance on the use of sarin gas in Syria suggests that he is ready to embrace at least some international Conventions – though his widely criticised unilateral rejection of the Paris Accord on climate change shows this is at best selective – and sees some role for the UN. However, as with NATO, he appears determined to see a more equitable burden sharing. This, in part, is motivated by the feeling that the US bears a disproportionate share, some 29 per cent, of the UN's peace-keeping budget, with focus in particular on the five largest budgets which cost over $1 billion each year. There is little doubt that unless others step up, either there will have to be a meaningful cut over the next few years, or the US will pull out of funding specific missions. These UN 'freeloaders' the Trump administration identifies are Russia and China. As for NATO, Presidents Obama and Trump have pointed to many European countries as freeloaders. Financial support, however, for UN activities will still be needed. Support for the UN over these difficult years ahead is not a soft option and UK funds will be required.

It is also clear that President Trump is ready to take radical decisions in a short time-frame, which complicates the management of sensitive global issues, such as immigration. On 27 February 2017, shortly after taking office, Trump faced the constitutional check integral to the US separation of powers. His executive order banning refugees from entering the US for ninety days, while other measures were put in place, and restricting travel to the United States from Iran, Iraq, Libya, Somalia, Sudan, Syria and Yemen was struck down by a US district judge in the State of Washington. Three judges then unanimously decided to uphold the decision, having found that the government had not provided enough evidence that urgently implementing the ban was necessary for the country's security. President Trump instantly appealed to the Supreme Court and tweeted in capital letters, 'SEE YOU IN COURT, THE SECURITY OF OUR NATION IS AT STAKE!' Within a few days, he thought better of that first reaction and announced there would be no appeal, but a new executive order. This took some time to re-emerge and was followed by a Hawaii federal judge blocking the revised travel ban in March and then extending his initial ruling. It is not risking much to predict that these will not be the last legal checks on Trump's presidential power. It may indeed be this external legal discipline that will limit his tweeting reaction and protect the presidency from Trump himself. The written constitution of the US and the constraining mechanisms within it are very powerful. The constraints are not just legal but also political. The individual states can and do frequently assert their independence of the federal government. We see this now over climate change, where more than half of them look likely to assert their right to stand by what had been agreed in the Paris Accord.

Trump was democratically elected President, predominantly by a large group of people who felt ignored by and unrepresented by the governing elite in the Republican and Democratic parties (a theme increasingly prevalent in global politics today). Though a Republican Party candidate, Trump acted independently and defeated a list of strong Republican candidates in open debate in their primaries. He then carved out of the Rust Belt states, the Tea Party movement and the religious right a constituency which he obviously intends to make his own, through tweets and visits, so he can pave the way for a second term in 2020. This is not a President who can or should be ignored by the liberal elite. He has to be engaged with. Prime Minister Theresa May was right to go and see him very early in his presidency, just as President Obama was right to invite him to the White House very soon after the election results were announced.

As for the UK, it is clear that President Trump approves of Brexit and is critical of the EU. The UK, however, should not count on these positions remaining unchanged. A US President, not least one who wins and continues to use the slogan 'America First', may change his mind quickly if he decides a position hitherto espoused is not in US interests. To some extent he did that on 2 April 2017, saying the EU had done 'a better job since Brexit'. Nevertheless, while we want him to reduce his hostility to the EU, his support for the UK's position could be very helpful. We should work with him to achieve a bilateral trade agreement, possibly even a multilateral agreement, if the North Atlantic Free Trade Agreement (NAFTA) is revised.

Maintaining human rights as a guiding light for policy means we in the UK have to respect the rulings of our own relatively new Supreme Court. This was challenged by some in relation to the debate around the invocation of Article 50 to start the formal Brexit process. Fortunately, respect for the law triumphed. It is a gain that, outside the EU, we can interpret human rights without the intervention of the EU's European Court of Justice. We will still have to adhere to the European Court of Human Rights (ECHR) in Strasbourg, whose convention the UK, as one of its main architects, ratified in 1951. The House of Commons noted in its March 2017 report on the UK's relations with Russia: 'In order to maintain international standards on human rights, the UK Government should not withdraw from the ECHR and should make clear that no such step is contemplated.'[5] Nevertheless, we must recognise that not every country will share our views on what constitutes human rights, and we must work within those constraints to make progress on the issues which face us.

For example, China, with the largest population of any UN member state, does not accept democracy as an essential aspect of human rights – let alone as a contributor to progress in the widest, economic and cultural sense. This was evident in the events of 1989 when the People's Liberation Army was turned against the people in a government crackdown, as Stein Ringen points out in *The Perfect Dictatorship*: 'The nature of the crackdown in 1989 is not well remembered, neither in China nor in the world. The challenge to the regime was not from students protesting but from a popular revolt with broad support in the population and with participation by various groups of citizens…'[6] What Deng Xiaoping had launched in 1978 was a process of economic, rather than political reform. What China has begun under President Xi Jinping is an all-important anti-corruption drive based on upholding their laws inspired by their communist beliefs. He is correct in insisting on greater respect for the rule of law within China and particularly to ensure their market economy thrives. Respect for the law in China could pave the way for greater respect for justice and international law outside the country. In this context, respect for the UN Convention on the Law of the Sea, of which China is a signatory (though the US is not), is likely to be a big test, as discussed in greater detail later. The UK, given its unrivalled history as a maritime nation, is in a unique position to champion and uphold the Law of the Sea in all international forums, and persuade the US it is in their interests to become a signatory.

The Russian Federation espouses a 'managed' democracy within a still broadly market economy, but has not yet developed a rooted respect for human rights. Their clamping down on potential opposition movements and leaders remains a concern. In the 1990s in Russia, there was a developing debate to define stricter legal boundaries in their market economy. Sadly, that debate has languished as their government showed less and less respect for upholding and enhancing the law. There are still very unattractive practices in Russia and the government is not bound by impartial courts of law. The annexation of Crimea, discussed in more detail in Chapter Five, was a particularly serious breach of international law. Nevertheless, it is through a market economy that the best hope lies for Russia to emerge as a nation governed by justice and law in all aspects of its life. It is absurd for the UK to give up on pursuing this considering how recently the USSR was a command economy, and not ready to contemplate any fair and free elections.

There are a considerable number of other countries in the UN, too, who neither espouse nor intend to espouse democratic government under the rule of law as the 'be all and end all' of their existence. It is unwise, therefore, for those who believe in a policy of human rights to regard democracy in the conventional Western sense as the only way of improved governance. For most countries, democracy will remain an ultimate goal, and what matters first will be a form of constitutionally based government. What is vital is that, by extension, it becomes possible for such governments and individuals to be removed from office by votes cast freely. The nature of a true democracy is that it cannot be judged in a pro-forma way. Structures may appear democratic which, in practice, are not in the slightest; and conversely, systems which appear to Western eyes as undemocratic may have more democratic aspects than they are given credit for, such as the consultative councils in some Middle Eastern countries. Democracy has to be rooted, wanted by the population and owned by the citizens, not the ruling class. The true test of whether a country is a democracy is whether its government can be legitimately removed by the decision of its citizens.

In 2011, the emergence of what came to be called the Arab Spring showed that the aspiration for democracy existed alongside calls for human rights. It came from the Arab people in large numbers in countries considered by many Western political leaders as being particularly resistant to democratic change. The chance for combining human rights and democracy was tempting – almost certainly too tempting – and so, encouraged by instant demands for reaction and new policies, Western democratic leaders exhibited little constraint in going with the flow of criticism on the street. In retrospect, it has been claimed that it would have been better if President Obama and Prime Minister Cameron had, in their different ways, been more restrained in supporting rapid and major change. It is argued they helped – though one should not exaggerate their influence – initiate a very radical and, in many cases, traumatic period. War prevails in Yemen and Syria. The civil war in Libya continues at a less intense level, but chaos is still close. Only in Tunisia can the Arab Spring be claimed as successful, and even this some claim is too optimistic.

Few would argue the West should respond in the same way or with the same enthusiasm if such a movement was to ignite again in the Arab world or elsewhere. Popular movements saw the overthrow of the governments in Egypt, Libya and Yemen; civil uprisings in Syria and Bahrain; major protests in Algeria and Iraq, Jordan, Kuwait, Morocco and Sudan; and lesser protests in Mauritania, Oman, Saudi Arabia and Djibouti. It was hard, initially, to discern which element should be encouraged – whether democracy was more important than stressing human rights – let alone to try to determine which should come first. In retrospect, a simple call for a greater degree of justice, leaving open the decision as to the degree of change, would have been more prudent and perhaps more successful. Certainly the Arab world is in a far worse state in 2017 than it was in 2011, and the prospects of that improving greatly in the near future are not high. Could it have been different? The wise, retired diplomat Frank Wisner tried delivering to President Mubarak of Egypt a two-part message from President Obama that he should not allow his security forces to crack down on the demonstrators, and that he should set a timetable for a transfer of power. But as Tahir Square erupted in violence, Wisner spoke through a video link to a security conference taking place in Munich which Hillary Clinton was attending. Obama rang Clinton and asked, 'What was Wisner doing speaking ... why was he saying different things than I have?' In Clinton's words, 'he took me to the woodshed'. She was told to put a stop to mixed messages.[7] An orderly transition was now even further from the US agenda.

Evolutionary reform has the best outcomes, but there is an inevitable impatience which suddenly breaks through when progress has been held up by repression. Evolutionary change was underway in Egypt within the Mubarak regime and the Muslim Brotherhood, pushed correctly by two US Secretaries of State, the Republican Condoleezza Rice and the Democrat Hillary Clinton. After Mubarak was ousted, for the best of intentions pressure from Washington and elsewhere was for Morsi to succeed, even though he was only third-in-line within the Brotherhood. He proved to be too weak. Would a more powerful leader have compromised more? Was it wise to try to impose this choice? There is room for a detailed retrospective study of what went wrong in Egypt. There are other potential questions about Egypt's role in the region – could it be the source of bringing order back into Libya? It used to be speculated that the two countries could come together in a federation. Is that inconceivable? Can Egypt help Gaza by providing more space in Sinai (see Chapter Six on the Middle East)? Whatever happens, the Egypt–Israel Peace Treaty signed in 1978 has remained and must remain in place. President Trump met with President Sisi in the US early in his administration and made it clear that he was ready to work with him. This presents choices for the

UK. Do we stand aside from working with Egypt over ISIS? Do we continue our criticism of the Egyptian government's handling of dissent and of their approach to the Muslim Brotherhood? The answer is surely that we must engage fully on all aspects.

Looking back over the period since 1945, the biggest and most liberating changes came from the abandonment of colonial rule in the Indian sub-continent and elsewhere; the introduction of one person, one vote in Southern Africa; the ending of apartheid in South Africa; and the fall of communism in Eastern Europe and its replacement with democracy, encouraged by the EU. The right to be free and to live at peace with one's neighbours and to experience a sustained and genuine liberty with economic progress has been the welcome success story of many countries.

Overall, the mood in established democracies worldwide in the years following the Arab Spring is one of caution over encouraging desirable, but revolutionary, changes. There is even greater caution over conflict resolution, particularly over unilateral or multilateral military interventions. Since 1945, the five veto powers on the Security Council have all experienced stunning defeats and major setbacks: China over North Korea; the UK and France, acting together over the Suez Canal in 1956 and more recently over Libya; the US over Vietnam and alongside the UK in Iraq in 2003; the Soviet Union over Afghanistan. It is wrong, therefore, to believe we are still living in a world of ever-greater superpower dominance, rather the reverse. Isolationism, always a factor in US foreign policy, might be on the way back. A new scepticism about humanitarian intervention had already emerged from President Barack Obama in the latter years of his presidency. Some call it 'off shore balancing', others 'retrenchment'. Obama has used neither term, but in an interview with Jeffrey Goldberg in *The Atlantic* in March 2016 quoted at the start of this chapter, his views were expressed with clarity and a certain defiance of 'the Blob', the name given by one of his closest advisers for the US foreign policy establishment.[8]

Under the Trump administration there are some signs that the

Americans will be more selective in their intervention but not isolationist in their military stance – a position compatible with their large projected $54 billion increase in defence spending – while reducing aid and environmental spending. The Trump administration, interestingly, may find itself more comfortable with the UN Security Council than the UN as a whole. The realpolitik of the five permanent members all having the veto means that the UN Security Council can be a place where deals are done. When the Security Council becomes blocked, as it is over Syria, it has devastating consequences. The General Assembly is likely to continue to grow in importance the more the Security Council fails. UK resources post-Brexit must be directed to meet essential UN tasks in the event of any US cutbacks.

The crucial political figure in 1945 for widening acceptance in the US for a United Nations was Senator Vandenberg. He had said acceptance of the UN Charter in 1945 would never threaten the US Congress's own claims to sovereignty. In 1946, the Soviet Union cast their first veto in a dispute over the successor regime when the French withdrew forces from Lebanon and Syria. To Senator Vandenberg, the Soviet action was not a smack in the face but rather confirmation that 'the system worked'. If President Trump does establish a dialogue with President Putin, as they should both be encouraged to do, we might see the Security Council operating as it did for a while with President Yeltsin and for an even shorter period under President Medvedev. It is certainly in the interest of British foreign policy to push for this development and not appear nostalgic for the supposed certainties of the Cold War. Reagan's personal style worked well with President Gorbachev. Like many areas of policy associated with Trump, the outcomes may be unpredictable but they must be explored. It looked as if any initial talks between the US and Russia would make the most rapid progress on nuclear arms control, but then it was suggested early progress could be made on Eastern Ukraine, and Israel and Palestine. North Korea was a case which rapidly moved up the agenda, given the increasingly aggressive stance being taken by its dictator, Kim Jong-un. Initial priorities will inevitably change, but there are aspects of Trump's approach that are refreshingly direct; at least he is not locked into some of the deep-seated Congressional attitudes. Long-term solutions to many of these issues will need to involve the UN in some form or another, not least over Syria.

While the UN Charter has withstood the passage of the years surprisingly well, the geopolitical evolution since the end of the Cold War has left the UN's key structures looking increasingly outdated; and regrettably, it appears as if they will be static well into the twenty-first century. Reform is needed to reignite commitment to the UN by all member states. A Security Council in the twenty-first century that does not have, at the very least, India, Japan, Brazil, Germany and an African country as permanent members, albeit without a veto, is very clearly unrepresentative. We would all benefit from that additional geographical authority coming to the Security Council, and the new UN Secretary General, Antonio Gutteres, should be given every possible support by the UK in making this happen. It is, however, a fact of life that China does not want Japan to be a permanent member of the UN Security Council and, though unspoken, that perception lurks behind all the manoeuvring in the Security Council, since they are widely believed to be ready to veto reform. Other countries also have unstated objections to these reforms and, as yet, the issue has not reached the Security Council in a resolution that dares China to veto. After two decades of stalled action on Security Council reform, many speakers in a General Assembly debate on 7 November 2016 pressed the need for the process to be moved forward, but there remained too many differences of opinion on the five areas of reform: membership categories; the question of the veto held by the five permanent members; regional representation; the size of an enlarged Council; and Council working methods. Discussions on reform are increasingly seen as a yearly ritual yielding scant results. There was, however, forceful support for an initiative aimed at preventing the use of the veto in cases of mass-atrocity crimes which, without Treaty amendment, may become a practice, but possibly not an invariable practice.

If Putin can get on with Trump, it may open the possibility both of

Russia returning to G8 – initially, perhaps, for specific issues – and of China being admitted. In both this grouping and the UNSC, the UK already has membership in its own right which, on some issues, we are likely to be freer to exploit post-Brexit.

It is at least possible that historians, looking back from the vantage point of 2045, will conclude that the first fifty years of the UN's history was more dangerous, yet more ordered, than the second. Experience of those two devastating world wars was so profound that most were content for many years to accept the implicit restriction in the Charter not to intervene in the internal affairs of another member state.

Those first fifty years after the UN's establishment in 1945 saw many challenges to its authority. The first landmark event was the war in Korea that started in June 1950. Intervention by the US using the UN was made possible only because of a temporary boycott of the Security Council by the USSR. We now know it was a proxy war. In Moscow in April 1950, Stalin had given the green-light to North Korea to start it as did Mao in May in Beijing. But for years, the Chinese and the Russians went through a ritual of blaming each other for starting the war. Both were surprised by the US's intervention over Korea and in the support they had from the UK. On the Taiwan straits, the US got into a habit of responding by exercising with the US Seventh Fleet. China took military action over both Taiwan in 1954–58 and the Indian border in 1962. There was a border conflict between the USSR and China over the Ussuri River in 1969–71, but today the border is stable, after many minor adjustments having been made by agreement.

The wars in Indochina in the 1950s led to the mistaken US involvement in the 1960s in the ideological war in Vietnam over communism or democracy across the divide between the South and the North. This was a war that the UK refused to become a party to, although without overtly criticising the US. We should pursue the same selective policy post-Brexit today in not becoming a military protagonist against China in the South China Seas over their island development policy. Of course we must stand by the Law of the Sea, but we can uphold that best by continuing to advocate non-military solutions. Going back to the Far East is not a licence for the Royal Navy to engage at will with the US Navy, and they should be under clear political constraints.

The US will pursue its national interests, often in great secrecy. While the war in Vietnam was still underway, on 9 July 1971 President Nixon sent Henry Kissinger privately to Beijing. This was followed seven months later, on 21 February 1972, by Nixon arriving in Beijing to meet Mao. As the Vietnam War wound down, the Chinese/US reconciliation created the climate for an economic transformation in South East Asia. In historic terms, it was a realignment; but at a deeper level, the China that has emerged is becoming very different. For example, there have been events as diverse as a progressive involvement of China in UN affairs; a massive increase in China's trade; the highly successful Beijing Olympics; and the unveiling of a statue of Confucius in Tiananmen Square.

We should never forget that events in one part of the globe impact in another. In the late summer of 1956, the UK and France clandestinely combined with Israel to invade the Suez Canal. This was disowned by President Eisenhower and economic sanctions were threatened if British troops did not stop fighting along the Canal, a demand to which Prime Minister Eden felt he had to accede. Yet within days, the USSR saw an opportunity to invade Hungary, but not before Khrushchev flew to consult Tito in the middle of the night and got his approval. Over Hungary, not even John Foster Dulles, the toughest of all US Cold War warriors, who had talked of the rollback of Soviet communism, ever seriously contemplated NATO fighting the Soviets. This continued to be NATO's position following the Soviet invasion of Czechoslovakia that, in 1968, came as a complete surprise to our own Joint Intelligence Committee (JIC).

Change came slowly, starting with *Ostpolitik* between West and East Germany, then détente, and US and Soviet arms control agreements and the Helsinki Final Act in 1975. These changes were accompanied by a new recognition that the situation over human rights was a legitimate concern for all signatories. Unfortunately Gromyko, the long-serving Soviet Foreign Minister, chose to demand of his UK counterpart that, as a result of Helsinki, the three Baltic States could no longer be considered not to be part of the USSR. That mistaken view is still held by key strategists in the Russian Federation. The emergence of Charter 77 in Eastern Europe, and the emigration of Russian Jews, was a good consequence of Helsinki and a portent that countries, hitherto under tough Soviet influence, could embark on public protest with a little more confidence. The Soviet invasion of Afghanistan in late 1979 was a profound mistake, as many invaders down the centuries have found to their cost, and it contributed to the collapse of the USSR.

When Argentina invaded the Falkland Islands in 1982, in defiance of self-determination – an important UN principle – the UK had to respond militarily in self-defence. We are slowly improving relations with Argentina commercially and diplomatically. Patience is the path to take, and we will have to use all the same virtues over Gibraltar from 2017. We will again have to be resolute and determined, but also not fixed in our readiness to examine with Gibraltar's citizens sensible suggestions as we did in 2002 with Spain.[9]

The Cold War struggle after 1956 was not primarily military; the fundamental East/West clash became ideological, between both totalitarianism and democracy, and the command economy and the market economy. The Cold War ended in Berlin, the place it began, which had survived as a Western enclave only as a result of the Berlin airlift of 1948–49. The fall of the Berlin Wall in 1989 owed much to Gorbachev's refusal to intervene and buttress the East German government with Soviet power, at a time when the Soviet Union itself was in deep-seated economic decline; and East Germans, many of them Berliners, were suddenly and unexpectedly allowed to pass freely through to the West via former Warsaw Pact countries.

This brief history demonstrates that there was never a period marked by non-interference in the internal affairs of an individual UN member state. Yet despite this, non-intervention, as spelt out in the UN Charter, was raised to the status of a diplomatic principle in the confrontational atmosphere of the UN Security Council in New York. It was repeatedly invoked in the Security Council, and more vehemently in the General Assembly. The UN Charter for the initial years protected any regime, however vile, from any form of external military overthrow. In reality, it was not the establishment of a principle; rather the recognition of an uncertain peace presided over by two superpowers with protective spheres of influence – itself a manifestation of realpolitik. A *droit du regard* for each superpower was openly espoused by the USSR to allow them to conduct themselves as they wished within their own sphere and this has been reasserted by President Putin. It is a doomed strategy which he or his successors will have to rethink. The US has been far less overt in espousing its own sphere of influence. But it goes back a long way and it lay behind the Bay of Pigs disaster in 1961, when a newly elected President Kennedy, on a bizarre cocktail of drugs for pain and recreation, humiliated himself and the US by backing a Cuban guerrilla landing up until the point of it needing overt US support, which he refused to give.[10] Eisenhower would never have handled it in the same way. Yet Kennedy, in dramatically better personal health by the autumn of 1962, handled the Cuban missile crisis with great personal skill. Vietnam, where the US lost out under President Johnson, was an example of a power projection led by a politically skilled but militarily flawed President that slowly failed; and in the process fostered a mass protest movement in the US that boosted attention to human rights. The US record of clandestine intervention in many countries in Latin America, which for too long had been founded on disrespect for human rights and lip service to democracy, also began to be scrutinised.

The attitude to interventions took a new turn in the 1990s as the US emerged as the sole superpower following the collapse of the Soviet Union. Looking back over the last quarter-century has given rise to much soul-searching about when and how intervention in the affairs of another state is justified. In her January 2017 speech mentioned earlier, Prime Minister Theresa May, speaking of the need to defend our interests, stated:

This cannot mean a return to the failed policies of the past. The days of Britain and America intervening in sovereign countries in an attempt to remake the world in our own image are over. But nor can we afford to stand idly by when the threat is real and when it is in our own interests to intervene. We must be strong, smart and hard-headed.

It is important to explore what these 'failed policies' were; how they can be avoided in the future; and what the criteria should be for future interventions, which this speech clearly envisages. As a starting point, the British and other governments should consider the physicians' fundamental principle of non-maleficence: being mindful of taking action which risks doing more harm than good.

In August 1990, Saddam Hussein's troops invaded Kuwait. By February 1991, President Bush Sr had forged a multinational coalition that confronted and forced Saddam Hussein to abandon Iraq's occupation of Kuwait. This success, with a coalition of forces which included Egypt, Syria, Jordan and Saudi Arabia, combined with the collapse of the Soviet Union, paved the way for what became known in many circles as 'the new world order'.

For a while in early 1991, after what appeared a clear-cut victory, a new mood of hope recaptured the idealism of the UN's founding fathers; everything seemed possible, even the reinstatement of the Military Staff Committee, the first casualty of the Cold War in July 1948. The issue of the Military Staff Committee is something that may become a subject of discussion in the attempt to re-examine Article 26 of the UN Charter which covers the establishment of a system for the regulation of armaments. A UN Report entitled 'Rethinking General and Complete Disarmament in the 21st Century' puts an emphasis on Article 26 of the UN Charter.[11] It is a joint publication between UNODA and the School of Oriental and African Studies (SOAS) at the University of London, and was launched in New York in October 2016. This UN report conclusively shows that after seventy years, the UN Security Council (UNSC) has still not acted upon its *de jure* obligation under Article 26, tasking it with the responsibility to formulate concrete proposals for the regulation of armaments. For an international body entrusted with the duty to preserve international stability, it is worrying that the Security Council devotes so little time to the threat represented by conventional weapons systems. Weapons of mass destruction lurk in the background of international policy making, particularly under the Non-Proliferation Treaty (NPT), but if we are truthful, we failed completely, despite trying, over Pakistan; the jury is out on whether we have slowed or stopped Iran. North Korea continues its tests of long range missiles capable of carrying nuclear warheads.

The optimism engendered within the international community over Kuwait was soon dashed, and the challenges of implementing interventionist policies began to loom large over the breakup of Yugoslavia in 1991, where once again Balkan rivalries, so evident in the tensions before 1914, came back to haunt Europe. Ever since the death of Tito in 1980, the long-asked question, 'What happens after Tito's death?', was left unanswered. Slowly, the latent nationalism was revived. The then UN Secretary General, Boutros Boutros-Ghali, initially had US support for a wider and more active role in the former Yugoslavia in 1991–92. But US support withered following the humiliation of the US-led UN intervention in Somalia.

In the Balkans it is easy to forget that the US in 1990, under President Bush Sr, wanted to maintain the unity of Yugoslavia, mainly because they did not wish to do anything to encourage the break-up of Gorbachev's Soviet Union. The US Secretary of State, James Baker, visited Belgrade in June 1991 and spoke for NATO and the CSCE when he warned Croatia and Slovenia not to declare independence. But only four days later Croatia and Slovenia declared independence, ignoring his appeal. Both countries felt sufficiently confident in doing so because they calculated, correctly, neither the US nor the European Community (EC) were prepared to take military action to stop them. They also knew they had the more-than-tacit support of Austria and Germany. The war in Slovenia in 1991 was over in a matter of days because there was no ethnic conflict with Serbs.

The fragmentation of Yugoslavia along its historical regional boundaries now suited Slobodan Milošević in Belgrade, the leader for a short time of all the Serbs, who attacked the Croats at Vukovar. The European Community, buoyed up by the belief that the 'Hour of Europe' had come, wanted to be involved diplomatically, while the US under President Bush Sr watched. When asked by the Dutch Presidency in their working paper of 13 July 1991 to contemplate changes by negotiation in the internal boundaries of the three republics – Bosnia and Herzegovina, Croatia and Serbia – emerging from the former Yugoslavia, the other eight EC states decided against, judging, unwisely, that it was inevitable that these internal Yugoslav boundaries should automatically become international boundaries. It would have been difficult, but not impossible, to make minor adjustments. The wisdom behind the Dutch position was later demonstrated by the 'velvet divorce' when, with no support from any other country and a lot of criticism, Czechoslovakia split into two by agreement on 1 January 1993.

In pushing for recognition of Croatia in December 1991, Germany and some other EC countries ignored the advice of their own peace negotiator, Lord Carrington, who was against premature independence for Croatia. This made it inevitable that pressure would grow for recognition later of Bosnia and Herzegovina. The UK and French position hitherto had been united against recognition of Croatia, but France decided to concede to Chancellor Kohl and Foreign Minister Genscher; and the UK felt they had to follow in December 1991, in recognition of the support Kohl had given to John Major during the Maastricht Treaty negotiations, thereby allowing the UK to opt-out from the Eurozone. It is dangerous to trade off such very different issues, but it is a fact, regrettably, of international politics. Then the world recognised Bosnia and Herzegovina without putting in a peacekeeping force before the spring 1992 referendum was called, in which the Bosnian Serbs refused to participate.

The incoming Clinton administration paid lip service to supporting the Vance Owen Peace Plan (VOPP) while denigrating it semi-publicly. The former US Ambassador to Yugoslavia wrote in

1996, 'During the first year of the Clinton administration, policy toward Bosnia revealed little resolve, determination or consistency.'[12] As for the EU, it tried very hard and was supportive of the VOPP, but it showed, then as twelve states and later as fifteen, that it was not an organisation that could fight wars – that was only possible through NATO. Nevertheless, the EU did field a team of monitors that did useful work. On 14 February 1993, after a confrontation with the EU, Russia and the UN, Warren Christopher, US Secretary of State, accepted the VOPP but in so doing gratuitously and publicly ruled out any form of military enforcement through NATO: an irresponsible message that brought huge relief to the Bosnian Serbs. Thereafter the UN held a humanitarian mandate which was constantly enlarged on the basis of UNPROFOR accepting more intervention but without adequate resources.

The UN role in Bosnia and Herzegovina increasingly became the scapegoat for President Clinton's refusal to put US forces on the ground with French and British forces as part of NATO to enforce a peace settlement on the Bosnian Serbs in May 1993. The war in Bosnia and Herzegovina raged from 1992 to 1995. A US doctrine developed during this time that one must be able to say no to UN interventions and this in turn led tragically in 1994 to the US blocking in the Security Council UN action in Rwanda, which we will return to later.

The policy of so-called 'safe havens' which, fatefully, included Srebrenica, was imposed on UNPROFOR by four of the P5, China not being involved. The UN commanders had asked for 31,500 thousand troops to implement the Joint Action Plan which superseded the VOPP and they barely got 6,000. Diplomacy continued in the EU–UN framework but the Bosnian Serbs under General Mladić, knowing that they were not going to face NATO troops, grew ever more confident. They took hostages, including UN troops, and all sides broke ceasefire agreements while the ink was still drying on the signed documents. The UN was criticised, often unfairly, by all sides. In the summer of 1995 a Bosnian Serb genocide – as it was judged to be on 26 February 2007 by the International Court of Justice – took place in Srebrenica, with over 8,000 male Bosnian Muslims, many of them boys, killed. The Dutch UN troops were the scapegoats for the folly of the US, UK, French and Russian Security Council policy of 'safe havens' that had operated with growing concern for the safety of the people supposedly being protected since the spring of 1993.

The best time for outside military intervention in the Balkans was early in the conflict in the summer and autumn of 1991, when Vukovar was continuously shelled for three months by the Serb Army and Dubrovnik was shelled from the sea by what was left of the Yugoslav navy. Had NATO or a well-equipped Rapid Reaction Force, on behalf of the Security Council, intervened from the air with strikes on Serb artillery and aircraft (as happened towards the end of the wars, leading to the Dayton Peace Accords), severe damage could have been done both to Serb forces in the flat, open territory around Vukovar and to Serb ships on the Adriatic. But Yeltsin would never have accepted such use of force in the UN. The political vulnerability of the Russian Federation government at home was a reality everyone had to take into account. The political will to use NATO and face down Russia was absent in both the US and Europe. The UN officials did their best; soldiers in blue helmets lost their lives. Once again, the UN filled in for the inadequacies of a world order that, though purported, did not exist.

A no-fly zone (NFZ) over Bosnia was eventually, and somewhat tentatively, enforced under NATO but with huge constraints, and it did not start to tilt the balance of fighting until after Srebrenica in late August 1995. The US government for years talked about 'lift and strike' – lifting the arms embargo for the Bosnian government while striking at Serb positions from the air – but refused to face up to the need to pull back or withdraw UN humanitarian forces to do so. After formally announcing that this was their policy on 1 May 1993, Clinton backed off it within a few days in Washington while his Secretary of State was still explaining the policy in Brussels.[13]

Over Kosovo in 1999, NATO resorted to what was termed a humanitarian military intervention to stop Kosovo Albanians being forced out of their homes and across frontiers. This action was taken without the authority of the UN Security Council because the Russians, under President Yeltsin, had made clear they would veto any authority sought in the UN, but they indicated they would not interfere over a humanitarian intervention on Kosovo. Contrary to many claims at the time and since, the NATO bombing was never as effective on Serb troops and positions within Kosovo as claimed. The study, 'NATO's Air War in Perspective', should be a mandatory read for all interventionists.[14] A US Air Force review claims that only fourteen Serb tanks were destroyed, not 120 as initially reported; eighteen armoured personnel carriers, not 220; and twenty mobile artillery pieces eliminated, not 450. The Serbs constructed 'fake' artillery from logs and old truck axles and 'surface to air missiles' made of paper.

NATO pressure built up on Milošević only when strategic positions within Serbia itself, like bridges over the Danube, were bombed. But this was far less easy to claim as having a humanitarian justification. Eventually, after a long bombing campaign of seventy-eight days, Russian diplomacy with Prime Minister Chernomyrdin helped by the Finnish President, Martti Ahtisaari, forced Milošević to pull his forces out of Kosovo. No one admits exactly what the crucial pressure was that made Milošević anger his own forces by ordering them to leave Kosovo, even though they had not been defeated. The probability was that Yeltsin authorised Chernomyrdin to say that all gas pipelines to Serbia would be turned off. But in those days – in contrast to later years – for commercial reasons Gazprom never came close to admitting using pipeline pressure for political ends; if it was done, it was done quietly and denied publicly. This pipeline pressure would have been both more immediate and more critical pressure in Belgrade than the vague hints from President Clinton when asked by Prime Minister Tony Blair to deploy ground troops as part of a NATO intervention. The settlement reluctantly accepted by Milošević in Serbia sealed his fate. He was no longer the man who was standing up for Serbs in Kosovo, the very policy which won him power in the first place. He lost an election, was pushed out of power and then sent to The Hague by the government in Belgrade. He was there charged with war crimes, but died before his trial was completed.

Rwanda is another example of a tragically inadequate international response to conflict. On 6 April 1994, President Juvenal Habyarimana of Rwanda and President Cyprien Ntaryamira of Burundi were killed when their aircraft was shot down as it approached Kigali, the Rwandan capital. Within hours, violence broke out in the city and the surrounding communities. Extremists from the Hutu ethnic group soon began executing less extreme Hutu and members of the Tutsi ethnic minority. Local political leaders, police, and soldiers went from house to house with lists identifying those to be killed. Attempts by the commander of UNAMIR,* Lt General Romeo Dallaire, and the special representative of the UN Secretary-General, Jacques Roger Booh-Booh, to bring the parties back to peace failed. The situation spun out of control as UNAMIR was repeatedly weakened, first by the pull out of the Belgians, who openly advocated a complete withdrawal of UNAMIR. Then a timid response was asked for by other participating nations, except Ghana, with governments instructing their UNAMIR contingents to protect themselves at all costs. Some UNAMIR soldiers stood by while drunken and armed thugs hacked women and children to death. The UN Security Council along with the US, after the intervention in Somalia, was fearful of another mission failure. Ready to say no, the Security Council found itself so hampered by the sovereignty issues raised by member states that no decisive action to intervene was taken. Within three months, UNAMIR was reduced to 450 personnel. Some 800,000 Rwandans, mostly Tutsi, were thought to have been killed; 500,000 Rwandans were displaced within the country, and over two million Rwandans fled to surrounding countries. The three months of carnage in Rwanda were far worse than four years of killing in the former Yugoslavia, yet initially it received far less press and media coverage.

The Carnegie Commission on Preventing Deadly Conflict, the

---

* UN Assistance Mission for Rwanda, established in 1993 to assist in the implementation of the Arusha Accords, which were signed to bring an end to the Rwandan civil war.

Institute for the Study of Diplomacy at Georgetown University and the US Army undertook a project with an international panel of distinguished senior military leaders to assess whether General Dallaire's plan for a UN-led military intervention force could have substantially reduced the killing. They concluded that a modern force of 5,000 troops, drawn primarily from one country and sent to Rwanda sometime between 7 and 21 April 1994, could have significantly altered the outcome of the conflict.[15]

The lesson the Carnegie Commission drew was that 'in an enlarged Security Council, member states should be prepared to accept as the price of being on the Council the obligation to contribute to the deployment of a well-trained and well-equipped Rapid Reaction Force for short-term missions'.[16] It is essential that such a force, which the Carnegie Commission felt should have a core of no fewer than 5,000 troops from the Security Council members, should be able to be deployed to anywhere in the world where it is needed for the maintenance of peace. The Commission wanted the political machinery, and the logistical and financial structures, to be put in place to enable deployments 'within days'. The fact that still, in 2017, no such global RRF has been formed to assist the Security Council, despite experience in the Balkans, Libya, Rwanda, Sierra Leone and South Sudan, is a sad demonstration of the lack of political will. As always, the biggest problem is logistical support for early deployment. This requires heavy lift aircraft and a naval, aircraft carrier-based force capable of worldwide deployment of aircraft and helicopters, escort vessels and troops who train and live together. Troops are still gathered together by the UN on an ad hoc basis and deployment takes months. The Danish Rapid Reaction Force is an advance, but it has a limited range of operation.

The UN needs to be able to rely on a force that is instantly available for global threats and of such a sufficient sophistication that it can overcome initial resistance. We believe this should be a key initiative for a new global British foreign and security policy involving heavy lift aircraft from identified countries. Given that the Royal Navy will have two aircraft carriers, a naval RRF could be poised to make a significant contribution by 2020 and that might also involve the French, who have a single aircraft carrier (see also Chapter Two). It is interesting to note that in June 2017, France expressed an interest in joining the 'Five Power Defence Arrangements' which bring Australia, Malaysia, New Zealand, Singapore and the UK together in an Asian defence grouping established in 1971 to protect Singapore and Malaysia against Indonesia, but is now focusing more on counter-terrorism and maritime security. A French official was quoted in *The Times* saying, 'It makes sense because France wants to remain a power in Asia and because Britain is our closest military friend. With Britain out of Europe, who is to be our partner? Germany is not the same.'[17]

After the failure of Afghanistan, Iraq and Libya, any discussion in 2017 about future UK military intervention, as distinct from a UN supported RRF, has to go back and examine what was done successfully when Kuwait was invaded by Iraq in 1990. A successful intervention was less of a foregone conclusion than many realise. With Iraqi land forces, tanks and airplanes already in Kuwait, President Bush Sr was faced with an alarming situation: Saudi Arabia was very close to being invaded and was asking for help. In advance of the multinational effort, Bush decided to fly American troops into Saudi Arabia with the agreement of King Fahd to man their border with Kuwait, initially without much logistical back-up, or support in depth. In taking this decision, Bush risked a humiliating initial defeat by the far greater Iraqi forces coming over the border into Saudi Arabia.

The multinational operation to force the Iraqi troops out of Kuwait took place later in 1991, with the full authority of the UN. It was not just a US force with help from the UK, France and a few other European countries, but a multinational force with Saudi, Jordanian, Egyptian and Syrian troops. This had to be handled with delicacy. There was a Commander-in-Chief from Saudi Arabia, Prince Khalid bin Sultan, and a military Commander-in-Chief of America's forces, General Norman Schwarzkopf, with the British forces, led by General Sir Peter de las Billière (an Arabic speaker and former SAS chief), under his command. It had one central task: to force Iraq out of Kuwait.

While the multinational force was victorious, it never moved on to the capital, Baghdad, to push Saddam Hussein out of power. Regime change was explicitly not a military objective, in the main because the US and UK had considered beforehand whether Iraq would be more or less stable after being forced out of Kuwait if Saddam Hussein was then toppled and Baghdad occupied. The professional judgement in Washington and London was that it was better to contain the Ba'athist regime rather than risk chaos after its removal. This judgement was very different from the decision made by George W. Bush and Tony Blair when attacking Iraq in 2003. They both assumed that there would be no untoward consequences of toppling Saddam Hussein, despite reservations of advisers which we shall come back to later. They assumed that Saddam Hussein must have resumed programmes for nuclear, chemical and biological weapons, developments originally discovered by UN inspectors in 1991. As politicians, it is odd that they did not understand why Hussein would choose not to provide chapter and verse to hostile neighbours like Iran and Saudi Arabia to demonstrate that he had got rid of nuclear weapons.

In 1991, humanitarian principles lay behind the ceasefire announced by General Colin Powell, the US Chief of Defense Staff at the time. Halting the developing 'turkey shoot' from the air on Iraqi forces fleeing Kuwait was an honourable expression of the most precious human right – the right to live. But Powell and his field commanders had not put in place a detailed ceasefire and disarmament programme. Most TV watchers were very pleased when the ceasefire was introduced; but a just war can, and should, demand a just end. The lesson of 1991 in Iraq is that the rapid and unplanned manner in which the war ended sowed the seeds of all the frustration that led up to the later invasion in 2003. Not enough thought was given to the just demands and safeguards that would need to be accepted by Saddam Hussein and his own generals in the field.

The UN Security Council's authority and its political will were thereafter persistently ignored by Saddam Hussein from 1991–2003, in particular in relation to the Kurdish people in Iraq. In retrospect, had there been an insistence in 1991 on an unconditional surrender by Saddam Hussein's generals, there would probably have been no need for operation 'Provide Comfort' to save the Kurds, and Saddam Hussein would in all probability have been forced out by his own army, without the need for further military intervention. The UN's ceasefire provisions were not fully enforced; for example, helicopters were allowed to continue to fly unchecked. Many of the specific UN resolutions over the next twelve years were visibly flouted. The US/UK invasion of Iraq in 2003 was, in part, a response to a growing frustration with economic sanctions being evaded by cynical decisions of which those from France, Russia and even Germany were the most deplorable. The notorious oil-for-food programme, which UN officials were party to under Kofi Annan and which was later strongly criticised in the Volker Report commissioned by the UN, is another example.[18] Nevertheless, the US and UK maintained the NFZ for twelve years to protect the Kurds from the air, under repeated attack from Iraqi ground-to-air missiles, while other countries broke UN sanctions for commercial gain. Yet the ill-fated military intervention in 2003–2011, by any test of 'do no harm', was a miserable failure. The price paid by the civilian population for the removal of Saddam Hussein was far too high in terms of lives lost and people maimed and harmed.

Again, as with the situation in 1991, many of the problems arising from the 2003 intervention arose from not anticipating the consequences of the initial military action, or, if they were anticipated, not providing the leadership or resources to deal with them. The then British ambassador to Washington has written about the 'titanic struggle' for six months to keep Britain 'onside for war' and how 'there was little energy left in No. 10 to think about the aftermath. Since Downing Street drove Iraq policy, efforts made by the Foreign Office to engage with the Americans on the aftermath came to nothing.'[19]

The results of this lack of foresight are all too well known, and we are still living with the consequences. Britain's former Ambassador to the UN, Sir Jeremy Greenstock, who was sent from New York to Baghdad in 2003, said of the days following victory:

No one, it seems to me, was instructed to put the security of Iraq first, to put law and order on the streets first. There was no police force. There was no constituted army except the victorious invaders. And there was no American general that I could ... establish who was given the accountable responsibility to make sure that the first duty of any government – and we were the government – was to keep law and order on the streets. There was a vacuum from the beginning in which looters, saboteurs, the criminals, the insurgents, moved very quickly.[20]

The fundamental issue was the inadequate number of troops deployed initially, and the failure to subsequently increase force level. This was flagged just before the invasion by General Eric K. Shinseki, the US Army Chief of Staff, when he went before the Senate Armed Services Committee on 25 February 2003. He said that based on his experience of peacekeeping in the Balkans, post-war Iraq would require 'something on the order of several hundred thousand soldiers'. This was the reasoned estimate of a lifelong military man who had lost most of a foot in Vietnam, led NATO's Peace Stabilization Force in Bosnia, and commanded both NATO's land forces and the US Army in Europe. President Bush and Condoleezza Rice, the National Security Advisor, should have insisted on the White House reviewing the planned force levels after Shinseki's assertion. Instead, Shinseki was contradicted a few days later by Paul Wolfowitz, who told the House Budget Committee that this estimate was 'wildly off the mark', explaining that 'It's hard to conceive that it would take more forces to provide stability in post-Saddam Iraq than it would take to conduct the war itself and to secure the surrender of Saddam's security forces and his army. Hard to imagine.'[21] For those experienced in post-war conflict, it was, on the contrary, all too easy to imagine why more forces would be needed in the aftermath. This was particularly the case for the UK military in view of their experience in both Northern Ireland over three decades, and Bosnia and Herzegovina from 1992 to 1993 where the government's largely Muslim forces and the Croatian forces were building up but were too weak compared with the Serbs. However, there was no such outspoken private concern expressed by the British military over Iraq, as judged by a reading of the Chilcot Report. Instead there was a reluctance to deploy from Basra to Baghdad in May 2003 when suggested to the Chiefs of Staff by Ambassador Sawers, sent specifically to Baghdad by Prime Minister Blair, the senior UK military commander and General Richards, sent out by the Defence Secretary to report back. It was the one chance for the UK to act militarily and politically to change the climate in Washington, which was readying to bring US troops home. It was a tragic error, for which the Prime Minister who wanted it done and the Chief of the Defence Staff who was opposed to it bear very heavy responsibility. It was the incident above all which demonstrated the need for the National Security Council, established in 2010 and described in detail in Chapter Four.

In learning lessons from the situation in Iraq, we must also look back to the political landscape before the Iraqi invasion of Kuwait. A massive error was made in the 1980s involving Iraq that, in a way, determined how 1990–91 was handled. The eight-year Iraq/Iran war had been allowed to drag on by the Security Council members. The Security Council engaged in no serious diplomacy to end it; rather they helped perpetuate it, expecting that it would burn out the Iranian Shi'ite revolutionary fervour. The UN asked Swedish Prime Minister Olof Palme to try to mediate, but since he had little support, he failed, as expected, and that fed rather than quenched the fervour of the Republican Guard in Iran. The Western democracies and the Soviet Union all knew that Iraq, under Saddam Hussein, was using poisonous gas against Iran in that war, and indeed, in 1988 Hussein had actually used gas against his own people. The condemnation in the UN was equivocal, and it is a lasting mark of shame that the Security Council tolerated the use of gas by Iraq. Let us hope that both the 2013 decision to involve the UN in removing substantial quantities of, and what was hoped all, sarin gas from Syria and the 2017 US strike against the airfield in Syria which they identified as the base for the Assad forces that delivered gas against their own citizens (see Chapter

Four), are signs the world has recognised that there must be zero tolerance regarding the use of gas and hopefully all weapons of mass destruction (WMD), whether chemical, biological or nuclear.

What does all this say about the UN moving into the twenty-first century? The UN did have modest success in the twentieth century, with peacekeeping in the Middle East and to some extent in Africa. The first ever preventive UN deployment in 1992 in Macedonia was a precedent worth reinforcing. Preventive diplomacy in the CSCE and NATO also helped the slow process of adjusting popular opinion, which is still going on, to accommodate a Muslim–Albanian minority in Macedonia. In 1999, following the UN-sponsored act of self-determination, Indonesia relinquished control of the territory of East Timor, which became a new sovereign state in 2002. In Haiti, the results have been mixed, but no other body than the UN had any locus there, and successive US administrations have wanted the UN to continue to take the lead. UN interventions over the years, whether military or humanitarian, have had identifiable weaknesses as well as strengths. Overall, the record is a mixed one. UN military interventions have, in almost all instances, saved lives, but in some they have also cost more lives than they have saved. The overriding principle of any intervention must be to 'do no harm'. When that principle is violated, the Security Council should have the humility to admit it and learn lessons for the future. On occasions when the UN has called on regional powers to exercise military strength, with the exception of the Kuwait experience, this has largely been in relation to missions such as that in Bosnia and Herzegovina, which initially was a humanitarian operation, starting with keeping Sarajevo airport open, getting aid convoys through roadblocks and similar activities. Non-UN interventions have been dominated by political, rather than military, thinking. Most such interventions have come from the US with help from the UK and sometimes other European countries, and have often run against the grain of the culture in which the intervention has taken place, with Iraq being the dominant case.

It is a significant and potentially welcome development that what the press calls a 'Muslim NATO' is starting to emerge. The problem is, however, that the Shia are not involved in this force, and many states that are, in some circumstances, would be happy for it to be targeted on Iran. But given wise leadership, it could develop more into a regional peacekeeping organisation with Shia participation. Kamal Alam from the Royal United Services Institute (RUSI) recently wrote that its new commander, the Pakistani General Raheel Sharif, is a very popular General and former head of Pakistan's army: a capable man who 'has respect for running the biggest non-NATO westernised army'. President Trump has also backed the force. The key support comes from Prince Mohammed of Saudi Arabia, second-in-line to his father, King Salman. This development could mean the UN delegating authority in Yemen to a Muslim peacekeeping force, which would be a shift in approach; indeed, Alam said since, that 'Brute force hasn't worked in the Yemen, proxies haven't worked in Syria and Saudis have no presence in Iraq.'[22]

Apart from the principle of doing no harm, there is another principle to assess carefully: that is, the rational chances of doing good. With this in mind, a new focus on the UN, if the US retreats, as some believe will happen, should create many more opportunities for the UK to act not just as an independent voice, but as part of a new Rapid Reaction Force called into play by the Security Council. It would raise our global profile, while reinforcing our trading position, commercially making more new contacts and improving our prosperity. In the Security Council, we have the responsibility to act but also the freedom to choose and advocate restraint where the impulse 'to do something' has dominated the rational case for non-intervention. We will not see a dramatic shift in policy in the UK, but there are recent examples, such as over policy towards Ukraine, where the UK could and should have been far more active than we were over the negotiating of the EU–Ukraine Association Agreement, whose provocative language contributed to the deterioration in relations with Russia – as we shall explore in Chapter Five.

Aside from direct military intervention, sanctions have been another tool wielded to enforce policy decisions peacefully, whether through the UN or otherwise. Some of the most longstanding were the sanctions imposed from 1965 to 1980 against those who rebelled against the nominal authority of the UK in Southern Rhodesia. They consisted of an arms embargo, an oil embargo (which the Bingham Report revealed had been undermined by the actions of major British oil companies) and many other specific economic sanctions. Over South Africa, a mandatory UN arms embargo was applied for thirteen years after the horrific death in 1977 of the black conscience movement leader, Steve Biko, before it was lifted in 1990. Minor economic sanctions on South Africa were also imposed with some – limited – effect. However, it was not until the Swiss banks clamped down on investment in South Africa in the middle 1980s that white South Africans in government concluded that a rapprochement with Nelson Mandela was necessary, took him off Robben Island and began a private dialogue well before his release. This long drawn-out equivocal process had a magnificent end result with Mandela peacefully introducing majority rule.

The most controversial of all sanctions, which was rightly never accepted by the Security Council, was the Arab boycott of Israeli goods, which covered oil supplied to Israel after the war in 1973. The campaign to sanction Israel over their settlement policy has been reinvigorated (see Chapter Six). Another controversial embargo was that applied in 1991 to supplying arms to all of the former Yugoslavia that lasted, even while being clandestinely breached, until 1995. Sanctions continue to be used as a tool of diplomacy, as they satisfy the immediate public pressure on governments to be seen to be doing something. They had a serious purpose when imposed on Russia over its actions in Ukraine, but as yet have had no real impact on Russia's stance. The Minsk process involving France, Germany, Russia and Ukraine has so far achieved little, despite offering for Russia a route to the removal of sanctions. An overall serious and well thought through regional stability negotiation under P5+1 (Germany), which was successful in the case of Iran, may now offer the best prospect of a solution, and should be quietly explored by the UK. Some will argue over involving China, a non-regional power, even though it is a permanent member of UNSC. This concern in part is on the grounds that China faces its own potential territorial disputes, such as over Tibet. But many other countries face that problem. China's presence may be a reassurance in this particular negotiation to Russia, but the clinching arguments for their involvement are twofold: China is now the second most powerful country in the world and starting to demonstrate a maturity that comes with more and more exposure to global issues, but also, very importantly, there is an automaticity about their presence that avoids ad hoc discrimination amongst the five. Germany's involvement is justified as it is clearly a major influence in the region, and showed its worth in this combination in the Iran negotiations. An overall regional negotiation under P5 offers the best prospect of a solution (see Chapter Five).

While sanctions, particularly financial sanctions, can have significant effects in economic terms, the efficacy of using them to prevent, or more frequently to moderate, wars or change policy stances has, with a few notable exceptions, been disappointing. These sanctions often consolidate entrenched positions and galvanise populations in support of their leaders. Nevertheless, sometimes imposing sanctions is better than taking no action, and sanctions cannot be dismissed merely because they will be circumvented. They are a limited means of expressing concern for upholding a principle, including those relating to human rights, if there is not the will or the capacity to use force to reverse the policy that is being objected to.

If we consider human rights as a whole worldwide, there has been measurable progress since 1945 and, as discussed earlier, it is critical that the UK continues to take a leading role in developing this agenda. The Genocide Convention was adopted in 1948, though it took many countries a long time to ratify – the US, for example, only ratifying in 1986. The world might have hoped then that we had put the Holocaust and the Gulag, separate and distinct forms of terror, behind us, but tragically that was not the case. Developing the ways in which we deter such actions in the future, or intervene to stop them, or indeed deal with regimes which persist human rights abuses, should remain a critical element of UK foreign policy. But in order to confound the sceptics, the sanctions need to be effective, since purely cosmetic sanctions damage the credibility of the policy.

Over three years from 1975, it is estimated that the Khmer Rouge killed between one and a half and three million fellow Cambodians out of a population of seven to eight million. In Cambodia, it took until June 2011 for the Extraordinary Chambers in the Courts of Cambodia (ECCC) to start the trial of a former head of state, Khieu Samphan. In Zimbabwe, in October 1980, Prime Minister Robert Mugabe signed an agreement with North Korean leader Kim Il-sung to train a brigade of Zimbabwean troops. This 5th Brigade went on to massacre large numbers of civilians in Matabeleland, which was also shamefully ignored by the world. The world did react to the Rwandan genocide in 1994 and to the Srebrenica massacre in 1995; and these reactions and the subsequent court judgments have done much to restore faith in the Genocide Convention.

In March 2009, the UN Secretary General, Ban Ki-moon, visited Sri Lanka and persuaded President Rajapaksa to establish an independent investigation of alleged human rights abuses. The President did not fulfil that commitment, but the Secretary General went ahead in 2010 and set up his own independent panel of experts. Their critical report, published in March 2011, documented how thousands of people lost their lives in three months at the beginning of 2009, for the most part as a result of government shelling. It also criticised the Sri Lankan government's own Lessons Learnt and Reconciliation Commission (LLRC) as neither impartial nor independent.

The Security Council has long accepted that a regime can be the target of sanctions as well as a head of government, but while a head of government who personifies its horrors and defects can technically be replaced under the pressure of specific UN sanctions, there is a reluctance to act. To enforce the stepping down of a head of government or regime, it is down to the UN Security Council to endorse a wider definition of a 'threat to the peace' within a broader interpretation of the Charter, but it is rarely done. Russia, at present under non-UN sanctions, is the most hostile government, but China is not far behind. The P5 countries must find a way forward on this complex issue. It is a global priority and the UK should take the lead linking it to a widening of UN Security Council membership.

Far better would be a world that took more seriously the dangers of selling arms to countries that are governed by regimes that practise torture, imprison their critics and trample over their citizens' human rights. Arms sales besmirch the reputation of too many countries. According to the Stockholm International Peace Research Institute, Britain is the sixth biggest arms exporting nation behind the US, Russia, China, France and Germany. Estimates of the number of jobs provided by the British arms industry range from 170,000 to 300,000 and indeed higher, but it is undoubtedly a significant number, and many of these are high-tech and skilled jobs. The more we can sell, the easier it is to reduce unit costs of defence equipment for our own purposes. The government claims in its 2015 Strategic Defence and Security Review that what it calls 'responsible' arms exports 'are essential for our security and our prosperity'. The UK government is mainly criticised at present for supplying arms exports to Saudi Arabia that have been used in Yemen. The Campaign Against Arms Trade (CAAT) has started a judicial review aimed at halting all UK arms sales to Saudi Arabia because of Yemen. In 2016, the then Business Secretary, Sajid Javid, apparently seriously considered suspending Yemen related arms sales. The rules about granting licences in the UK are tough, and licences should not be granted if there is a clear risk that the exports might be used in 'a serious violation of international humanitarian law' or for 'internal repression'. Some of the most difficult decisions relate to crowd control questions, and this was an issue in Iran under the Shah in 1978. There have also been questions about civilian protests in Bahrain and Egypt, where the UK government did revoke licences. In Chapter Six, we refer to the controversial UK and European ban in 1973 on all sales to both sides during the Arab–Israeli war. In some ways having the decision-making about arms sales more open to question in the courts is a good thing, for it demonstrates to the country purchasing equipment that the decision is not discretionary on a British government and that ministers can be constrained by law.

The UN summit of heads of government in 2005 saw an agreement to apply the principle of a 'responsibility to protect' or, in shorthand terms, R2P or RtoP. Disappointingly for some, this never materialised into a Charter amendment. It may be an issue which the UK and France could pick up and take leadership over in order to bring more clarity and certainty. But no progress will be made until we resolve with Russia the issues surrounding Ukraine. R2P was more the outcome of deft diplomacy and global liberalism trying to rally world opinion after the appalling handling of Iraq following the invasion of 2003 and, to a lesser extent, the situation in Afghanistan. Since the leaders did not also advocate amendment of the UN Charter, it was implicit that they judged R2P could be achieved within the existing Charter. It may appear reasonable, therefore, to assume that they were endorsing the responsibility to protect, as overriding the Charter's wording about respect for national sovereignty; but that was not the interpretation of many states, and certainly not Russia's.

It needs stressing that a UN Security Council resolution – passed by the requisite majority of nine with no vetoes – which demands that a head of government step down, with the threat of military action under Chapter VII of the Charter if they do not, is legitimate. Similarly, a threat to invoke such a provision if the head of government does not start protecting their civilian population and living up to the requirements of the Charter and the Universal Declaration on Human Rights is legitimate. A threat to peace, which is a political, not a legal, judgement, can therefore override the Charter's injunction not to interfere in another state's internal sovereignty; but this is more theory than practice, and the failed interventions in pursuit of regime change in recent years will not make such action easier to take.

The Security Council tried to interpret 'the responsibility to protect' when dealing with the genocide in Darfur in 2008 and that debate will influence the UN for long into the twenty-first century. The Security Council faced an immensely difficult challenge, because the African Union (AU) was both weak and divided over Darfur. The leaders of the Sudanese government had shown a brutality and defiance of the UN that boded ill for the future. But there was in AU eyes insufficient evidence for the Security Council to ascribe all the problems within Sudan to a single, despotic leader, President Omar al-Bashir.

In 2009, the ICC issued an arrest warrant for al-Bashir on counts of war crimes and crimes against humanity, but ruled that there was insufficient evidence to prosecute him for genocide. However, on 12 July 2010, after a lengthy appeal by the prosecution, the Court held that there was indeed sufficient evidence for charges of genocide to be brought, and issued a second warrant containing three separate counts. Al-Bashir is the first sitting head of state ever indicted by the ICC as well as the first to be charged with genocide, yet the warrants were never executed by the Sudanese government; particularly since the court's decision was opposed by the African Union, the League of Arab States, the Non-Aligned Movement, and the governments of Russia and China.

One situation where a carrot and stick approach on the part of the international community perhaps surprisingly appeared to have worked, at least in part, was when dealing with Colonel Muammar Gaddafi of Libya. Indeed, the approach culminated in his agreement in 2003 to renounce weapons of mass destruction. This was the result of a sustained diplomatic effort over many years, backed by sanctions. It is suspected that President Clinton and then President George W. Bush, acting with Prime Minister Tony Blair, gave assurances to Gaddafi that if he abandoned nuclear weapons he would not later be toppled from power by military intervention from outside the country. Gaddafi started to abandon support for terrorism. It was a gamble, but one worth taking. Gaddafi even agreed in 2004 to pay $35 million in compensation for victims of the Lockerbie air disaster. Compensation was not paid to the UK victims of the Canary Wharf bombing by the IRA in February 1996, using half a tonne of semtex supplied by the Libyan government. In July 2006 the United States dropped Libya from their list of terrorist countries. Then, as the Arab Spring took hold in 2010, there were protests and demonstrations. Gaddafi and his sons had a choice: they could listen, adjust and negotiate, or repress. Depressingly, they threw caution to the wind and threatened to use force of considerable severity against the opposition movement who were poised to take the second city of Benghazi.

The spectre of another Rwanda or Srebrenica loomed in Libya. In the light of a specific request from the Arab League for a no-fly zone, UNSCR 1973 was passed on 17 March 2011, authorising UN members to 'take all necessary measures … to protect civilians and civilian populated areas'. The French flew against advancing Gaddafi forces. The US fired over 200 Cruise missiles and aircraft to destroy Libyan air defences and then stepped back, leaving the French and British to lead within NATO (described in Chapter Four). There was no Russian veto in the Security Council over the no-fly zone, sanctions or asset freeze. Humanitarian considerations were genuinely uppermost. It was always possible that Gaddafi, as a head of government, might be forced out of office. But for this to happen, UNSCR 1973 demanded a ceasefire and was framed 'excluding a foreign occupation force of any form on part of Libyan territory'. The terms of this resolution were pretty strictly applied and NATO's conduct of the operation, as a consequence, meant many months passed before Gaddafi fell. It was initially a constrained intervention. The Libyan people did all the fighting on the ground, helped by some well-trained Qataris; the balance was tipped by NATO air power in favour of the opposition forces. UN Security Council Resolution 1973 would never have been brokered without a direct plea for action from the Arab League. Yet the Libyan no-fly zone intervention did show, despite many difficulties, that a citizen army can not only defend themselves but beat back well-equipped forces, if helped by UN authorised air-power that can tilt the balance of fighting on the ground by well-targeted bombing and strafing from the air. But Libya showed once again that, without military intervention on the ground by UN member states' armed forces in addition to help keep the peace, we run a very real risk that only an initial attack with little or no ground involvement produces chaos not peace. How long a period of chaos will follow in Libya, no one knows. It is in this sort of case in the Middle East that the new 'Muslim force' may be helpful in mounting intervention with UN authority on the ground.

Regime change in Libya did not lead to a stable replacement government. While it had been undertaken as an emergency effort to save lives and to respect human rights, there were in effect no peacekeeping troops to stop local groups fighting each other. It may become a democracy, but there is no UN authority to stipulate that a successor regime in Libya must be a democracy, and its future is anything but settled in 2017. The UK must have the courage and coherence not to support this cycle of no-fly zones, no external peacekeeping force and rebel infighting bringing greater chaos. The advocates of following that same pattern over Syria were loud and vigorous but, for a variety of good reasons, they have been correctly overruled. Boris Johnson was brave to risk his reputation by going to Libya in May 2017 to try and boost the somewhat unlikely chance of the meetings between Prime Minister al Sarraj and General Haftar following much welcome diplomacy between the Egyptians and the UAE. A post-Brexit UK must be ready to take risks for peace. Our influence in other richer Arab countries will deepen as we are seen to identify with their problems and show an interest in helping find Arab solutions. Respect can be built up by demonstrating a readiness to get down in the dust and turmoil of much of our modern world. The UK will get a better hearing in Cairo for criticisms of their human rights record after undertaking this visit. As will ideas for how Egypt can help bring peace closer in helping Gaza. We examine policy making in the UK over Libya and Syria in Chapter Four.

As well as the traditional areas of focus of peacekeeping and conflict prevention, one of the major relatively new issues facing the UN is going to be how to ensure effective compliance with the 1982

UN Convention on the Law of the Sea (UNCLOS). This will have an impact on many core policy areas, from global security to global warming, and issues such as fishing rights and conservation. It is very obvious that President Xi Jinping is determined to assert China's claims to disputed islands in the South China Sea (discussed in more detail in Chapter Seven), and China is also becoming more assertive in the East China Sea and in the Pacific. There are also other areas – notably the Polar Regions – in which maritime rights are increasingly an area of focus. Whether in the South China Sea, the Pacific, the Arctic Circle or Antarctica, it is virtually certain that sometime in the next decade, there will be a serious challenge to the UNCLOS, which could – unless handled with great care – result in conflict.

In 2017, the European Parliament made it clear that fishing would be an important element in any Article 50 exit agreement. They would expect their negotiator Michel Barnier to ensure that 'Every agreement that guarantees UK access to the EU domestic market has to guarantee an access to the UK fishing grounds for the EU fleet.' While these specific negotiations are outside the scope of this book, it is clear from what Denmark's Foreign Minister, Anders Samuelson, said that they will invoke the fact that the Danish fishermen have historically been fishing across the North Sea. They plan to use the UN Convention on the Law of the Sea, to which both the UK and Denmark are signatories, which instructs states to respect the 'traditional fishing rights' of adjacent countries within sovereign waters. There is also the London Convention on Fisheries signed in 1964, which also recognises historical rights of access to the waters of the UK. Around 85 per cent of the current catch of the Danish fleet is in UK waters and 80 per cent of the fleet from Normandy.

This EU–UK fishing issue is therefore likely to raise important international legal issues in the North, Celtic and Irish Seas. The British government's position is that leaving the EU is a real opportunity to 'review fisheries management in the UK', and they will be working hard on management issues to achieve the 'best possible deal for the whole of the UK fishing industry'. In 2015, EU vessels caught 683,000 tonnes (£484 million revenue) in UK waters and UK vessels caught 111,000 tonnes (£114 million revenue) in member states' waters.[23]

By 2009, some 157 countries acceded to the Convention, leaving countries that had not acceded bound by the 1958 Geneva Conventions. The new Law of the Sea is based on common sense, since the state's powers and jurisdiction decrease the further one goes out from the coast. There is full territorial sovereignty in what is referred to as internal waters and limited 'acquitorial' sovereignty in what is referred to as the territorial sea, with limited jurisdiction in the exclusive economic zone (EEZ) and continental shelf, which can extend to 200 miles and in special cases 350 miles. There is a UN Commission on the Limits of the Continental Shelf (CLCS). All this is calculated from the mean low-water line. But where there are deep indentations and inlets, the classic example being Norway, or a chain of islands or a big bay, closing lines are drawn. In some cases, shipping lanes can be created by the coastal state. It does not take a genius to realise that this all creates a measure of uncertainty and of contention, particularly for a large country like China that was not fully involved in the international debate while much of this law was created.

There is, in addition, a number of other bodies with sometimes overlapping remits. These include the International Whaling Commission, around which Japan has created an exemption by using the related Convention which allows the killing of whales for scientific purposes. While Japanese whalers hunt in the South Pacific, however, most countries protect whales. Indeed, there is an agreement on the Conservation of Small Cetaceans of the Baltic, North East Atlantic, Irish and North Sea (ASCOBANS); the International Maritime Organization based in London that protects areas of concern against pollution from ships; and the International Seabed Authority, based in Kingston, Jamaica which is responsible for the equitable sharing of deep sea bed mining activities.

On top of this, global warming presents many problems for the marine environment. The melting Arctic ice sheets result in their margins shrinking. Mineral deposits are being newly discovered. We are seeing new sea routes opening up, such as the Northwest Passage and the Northern Sea Route. The Arctic littoral states, US, Russia, Canada, Norway and Denmark, are trying to extend their territories by claiming submerged prolongations, and there are disputes over the continental shelf. The role of plankton becomes important in regulating concentrations of CO_2. The Indo-German 'Lohafex' marine iron fertilisation research project of 2009 involved geo-engineering. People have different views on iron providing plant nutrients,[24] allowing plankton rich in CO_2 to sink to the sea bed.

The UK is well placed to use our limited locus in these maritime areas to help avoid conflict. Accordingly, the UK should build up the necessary legal expertise, knowledge and skills to contribute constructively to the maintenance of peace in these areas surrounding the Law of the Sea. To do so, the UK should establish a UN unit with a special locus on dealing with all aspects of the Sea and the maritime environment generally.

It will be very important to reassess the deployment of FCO diplomatic resources post-Brexit between London and New York, and to deliberately establish new schemes to widen the base of diplomats and allow more of them who have spent a high percentage of their time on EU business to gain UN experience in New York and London. If this distorts global staffing structures for a few years, that is a price worth paying. There was a time in the 1970s when the UN department in the FCO was a major resource for the Foreign Secretary in dealing with UN issues in New York, but it appears this UN oversight has since been cut back far more than is wise. London also has the advantage of a certain distance from the political hothouse atmosphere surrounding the Security Council in New York. Indeed, that distance used to be valued by Foreign Secretaries as they tried to decide both how to vote in the Security Council and how to estimate voting intentions. In this process, where each nation holds its cards close to its chest, it is important to be able to go back to capitals rather than relying solely on New York representatives who do not always reflect their government's innermost considerations.

An increased focus on driving our foreign policy through the framework of the UN, and the Security Council in particular, should not see the UK lessen the importance it gives to other international fora. On security, our leading role in NATO, which we shall come onto in the next chapter, will remain critical, as will the relationship with have with our 'Five Eyes' intelligence sharing partners – Australia, Canada, New Zealand and the United States. Our membership of the G7 and the G20 will remain a key focus for political and particularly economic dialogue, and we should also seek to reinvigorate the relationship with the Commonwealth. Many of our twenty-seven EU partners are also partners in these groupings, notably NATO, and this should ensure we are not perceived to be turning our back on Europe after Brexit, but EU representation will need to be considerably reduced, and there is little if any scope for a '27+1' approach. Experience has shown, agreeing a coherent and effective foreign policy became harder as the EU expanded. In a group of twenty-eight it had become even more challenging, and we should be extremely wary of seeing formalising EU foreign and security policy linkages as worthwhile. Existing structures provide credible fora for continued UK involvement in wider European foreign policy making. After Brexit, we must use our freedom to engage with the appropriate partners for the situation at hand, and as we demonstrate through the book, these will vary according to the circumstances.

Whatever decision is taken on resourcing UN-focused activity, we must maintain our track record of appointing exceptionally talented diplomats as our Permanent Representative in New York. As yet, not a single woman has held that role, but hopefully that will soon happen. The nature of the job requires the holder to establish good working relations with the other four permanent members of the Security Council. The key has been in the past, and will remain for the future, virtually always to work closely on drafting with the French and often the US. We will work closely with the vice president of the Commission in Brussels through our Ambassador to the EU, and that post, along with the Permanent Representatives to the UN and NATO, will remain the top three diplomatic positions for multilateral diplomacy. They will be expected to give a high priority in coordinated action across the UN, NATO and the EU.

They will also be expected to give a high priority to cooperation designed to fulfil the spirit and intent behind the words of Article 8 of the Lisbon Treaty:

1. The Union shall develop a special relationship with neighbouring countries, aiming to establish an area of prosperity and good neighbourliness, founded on the values of the Union and characterised by close and peaceful relations based on cooperation.
2. For the purposes of paragraph 1, the Union may conclude specific agreements with the countries concerned. These agreements may contain reciprocal rights and obligations as well as the possibility of undertaking activities jointly. Their implementation shall be the subject of periodic consultation.

For the next two years we will be operating under Article 50, but that will cease to have any relevance when the UK leaves the EU, no later than March 2019. After Brexit, Article 8 provides the guidelines for developing a continuing special relationship.

The Bruegel Group under the leadership of Jean Pisani-Ferry proposed a 'Continental Partnership', but that title runs into the not inconsequential fact that the UK is not part of continental Europe, and it also is too linked to the Article 50 negotiations. The UK and the EU have to feel their way to building a new relationship and it is premature to fix titles or assume structures. Better to let the situation evolve. One thing is for sure – a relationship between the EU and the UK based on 27 + 1 is not credible.

When the EU foreign ministers were trying to hammer out a policy for Bosnia and Herzegovina in 1994 with the US and Russia, we were both heavily involved in the creation of the Contact Group of the US, UK, Russia, France and Germany. Later Italy was added. The Contact Group concept had first been used in 1978 in the context of negotiations with South Africa over the need for UN monitored elections before bringing South West Africa to independence (as Namibia), as mentioned earlier. Eventually that came twelve years later, in 1990, on the basis of a UN resolution negotiated directly between the US Secretary of State, the British, Canadian and German Foreign Ministers, and a junior French minister, with the President and Foreign Minister of South Africa and its Chief of Defence and Cabinet Secretary. Structures have to adjust to circumstances. Large groups are not suitable for conducting serious business, especially in limited time frames.

What of a post-Brexit world? It would be foolish to pretend it will be much different from what it is now. The international laws and conventions that we have at the start of the twenty-first century are imperfect, but so is the world they seek to improve. They are the product of an emerging, but flawed world. A world that has tried through the UN, since 1945, to become ever-more civilised and coherent, but is facing threats from global issues unforeseen at the UN's birth – such as terrorism, cyber warfare and climate change – that also demand international cooperation to find solutions. A world that has chosen to root itself in the moralities and the cultures of many civilisations that embrace almost all races, religions and creeds. A world that, for all its failings, is an improvement on the world prior to the UN Charter and its first major follow on, the Declaration of Human Rights. A world which can still strive to define a universal and culturally inclusive variant of an enlightened political philosophy. It is a world in which a post-Brexit UK must involve itself more fully, but also recognise and avoid repeating mistakes, particularly those made in Iraq following the invasion in 2003. We need to offset any down-playing of the UN by the Trump administration and if necessary do so with money. We also need to demonstrate, where sensible, a sober evidence-based British commitment to use and build up the authority of the United Nations. While it may not create a very different world, it will prevent a much worse world developing.

CHAPTER 2

THE UK'S ROLE IN
GLOBAL SECURITY

To carry conviction, a realigned global British foreign policy needs to be matched by an appropriate military strategy and the means, in terms of service personnel and equipment, of carrying it out. It is imperative that UK politicians and military leaders undertake a fundamental reassessment of the nation's needs in 2017. With two big defence projects, the Trident nuclear deterrent replacement and the naval aircraft carrier programme, recently reaffirmed by Parliament on a cross-party basis, some major projects will have to be trimmed and the last thing a new global strategy needs is talk of defence cutbacks. To put in place an effective global foreign and defence policy and support a global commercial and trading policy, the UK has to challenge conventional thinking and find mechanisms to fund more for defence. The US Secretary for Defense, Robert Gates, demanded as long ago as May 2009 a shift on defence spending, given the new circumstances of fighting insurgents in messy unconventional wars. This shift would focus spending on mine-resistant vehicles, surveillance drones and medical evacuation-helicopters at the expense of high-cost technically sophisticated weapons such as new tanks, bombers and aircraft carriers. In light of the challenges facing us post-Brexit and our future foreign and defence policy aspirations, it is essential to examine all our options afresh, and make the budgetary commitments required to meet them.

This will be hugely enhanced if there is as great as possible agreement on all aspects of post-Brexit policy amongst the different political parties within the UK. It has been a strength of the conduct of British foreign and security policy over the last century that, for most of this period, we have been able to rely on a broad measure of cross-party support. After the announcement of our withdrawal from East of Suez in 1968, we have slowly returned to the Gulf and fought two wars in and around Iraq and fought in Afghanistan. We have seen NATO transformed to a global alliance and the days of the old NATO wording about 'out of area' deployments are long gone. It is, for example, logical and correct to follow NATO involvement in Iraq with a broader action to deal with ISIS. As a percentage of GDP we now spend, at 2 per cent, far less on defence than we used to do. Yet, as part of our foreign and defence policies, we are facing more challenges, such as defeating ISIS and tackling wider international terrorism.

Professor Christopher Hill, in his 40th Martin Wright Memorial Lecture, writes 'The British discourse, for its part, continues to stress loyalty to NATO before that to the EU. But NATO is not a foreign policy organisation...'[1] In strict terms, that is accurate. Yet its permanent representatives are diplomats and its Secretary Generals have been politicians; the present incumbent Jens Stoltenberg is a former Prime Minister of Norway, his predecessor was the Prime Minister of Denmark and those before him have in the main been either Foreign Ministers or Defence Ministers. NATO's annual meeting is attended by Heads of State and Foreign Ministers. It was backed and supported by a British Foreign Secretary, Ernest Bevin, and blessed by a US Secretary of State, formerly General, George Marshall. Given the present uncertainties in Europe, NATO is a very appropriate forum for the projection of a new British foreign and security policy; not just because the two are inextricably intertwined, but because the single most urgent issue is to bind President Trump's administration into NATO with what Shakespeare graphically called 'hoops of steel'. In that respect, while Trump's selection of senior officials has undoubtedly given rise to controversy, his appointment of Rex Tillerson – who brings extensive experience of dealing with key foreign governments to the role of Secretary of State – and two highly experienced military figures James Mattis as Defense Secretary and Lt

Gen. McMaster as National Security Advisor (replacing Gen. Michael Flynn), are reassuring choices of people of real quality.

CHALLENGES TO NATO

For the first time since the mid-1980s, NATO faces challenges on its own borders, in the north and in the south. In the north, the Russian annexation of Crimea has stirred deep anxieties. Not unreasonably, the most concern is in the Baltic States, and on this there can be no equivocation by NATO. These three countries, Estonia, Latvia and Lithuania are covered, and must continue to be covered, by Article 5 of the NATO Treaty, which involves an automatic commitment to come to the assistance of member countries that are attacked or threatened. Early in 2017 it was confirmed that the US had offered additional safety assurance measures to these countries that were reported to amount to dozens of special-ops soldiers being stationed along Europe's eastern flank. The UK is making its largest long-term deployment to one of Russia's neighbours since the end of the Cold War with an estimated 800 troops with tanks, armoured vehicles and drones in Estonia. An additional 1,200 soldiers, with the vast bulk coming from Germany, but also from Belgium and the Netherlands, are being deployed in Lithuania. Spain is joining a Canadian-led battalion stationed in Latvia. There is a NATO-led Baltic Air Policing mission in which UK Typhoons, flying from the Amari airbase in Estonia, have participated on a rotational basis. These could quickly be deployed if tensions rose further. The US has also deployed F-15s from Lakenheath to Lithuania in the past at the height of the Crimean crisis. In practice, our army must have air support.[2]

In the south, Turkey's NATO membership is complicated by many factors, not least the civil war in Syria and the massive number of Syrian refugees that have crossed into Turkey. This means it has become in more direct contact with Russia than before. Russian–Turkish relations deteriorated after Turkey shot down a Russian aircraft infringing their air space in November 2015. It was very necessary for Russia to be in no doubt that Turkey invoking Article 5 of the NATO Treaty if they were to be attacked would be honoured by the rest of NATO. The relationship between Turkey and Russia has subsequently stabilised and by 2017 had become much closer: a welcome change. Turkey's relationship with its NATO allies has not been straight forward, as internal political issues often come to the fore. This has seen, for example, very heated and public exchanges between the Dutch and Turkish governments following an incident when Turkish ministers were prevented from entering the Netherlands at the time of the Dutch elections, to campaign on behalf of President Erdoğan's domestic policies. There have also been tensions on military questions, such as the use of İncirlik airbase, which is one of the main NATO bases involved in the campaign against ISIS which also has US nuclear weapons based there. The replacement of a large number of Turkish officers based at NATO HQ, some of whom had supported the attempted coup in 2016, has complicated this relationship.

The UK is right to see Turkey as an important partner, in terms of being both a NATO ally and a country with whom we have had longstanding and good relations. They know we value their alliance membership and bilateral relations. So coming out of the EU means the UK can offer an attractive bilateral relationship free from the tensions that Turkey has being only an associate member of the EU with little chance of becoming a full member. Prime Minister May's visit to meet President Erdoğan in Turkey in January 2017 was an important step in building this relationship, following on from one of the earliest foreign visits taken by Foreign Secretary Boris Johnson in 2016. Both visits were public opportunities for flagging up Turkey as a UK foreign policy priority and an important trading partner. This was evidenced by the signing of a modest sale of planes, the offer of British economic engagement and a future trade deal. Another key aspect which will require engagement is Cyprus. In the immediate circumstances of the Turkish constitutional referendum it was inevitable there would be a stalling of negotiations which were controversial within Turkey. A vital British task is to keep Turkey positive about a Cyprus settlement and, since Erdoğan has won the divisive vote allowing him to become executive President, ensure that he exerts his authority in favour of an agreement over Cyprus which will open up cooperation over oil and gas exploration in the surrounding seas.

Yet the human rights situation in Turkey, which the Prime Minister raised on her visit, and the increasingly autocratic style of government are making it harder to sustain public support in the UK for warmer relations with Turkey, and that means patiently explaining that as a large Muslim nation, it is a very important strategic partner, both inside and outside of NATO. Fortunately, the British public have long experience of weighing up these sorts of complex international issues if given a sensible lead. There is, for many on the left in Britain concerned about human rights, a salutary lesson from the period of the Greek junta of 1967–74. The then Labour government faced a difficult choice over whether to support Greece remaining in NATO, but Harold Wilson was clear; it was better they remained in NATO, allowing British soldiers and diplomats to use every contact – discreet or otherwise – to maintain contact. Portugal in 1967 was still under the dictatorship of Salazar, who died in 1968, only to be succeeded by another dictator, Caetano, but remained in NATO. Shortly after Labour came back into government in 1974 there was a coup in Lisbon and a junta was formed by seven officers. They were predominantly Marxists. Foreign Secretary Jim Callaghan had close links with a fellow socialist Mario Soares, who became Portuguese Foreign Minister in in the military-controlled provisional government. On 1 August 1975, after the Helsinki CSCE meeting, senior European social democrats Wilson, Callaghan, Brandt, Schmidt, Mitterrand, Craxi and Kreisky met with Soares in Stockholm and a robust line was established to protect socialist colleagues in Portugal from either communism or fascism. The US were pessimistic over saving democracy and it was Callaghan's achievement – with covert military assistance and direct talks with the military officer Ernesto Antunes who succeeded Saores as Foreign Minister – to maintain a semblance of democracy which held and developed. He also convinced Kissinger. In government, the Labour Party in the UK and the SPD in Germany were critical in holding the line and paving the way for Greece and Portugal (and Spain) to come into the EU.[3]

During all this time, there were many critics on the left concerned about human rights as they are rightly now over Turkey but the case for continued membership of NATO remains a sound one. While left opinion disliked the Greek military rule intensely and wanted Greece to be expelled from NATO, the successful transition to democracy under Prime Minister Karamanlis in 1974 was quicker and easier to accomplish because the Greek military, and particularly those in touch with other NATO officers, used their influence to return the country to democracy and quietly helped that process. NATO membership outlasts the span of power of individual politicians, and provides a critical democratic mooring in times of strain and stress.

By contrast, in central Europe, NATO politicians did not help the growth of stable democracies by frequently saying they wanted to expand NATO's borders to Georgia and Ukraine. It was an unwise commitment given the long history of many people in those countries with Russia. In effect it has had to be quietly dropped. Nor did it help when a NATO spokesperson writing to *The Guardian* on 5 March 2015[4,5] misquoted Mikhail Gorbachev in support of her contention that the Alliance gave no commitment not to take in new members. The question of expanding NATO even further than East Germany did not arise in 1990–91, because, as Gorbachev wrote, 'not a single east European country suggested it, even after the demise of the Warsaw pact in 1991. Western leaders didn't raise the issue either.' From 1993 Gorbachev criticised NATO expansion. Gorbachev's analysis of the present crisis in European relations is:

> One of its causes, though not the only one, is the unwillingness of our Western partners to take account of Russia's point of view, legitimate interests and security. Verbally, they applauded Russia, especially during the Yeltsin years, but in deeds they took no account of it. I am thinking mainly of NATO's enlargement, the plans to deploy a missile shield, and the West's actions in areas important to the Russian

Federation (Yugoslavia, Iraq, Georgia, Ukraine). They literally told us: 'It's not your business.' As a result an abscess built up, and burst.

That burst abscess has yet to subside. John Simpson, the hugely experienced BBC world affairs editor, wrote about a chilling story of how the Russian ambassador to Denmark, as recently as 21 March 2015, challenged in a Danish newspaper the Danish government policy. 'I don't think that Danes fully understand the consequences if Denmark joins the American-led missile defence shield ... If they do, then Danish warships will be targets for Russian nuclear missiles...'[6] However, whatever the provocation as seen by either side, to try to cast the present situation with Russia as a return to the old days of the Soviet Union at the height of its Cold War powers is both premature and fatalistic, as we discuss further in Chapter Five.

Nevertheless, holding the US to their NATO commitment to come to the defence of any other NATO country under Article 5 of its founding treaty is the priority for the UK's foreign and defence policy. All other UK military deployments around the globe are secondary and that has to be faced. The size of the UK's defence budget and cost of nuclear deterrent are matters we must be ready to discuss fully and frankly with the US, as we have done in the past. We need to be convinced that our defence spending priorities are the correct ones. In 2017 we face a possible request to keep forces in Afghanistan. We need to decide with the US whether this really is a priority for the UK. The UK withdrew combat troops in 2014. Some 450 stayed in a support mission and in July 2016 that was increased from 450 to 500, all of whom are due to leave soon. If the US attaches great importance to our doing this for their NATO purposes, or other reasons, we should carefully weigh up the implications of continuing our involvement, but one only has to read *A Kingdom of their Own* to realise the depths of the corruption and the economic crisis in Afghanistan since 2014. The large US withdrawal of troops, and the fact that the shared power between Ghani and Abdullah is not functioning, leads to questioning whether another significant military deployment is justified.[7] Past tolerance of corruption under

Hamid Karzai has left its legacy too. But the real problem is Pakistan continuing to support the Taliban; while that goes on NATO's task is impossible. When NATO went in, it hoped US and UK influence in Pakistan would enforce a change of attitude but that has not come about. President Trump should confront Pakistan for one last time, and make clear that without their commitment to support NATO's efforts to restore stability in Afghanistan, there will not be support for further engagement. Otherwise we should stick to withdrawal and not maintain a hopeless mission for fear of more refugees into Europe.

In assessing what a global UK can take on in 2017 we must not forget that at the end of the Cold War in 1989–90, the UK had some 306,000 regular servicemen as well as 340,000 reserves. The army alone had 153,000, with three armoured divisions and an infantry division, including 1,330 main battle tanks. The Royal Navy had some fifty principal surface combat ships, including two carriers, together with twenty-eight attack submarines, two squadrons of Harriers and a marine commando brigade. The RAF fielded twenty-six operational fast jet squadrons, eleven reserve squadrons and a full complement of early-warning, intelligence gathering, transport, helicopter and maritime patrol squadrons.

Nor should we forget how well the collapse of the Berlin Wall went financially for NATO countries. We in the UK felt able to relatively safely slash our defence budgets. Those reductions to our conventional forces, however, went too far and need redressing in present circumstances, with the Russians building up their military capabilities. It has become very unclear whether the government is likely to retain a previous plan for the British Army to be reduced to 82,000 troops. *The Times* on 3 June 2017 had a story that the number could fall to as few as 65,000.[8] Others have claimed it could be between 60,000 and 70,000. A reassessment after the election seems likely. But the army was cut substantially in 2010 and 2011 from 102,000 – France has an army of 109,000. *The Times* in an editorial of the same date noted: 'The global projection of power is not a luxury for a country so dependent on the stability of trading routes and international commerce. Brexit will make this more important than ever.' We are in no doubt, as the rest of this chapter underlines, that a post-election review of the 2015 Strategic Defence and Security Review is essential.

The UK government is committed to NATO's 2 per cent of GDP defence spending target through to 2022. This is not enough. We believe, as argued later in this chapter, that figure should rise to 2.5 per cent by 2022 to ease the pressure on maintaining our conventional forces at an adequate level, though we recognise that it will probably have to be raised gradually. To do this, besides changing our spending priorities across the international spending budget, as overseen by the NSC (see Chapter Four), we need to spend on defence in a way that makes the best sense to the US, whose defence expenditure effectively represents around 72 per cent of the defence spending of the NATO alliance as a whole. We are very close to losing critical mass as a nation with our defence forces. With hard-headed vigilance over rising costs in 2017, a post-Brexit British government committed to deep-seated cooperation within NATO can establish a better balance. Nevertheless, there has to be some more money made available. This could perhaps be reassessed when all NATO members have reached the 2 per cent guideline, and, if the Russian Federation cuts back its very considerable increase in defence spending, perhaps as part of an agreement with the US. For the present we are grappling with an emergency in European NATO defence spending and there is no credible way of escaping our responsibility to, as the Americans would say, 'step up to the plate'.

THE UK'S NUCLEAR DETERRENT

At NATO's summit meeting in Warsaw in June 2012, our NATO allies made clear that by maintaining our independent nuclear deterrent alongside the US and France, the UK provides NATO with three separate centres of decision-making and that complicates the calculations of potential adversaries and prevents them threatening the UK or our allies with impunity. We in the UK have always seen our independent deterrent as inextricably linked to NATO's deterrent. That is how the US sees it too and it binds us into NATO's strategy in a way that no words could. Nevertheless, the cost of renewal is putting the defence budget over the next decade under great strain.

When Prime Minister Theresa May met President Trump in Washington on 26–27 January 2017, she would, if following past practice, have reaffirmed existing US/UK understandings over nuclear policy. This is a policy that has been followed ever since Prime Minister Clement Attlee met with President Truman on 7 December 1950 in Washington during the Korean War. At such meetings, new Prime Ministers can raise privately with the President many issues surrounding the British nuclear deterrent and its relationship to the nuclear and conventional weapons strategy of NATO. That dialogue is not pressing, but it needs to take place.

There is no predisposition in the UK government or amongst the vast majority of MPs, including Labour, to want to make economies on the nuclear deterrent, and this emerged strongly in the June 2017 general election. That and the overwhelming vote in the House of Commons makes it impossible post-Brexit to propose savings by going from four boats to three, even though there are arguments for this economy. The current cost of the new Dreadnought-class submarines (SSBNs), with intercontinental nuclear armed ballistic missiles (ICBM), is £31 billion with £10 billion in additional contingencies. The appointment of Treasury official Julian Kelly to take control of this budget is welcome, because it is essential this programme stays on budget. But while in the 2016 plan the overall MOD budget had £10.7 billion 'headroom' built in, the 2017 plan, according to a story in the *Financial Times*, has drawn down the entire amount.[9] In addition, there was another worrying reported cost overrun last year at the Rolls Royce facility in Derby where the nuclear reactors are built for the submarines, totalling £249 million.[10] These spiralling costs cannot be contained just by delaying other key programmes' delivery dates. There would have to be more realism and some damaging cancellations which would impact on our capacity to carry out new foreign policies.

Another aspect of the deterrent is the Atomic Weapons Establishment (AWE) at Aldermaston. Here the story is a good one. Cooperation with the US has vastly improved since the time of the 1958 Mutual Defence Agreement (MDA) between Lawrence Livermore National Laboratory, California, and Los Alamos in New Mexico. The process of collaboration has moved considerably in the UK's favour over nearly six decades. AWE's work is now at the cutting-edge of nuclear warhead design and development, and it is conducted with the benefit of exchanges on specific issues with the American nuclear weapons facilities, along with a small number of civilian contractors. These exchanges at the technical 'working level' were conducted through Anglo-American Joint Working Groups (JOWOGs), created through the 1958 MDA.* Following the 1963 Polaris Sales Agreement (PSA), these activities became linked to the strategic nuclear weapons programmes of the US Navy and their Special Projects Office (SPO) – now the Strategic Systems Project Office – through the Department of Defense, Atomic Energy Commission and Lockheed Missile and Space Company – the manufacturers of Polaris, Poseidon and Trident.† The 1959 follow-on agreement to the MDA made available Special Nuclear Materials, such as Tritium, which the US supplied to the UK and which have periodically taken place as 'barter arrangements' whereby the UK supplies the US Atomic Energy Commission with highly enriched uranium or plutonium, and the US supplies the UK with Special Nuclear Materials. Ultimately the MDA has been the enabler for the transfer of nuclear warhead designs and techniques between the US and UK and has meant Britain has been able to test

---

* The Joint Working Groups (JOWOGs) had first been set up as part of the 1958 MDA along with the Joint Atomic Energy Information Group (JAEIG), which provided a mechanism for passing information along with regular 'Stocktakes' or Reviews. These ensured that everyone employed in each specialist area worked to mutual advantage. Although the MDA was published as a government Command Paper the substance of the agreement remained hidden in a series of classified annexes. The same was also true for the 1959 US/UK agreement relating to nuclear materials and the specific terms of the 'barter exchanges' under the MDA. TNA, PREM 13/3129, S. Zuckerman to Prime Minister, 16 December 1964.

† Now Lockheed Martin. As with the UK effort, a large number of both government and private contractors each played a part.

devices at the Nevada Test Site. This collaboration could go much further now, even in the area of warheads.

US and UK exchanges are becoming, and should become ever more so, a two-way street. We see this over the Joint Strike Fighter production. It is time to finally put aside memories of the drying-up of information exchanges that took place in the 1950s and the problems over UK nuclear explosive testing between 1965 and 1973. The UK–US nuclear relationship is sustained by the UK being able to offer the US unique alternative technical pathways to develop and produce future nuclear weapons. This was one of the driving forces following the costly Chevaline programme and the later UK exploration of new ways to trigger a thermonuclear explosion through its Nessel test in Nevada in August 1979. This two-way series of exchanges from AWE and elsewhere to the US labs and nuclear weapons facilities helped enable the US to transfer technology for MIRV warheads. The MDA is dovetailed with the Polaris Sales Agreement and the 1980 and 1982 agreements to supply Trident and its associated technology and will be crucial considerations to all successor systems. Whether over Trident missiles, or the Dreadnought SSBNs, or other expensive equipment there is a future for more cooperation with the US and AWE is a shining example of the way to go.

On supersonic Cruise missiles and stealth technology, we know that the US Department of Defense is designing a new air-launched Cruise missile. The US Air Force's Long-Range Standoff (LRSO) weapon system is designed to be capable of penetrating and surviving advanced Integrated Air Defense Systems (IADS) from significant standoff range and hit strategic targets in support of the air force's global strike capability and strategic deterrence core function. Such a missile may be of considerable interest to the UK. The US, as is clear from the past, is likely to want to strike a bargain over waiving of costs involving nuclear equipment in favour of improving UK conventional forces for NATO.

There may come a time in relation to Scotland when it might be helpful if Britain could share even more US based facilities for Trident missiles including storage of our nuclear warheads, since we already participate in an ongoing rotation of missiles with the US Navy, whereby the missiles are less expensive for not being earmarked. Sharing facilities and dual use are all essential contributors to cost effectiveness. The complete independence of the British nuclear deterrent submarines on patrol stems from their command and control procedures; whether we are sharing manufacture and storage facilities in the US has become irrelevant.

No one can begin to consider the nuclear dialogue with Washington over the next few decades without studying the evolution of the agreements covering conventional defence made in the past with the US over, first, Polaris and then Trident. The UK has never had to pay the full development costs of either the Polaris or Trident ballistic weapon system and, in terms of value for money, we have been very generously treated by the US. At times the US has reasonably bargained a conventional military price for giving the UK access to their huge investment in nuclear deterrence. The Chevaline experience of going it alone in the UK in the 1970s over nuclear warhead development must never be repeated. The reality is that keeping in step with American developments is to be the guiding principle of UK–US nuclear deterrent procurement policy. It is a challenging thought but no one should preclude consideration of having some conventional warheads on supersonic, stealth technology Cruise missiles deployed on our SSBNs at some stage in the future. Dedicated submarines for nuclear deterrence alone may be a luxury we cannot afford. Of course, the SSBNs will continue to be deployed to hide virtually motionless in the oceans of the world, but in an emergency, to know that in a remote part of the world we have a conventional capacity available might make it easier to live with fewer nuclear powered submarines equipped with conventional warheads (SSNs). We have to encourage new thinking across the board on our total nuclear submarine spend.

The deal reached with Harold Brown, US Defense Secretary, and Margaret Thatcher in No. 10 on 2 June 1980 is worth examining for what may follow in 2018 or 2019. The US had agreed to waive the bulk of pro rata research and development costs of the Trident missiles in exchange for greater American usage for military purposes of the island Diego Garcia in the Indian Ocean. Britain paid a nominal $100 million towards R&D costs and agreed to cover the cost of manning air defence systems at US bases in the UK.

Then in August 1981 the new US Defense Secretary, under President Reagan, informed the UK that they had finally decided to upgrade the C-4 submarine launched ICBMs to the D-5. The cost of D-5 was raised by Thatcher with Reagan on 1 February 1982 and it was clear the administration wanted to help. Keeping within the US legal require-ment that development costs could only be waived in the national interest on 11 March 1982, before the Falklands War, Britain agreed to maintain a stronger naval capability than had been envisaged in John Nott's initial defence cuts and, in exchange for a waiver for the R&D costs of D-5, the Royal Navy would keep their amphibious capability with HMS *Fearless* and *Intrepid*. Margaret Thatcher was also prepared, in principle, to reduce to the minimum the number of missiles and warheads on our SSBNs.[11,12]

All this focus on equipment means little unless we also understand the basis for our nuclear deterrence strategy, an area on which there is much ignorance despite heated debates over the years. In 1977–79 under Prime Minister Callaghan, there was the most intensive debate about what constituted a minimum nuclear deterrent and whether we needed our own ballistic missile capabilities.[13] An argument was that it would be sufficient for a minimum deterrent to target Soviet cities with Cruise missiles, a counter value targeting strategy, rather than having the capability to attack Moscow itself. Attacking Moscow required being able to penetrate their anti-ballistic missile (ABM) defences, which Cruise missiles were not capable of doing. No decision was taken by that Labour government but, under Margaret Thatcher, the deci-sion was taken to replace Polaris with Trident, another ballistic missile system, and retain the capacity to penetrate ABM defences, which were still deployed around Moscow. We have in effect repeated that decision between 2006 and 2016 under Labour and Conservative governments.

In early 2009 the late Michael Quinlan, a former senior MOD civil servant and expert on the UK's nuclear strategy, published *Thinking about Nuclear Weapons*.[14] In it, he revealed that 'the most explicit conceptual account of what it was thought during the Cold War that the UK nuclear strategic nuclear force should be able to do is to be found in Defence Open Government Document 80/23 of July 1980'.[15] This probably remains the concept behind the UK deterrence in 2017.

Quinlan emphasised in his book that in paragraph twelve of the Open Document, the phrase 'threat to key aspects of Soviet state power' was of particular significance, though public commentary mostly did not pick this up. For a small country like the UK, which cannot survive – in any true sense of the word – even one significant nuclear strike, the vital need in deterring a first strike is to let any adversary know from the outset that they will pay a massive retaliatory price following any first strike. Quinlan says UK strategy shifted in July 1980 to 'counter force targets': in effect, military targets. That meant hitting Moscow. This was therefore very different from the 'counter value' targeting of cities without ABM defences. The 1978 Duff-Mason Report (withheld for many years), which examined 'counter force' and 'counter value', is described in *The Silent Deep*.[16]

The phrase 'key aspects of Soviet state power', used in the 1980 Open Document, was shorthand for the UK's ability to hit Moscow and thus to put at risk the capacity of the Soviet state to function, including – depending on the thickness of the concrete of their underground bunkers or their dispersal arrangements – the chances of survival of its leadership. If one is to use the word 'moral' in relation to targeting policy (a usage on which it is reasonable to have considerable reservations), it can be argued that the key criteria is that those who make the decision to attack another country with nuclear weapons should know that where they live could be targeted.

The White Paper of December 2006 judged that 'no state currently has both the intent and the capability to pose a direct nuclear threat to the United Kingdom or its vital interests'. But it offered three generic future scenarios in which the possession by Britain of a nuclear deterrent force would be relevant. These are the risk that 'a major direct nuclear threat to the UK's vital interests will re-emerge', a likely reference then to the Russian Federation; the risk that 'new states will emerge that possess a more limited nuclear capability', a likely reference to what we see now in North Korea. The other risk was that 'some countries might in future seek to sponsor terrorism from their soil'. By any standards, this is a more dubious linkage to justify the use of nuclear weapons. For a British national deterrent to be credible, the 2006 White Paper said the force needs to be invulnerable to preemption; that its range should be 'anywhere in the world'; and that the judgement of the minimum destructive capability necessary requires 'an assessment of the decision-making processes of future potential aggressors and an analysis of the effectiveness of the defensive measures that they might employ'.

To deter a decision to authorise a first nuclear strike best means that the leader threatening the UK with such a nuclear weapons attack should fear that they personally will be targeted in retaliation and that there is a likelihood, even if they have ABM defences around their capital, they may be penetrated by such a retaliation. Even if they are personally confident their ABM defences will work to save their lives, ruthless politicians want to stay in power and they know this is difficult if large numbers of the people they rule have been killed by a nuclear attack on their larger cities. Given the relatively small gains from hitting the UK with nuclear weapons, in terms of strategic balance they have to believe that it is not worth even contemplating since there is a very high chance of millions of their people in large cities, not necessarily their capital, being killed after they have launched an attack on the UK. These are deadly but in essence simple concepts to grasp. They are not offensive but defensive. The fact the capability exists is important as we reconsider the global role that has existed since the late 1940s to the present day.

It must never be forgotten that what constitutes nuclear deterrence is a political, not a military, decision. It is a fact that at an MOD meeting on 27 May 1976, it was suggested that rather than targeting ten cities in the then USSR, as we were doing already, five cities would be sufficient until the Chevaline programme was finished in the early 1980s, because of the inability of our then Polaris missile to penetrate

Moscow's ABM defences. It was felt at that time five cities could fulfil the criteria of minimum deterrence facing the USSR. Admiral Sir Edward Ashmore, the Chief of the Naval Staff, then wisely reminded the group that what 'constituted a credible development was political'.[17]

The political case is described by Tony Blair as what lay behind the 2006 White Paper:

> I could see clearly the force of the common sense and practical argument against Trident, yet in the final analysis I thought giving it up too big a downgrading of our status as a nation and in an uncertain world too big a risk for our defence. I did not think this was a 'tough on defence' versus 'weak or pacifist' issue at all. On simple pragmatic grounds, there was a case either way. The expense is huge, and the utility in a post-Cold War world is less in terms of deterrence, and non-existent in terms of military use.[18]

The fact that President Putin has admitted that he considered putting Russian nuclear forces on full alert at the time of maximum tension over Crimea shows it is unwise to assume that Russian nuclear strategies are anywhere near the same as ours. It is also a salutary fact that the nuclear threat has not gone away since the fall of the Berlin Wall. What is happening in North Korea is a powerful reminder of that reality. It is true that President Putin has already threatened to base nuclear forces in the Crimea and has deployed missiles capable of carrying nuclear warheads in Kaliningrad, the Russian enclave on the Baltic Sea that neighbours Poland and Lithuania. Nevertheless, the might of the USSR far outweighs that of the Russian Federation.

The most concerning wording in the 2006 White Paper when listing 'five enduring principles' is the third: '[a] continuing policy of strategic ambiguity regarding potential employment including the potential for first use'. In a speech in 2007, the then Labour Defence Secretary wisely pulled back on this wording and said that the British government 'would only consider using nuclear weapons in the most extreme situations of self-defence'.[19] This is legal wording covering the

United Kingdom in terms of international law, but also wiser wording. Threatening first use has no moral basis, nor strategic value. It should be erased not just from the vocabulary but from our strategic thinking. Ambiguity has its merits, but first use of nuclear weapons should not be one of them. It is doubtful, however, that many MPs in 2006 had any idea that they were endorsing first use. It can be argued that Russian strategy today envisages the first use of nuclear weapons in Europe, not just because they say so but because of their field planning and exercising.

But of more relevant concern is the growth of the belief amongst informed military opinion that Russian conventional forces are now able to punch a hole in NATO's conventional defences, particularly in the Baltic region. This is the case for increased NATO defence spending; to allow that new feature to consolidate would lead to a risk that NATO would be forced to make a choice over resorting to nuclear weapons at a far earlier stage than hitherto. It is essential that the UK puts money and effort into examining deterrence in its modern setting and its relationship to cyber warfare. It is very welcome that a further £6.4 billion has been added from the new cross-departmental budget, the Joint Security Fund. Cyber warfare accounts for the information systems spending, rising from £18.9 billion to £23.5 billion in the 2017 MOD long term budget.

The Sixth US Strategic Command Deterrence Symposium on 27–28 July 2016[20] looked at deterrence in its widest context. One conclusion of the symposium was that 'space is not deterred in space and cyber is not deterred in cyber, they must be considered in conjunction'. It claimed that the US 2010 Nuclear Posture Review had changed to focus more on deterrence than arms control and that the deterrence environment is much more complex since the end of the Cold War. Russia's approach to international relations and hybrid warfare is designed to stretch consensus in the Alliance. As an example, in the context of arms control, the Russian perception is that there is domestic pressure in some NATO members for disarmament, which tends to encourage the West to offer inducements, without any Russian reciprocation. The symposium saw hybrid warfare – characterised by misinformation, unconventional activity and ambiguity – as designed to be kept below the threshold which would involve conventional conflict, and carefully planned to avert state conflict, but supportive of an overall strategy.

As an aside, in an interesting assessment of counter terrorism, they stress it requires positive solutions, in the sense of continued economic and social solutions – which ties in with the arguments discussed in Chapter Three on supporting fragile states – rather than negative solutions such as imposed security restraints. They also conclude that we need a wider understanding of security: food, energy and offensive cyber usage, which they see as the weapon of the twenty-first century. In a section on the 'Deterrence of Violent Extremist Organizations' they assert they are not irrational and 'we might need to lose something of ourselves' in order to defeat them. This is a profound thought, and one to which politicians and diplomats, as well as military commanders, should give time for consideration.

The other response to President Putin's Russia, and it must not be shelved or derided, is to start a fresh dialogue in an attempt, which is by no means a forlorn one, that we can return to the situation we were in prior to 2013. Like others, we consider that date does mark a threshold for Putin's own attitudes, returning to the Presidency for a third term.

Despite Britain's commitment, as a nuclear weapon state signatory to the 1968 Non-Proliferation Treaty (NPT), to the eventual abandonment of all nuclear weapons, which we must pursue, it is wise for Britain in 2017 to continue as a nuclear weapon state, given our uneasy relations with some of the countries that possess or have access to nuclear weapons. In his well-researched book on Britain, the USA, NATO and nuclear weapons across the period 1976–83, Kristan Stoddart states about present thinking: 'the reasons for retention of the strategic nuclear capability provided by Trident emphasise that although the deterrence effect of nuclear weapons has diminished since the end of the Cold War the future remains uncertain.'[21]

Pakistan, China and India have all declared themselves nuclear states. Pakistan, helped by China to develop their nuclear weapons, today faces huge challenges from Taliban forces inside their own country and there are real concerns about the security of their nuclear weapons. It has been reported that the Pakistan nuclear programme was largely paid for by Saudi Arabia, and that nuclear weapons could be quickly made available to the Saudi government by Pakistan, though Saudi Arabia is a signatory of the NPT.[22] Israel is a technically undeclared nuclear weapon state, though its possession of nuclear weapons is widely reported. Iran can hopefully be held off acquiring nuclear weapons. The permanent five on the UN Security Council plus Germany (P5+1) achieved something very worthwhile in extraordinarily difficult circumstances in negotiating with Iran over halting its nuclear weapons programme. With the Middle East as unstable as it is currently, it would do great damage for President Trump to tear up this agreement as one of no value, while the independent assessment remains that Iran is respecting their signature and that there are no violations. It was a good sign that President Rouhani won re-election with 57 per cent of the vote in May 2017, the same time that President Trump chose Saudi Arabia as his first country to visit. Rouhani made clear his desire to re-engage with the West, saying 'today the world knows that Iranians have chosen the path of interaction with the world away from extremism and violence'.[23] Iran has to address strategic concerns about their roles in Yemen and in Lebanon. They must become part of the dialogue over the Middle East, whether in Iraq, in Syria or over ISIS. It does not make sense to isolate Iran after this victory. A Sunni–Shia conflict is preventable. But Rouhani has to be bolder now in curbing the military and the place to start that is Yemen, for it is there, rather than in Lebanon, that Iran is dealing directly with Saudi Arabia. At present, the Saudi Deputy Crown Prince, Mohammed bin Salman, rejects talking to Iran and has said explicitly: 'we will not wait until the battle is in Saudi Arabia. Instead we'll work so that the battle is for them in Iran'.[24] The visit of President Trump to Saudi Arabia is likely to mean a new readiness for the Saudis to help Egypt and engage on the Arab–Israel dispute. Here

Rouhani has to engage with Iraq to be constructive players over Syria and Lebanon.

The key military countries in the region are Iran, Israel and Saudi Arabia. In the post-Second World War period the challenge was to keep the Shah of Iran and the King of Saudi Arabia on speaking terms. Hard to achieve, but, for most of the time, that was successful until the Shah was ousted in 1979. The challenge for the UK is now to do everything we can to encourage the Trump administration to hold open the possibility of eventually talking with Iran (see Chapter Six). We will be in a far better position to do this if we are strengthening our defences and ready in a very difficult expenditure climate to find more money for NATO responsibilities.

In terms of nuclear weapons, the biggest challenge facing world leaders and, in particular, President Trump is the North Korean missile development which may very soon be able to strike North America. North Korea has withdrawn from the NPT. It is the only country in the world to have tested nuclear weapons this century, and has ballistic missile technology capable of carrying a nuclear weapon. What it has not developed, but is believed to be close to doing so, is a sufficiently miniaturised nuclear warhead which could be carried on a missile capable of reaching the USA. North Korea is, in all likelihood, developing a submarine-launch capability. No global deterrence strategy can any longer avoid facing the danger North Korea represents. It is credible that President Xi will decide that China must do more to control North Korea's activities in this area, but China's actions alone will not be enough. The Washington-based Institute for Science and International Security estimates that North Korea has fissile material sufficient to produce more than a dozen nuclear weapons[25] which it may be able to put on its long-range ballistic missile that can certainly reach Japan. We in the UK cannot, therefore, ignore what is happening in North Korea and indeed what could happen. We saw in Pakistan in the 1970s and 1980s how a country can allow its own experts to transfer their nuclear technology and expertise for money to other countries. The North Korean leader is quite capable of giving away nuclear technology or, more likely, weapons to what we would regard as terrorist organisations. President Trump rightly put these issues squarely to President Xi personally at their meeting in April 2017 in Florida, and the fact that China, in a unanimous Security Council vote on 2 June, supported extending UN sanctions against North Korea is a positive sign. With the election of new President Moon Jae-in in South Korea, there may be a window of opportunity for addressing the situation in a different way. In contrast with his predecessor, President Moon has spoken in favour of dialogue with the North, while still strongly criticising the North's nuclear programme. A joint strategy fully endorsed by all the key parties, which, as in the case of the negotiations with Iran, offers a combination of stick and carrot, would be a major achievement, and so time devoted to this is very necessary, rather than accept unilateral American action as inevitable. In this regard, we must engage more with Japan and South Korea, encouraging them to hold a fresh dialogue with the North.

The UK itself had in the past an opportunity to champion small but significant steps as an existing nuclear weapon state to strengthen the NPT, by taking our minimum deterrent further down that scale while retaining credibility. We have been doing this under successive governments, including that of Margaret Thatcher, in terms of megatonnage. We may still be able to justify doing more with the Dreadnought, building three rather than four, but for the present we are bound to proceed under existing plans, while not ruling out eventually building three. To go to three would also be a significant step in NPT terms but while relations with North Korea, and even Russia, remain uncertain, we are wise to continue to keep our options open.

To those who believe that there can be no progress when it comes to reducing nuclear arsenals, the Cuban missile crisis in 1962 still represents the most compelling case as to why we need more reductions and more safety regarding nuclear weapons.

We now know how dangerous the situation became. On 26 October 1962, Soviet troops in Cuba moved three FKR Cruise missiles with fourteen kiloton nuclear warheads to within 25 km of the US naval base at Guantanamo Bay. On the morning of Saturday 27 October, Secretary of Defense, Robert McNamara, asked what the Chiefs of Staff had in mind when they wrote about 'early and timely execution' of the air strike plan against Cuba. The US Air Force chief, General Curtis LeMay, gruffly replied: 'Attacking Sunday [next day] or Monday'. Fortunately, Khrushchev had already sent an urgent cable to the Soviet commander in Cuba: 'It is categorically confirmed that it is forbidden to use nuclear weapons from the missiles, FKRs and Lunas without approval from Moscow. Confirm receipt.'[26] Also fortunately, as already mentioned, President Kennedy handled the whole crisis with great skill and was ready to promise to remove US nuclear weapons targeted at Russia from Turkey if Khrushchev complied with his demands over Cuba and remained doing so for at least six months.

When former Republican leaders of the quality of Henry Kissinger and George Shultz argue today for a process of eventual elimination of nuclear missiles, President Trump should listen and act on their advice. In that process, missile defence may, if the technology further improves, very likely be the essential stepping-stone towards the long-term goal of elimination of nuclear weapons. This aspiration needs champions today in the US amongst the realist school of politicians; hopefully, the fact that Reagan embraced it should help Trump to do likewise. After the allegations over Russian interference in the US Presidential elections of November 2016, there is a danger that no dialogue takes place between Putin and Trump, though wisely they were talking over Syria in May 2017. At this stage, it is not possible to know where the Trump administration will end up but the UK can at least encourage, not distance itself from, Presidential engagement with Russia. Also, it is important that the process of law, not congressional partisanship, is used to settle the allegations and counter allegations about the extent of any Russian interference. The appointment of Robert Mueller as special counsel to investigate provides for the process of law and illustrates again the underlying strength of the US constitution.

There are some other strategic nuclear questions that need attention in NATO. It could not have been foreseen in its final communique

issued by NATO after the December 1996 Summit, that a deterioration in relations with Russia after President Yeltsin left office would
happen later in President Putin's period in office. Today, tensions are
higher but that can and may well improve, though it may take some
time. Hopefully, British Prime Ministers and officials are, even in
these difficult times, going to make clear Britain's continued support
for that part of the 1996 NATO communique which argued that there
is 'no reason to deploy nuclear weapons on the territory of new members.'[27] Effort needs to be put in with the Trump administration so that
this policy should remain. But it may be necessary to change some
other aspects – not just air force-related UK and NATO nuclear policy
in which the Trump administration's attitudes will be important.

The 2012 Chicago NATO Summit controversially agreed to continue
the Dual-Capable Aircraft (DCA), which is capable of carrying nuclear
and conventional weapons. The attempted coup in Turkey in July 2016
involved a number of officers stationed at the base where the nuclear
weapons for such aircraft are housed, and this may prove to complicate continued deployment. Nevertheless, the fact that the US nuclear
bombs are being updated and a new Joint Strike Fighter (JSF) aircraft
is being built provide important background context with regards to
satisfying the genuine concerns of the Baltic States, as well as those
of the Central and East European members of NATO. Reshaping and
developing a new NATO nuclear strategy may require re-examining
whether RAF Lakenheath in Suffolk should share NATO hosting of
US aircraft with the planned B61–12 free-fall nuclear bombs, along
with the Italian air base at Aviano – particularly if Turkey is not to
continue to host as had been assumed.

BLUE WATER DIPLOMACY

While not wishing to conjure up a return to the era of gunboat diplomacy, the Royal Navy, despite its limited resources, should now
be deployed judiciously as a critical adjunct to a revitalised global

diplomacy. In relation to our new aircraft carriers, this can range from the conventional security role, through to supporting a Rapid Reaction Force engaged in responding to military and humanitarian emergencies. We saw during Operation Barras in Sierra Leone in 2000 the advantages of an Amphibious Ready Group offshore with much of 42 Commando on board the helicopter carrying-vessel, with HMS *Ocean* accompanied by the aircraft carrier HMS *Illustrious*. Involving around 1,300 troops, it represents one of the most successful military interventions to-date; a skilful use of British military power working closely with, but under separate command from, UN forces.

The UK's nuclear-powered submarine fleet has long had a key part to play in reinforcing the UK's 'blue water diplomacy', though their prime responsibility is to mark and, if need be, sink enemy aircraft carriers, warships and submarines. The deployment of a nuclear-powered hunter-killer submarine as an underwater presence close to the Falkland Islands in the autumn of 1977 is a prime example of how these submarines can be used. The best account is in Aaron Donaghy's book, *The British Government and the Falkland Islands, 1974–79*, which covers all the relevant diplomatic considerations, as well as the naval arguments.[28] The most recent evidence released by the National Archives from Admiral of the Fleet Lord Lewin, which was given to the Franks Committee sitting in private in 1982, needs to be examined.[29] The Rules of Engagement drawn up by ministers in 1977 with involvement from the Foreign Office, Ministry of Defence and the Law Officer's Department, all of which were surprisingly not included in the official history of the Falklands War and whose very content was denied in public in 1982 by Admiral Lewin, all need to be addressed in an internal review within an NSC working party if submarine warfare's full geostrategic potential is to be realised in the future, equipped with Cruise missiles and torpedoes.

Fortunately, today, Britain and Argentina have reached a form of détente over the Falkland Islands, with both sides claiming to have made the first significant progress on the matter since 1999. This follows an end to the government of Cristina Fernández de Kirchner. During her time as President of Argentina, she often resorted to aggressive rhetoric and tried to use the issue of the Falkland Islands to rally support, particularly with China and Russia. Her successor, Mauricio Macri, who took office in December 2015, has looked to repair relations with Western powers including the UK and the US after years of isolation under the Kirchners. In a joint statement following a Foreign Office Minister's visit to Argentina in September 2016, the UK and Argentina said they would seek closer cooperation, including the removal of restrictions on the Falklands' oil and gas industry, and that they will pursue ideas for joint exploitation. Commitments were also made to increase the Falklands' trade, fishing industry and air links, thus overturning a previous strategy of commercial disruption. The territory is now able to set up flight connections with other countries in the region, and flight connections between the Falklands and Argentina are set to improve.

Unfortunately, the Falklands remains a sensitive and divisive issue in the UN and the Argentinian claim on the islands will not easily be revoked. The Falklands has to remain a priority for the MOD, even though Argentina's military capability today is a shadow of what it was in the 1980s. There are around 1,000 British personnel on the airbase in the Falklands at any one time and usually four Typhoon jets. These are very expensive weapon systems to continue to deploy. If the submarine geostrategic capability dispute referred to earlier is resolved, made easier by the deployment of Cruise missiles on SBNs rather than just torpedoes as in 1977, it would be easier to end the permanent deployment of as many as four Typhoons, particularly since the island's RAF Mount Pleasant runway has been extended, enabling larger jets to make the transatlantic journey and allowing more troops to be deployed at shorter notice if necessary. Analysts estimate our reinforcement capability has been enhanced so that another 1,000 British troops could be sent to the South Atlantic within days using an 'air-bridge' with Ascension Island, where the RAF has a base, which allows planes to refuel mid-way through the twenty-hour flight. A post-Brexit UK must look to restoring our traditional commercial links with all the countries of South America, while also ensuring that there are appropriate consultations with the Falkland Islanders to maintain their continuing understanding and trust on their legitimate fears about their security from any future attack.

The submarine service is correct to emphasise the 'seven deadly virtues of SSNs: flexibility, mobility, endurance, reach, autonomy, stealth and punch' – all very helpful features for putting into practice 'blue water diplomacy'.[30] This was demonstrated during the NATO humanitarian operation in Kosovo, when HMS *Splendid* fired twenty of the 238 Tomahawk missiles launched throughout the conflict. HMS *Tireless* was also involved in intelligence-gathering operations during the Kosovo crisis, monitoring radio transmission, intercepting communications and passing information to Allied forces.

The accuracy of the missile attacks during the Kosovo War meant claims that the three Tomahawk Cruise missiles which hit the Chinese embassy in Belgrade on 7 May 1999 did so 'mistakenly' were viewed sceptically. While it has been alleged that they were deliberately targeting the embassy, the line taken at the time was that they had been aimed at the Yugoslav Federal Directorate for Supply and Procurement (FDSP), which was located some 500 metres down the street. Immediately after the Chinese embassy was hit, the Clinton administration stated that the strike was accidental on account of faulty maps and intelligence. However, the *Observer*'s report of 17 October 1999 was the first in the UK to suggest that the attack had been deliberate, stating: 'the Chinese embassy was acting as a "rebro" [rebroadcast] station for the Yugoslav army (VJ) ... The Chinese were also suspected of monitoring the Cruise missile attacks on Belgrade, with a view to developing effective countermeasures against US missiles.'[31] It has also been alleged that the attack was based on intelligence that the then Serbian leader, Slobodan Milošević, was in the embassy at the time. The claim that 'outdated' intelligence information had been provided by the Central Intelligence Agency (CIA) was made by US Defense Secretary William Cohen, who claimed that '[one] of our planes attacked the wrong target because the bombing instructions were based on an outdated map'. However, sources within the US National Imagery and Mapping

Agency did not take kindly to the allegation that their mapping was to blame, with one official calling it 'a damned lie'.

Since then, submarine or service-ship-fired Cruise missiles have been deployed in Afghanistan and Iraq, and these missile attacks have had a significant tactical and strategic effect. On 7 April 2017, President Trump used Cruise missiles to attack a Syrian airbase to demonstrate to President Assad that he would not accept the use of nerve gas. He chose to inform Russia of his intentions, thereby letting them warn the Syrians and reduce the loss of life. The accuracy of the missiles once again demonstrated their effectiveness, and shows why the UK also needs this capacity.

The UK's current capability to back up our diplomacy with conventionally armed submarines is built around our fleet of *Astute*-class vessels. These seven boats carry a mix of Spearfish heavy torpedoes and Tomahawk Block IV Cruise missiles, the latter costing £870,000 each. The Tomahawk missiles are capable of hitting a target to within a few metres, at a range of up to 1,000 miles (1,600 km). Three boats, *Astute*, *Ambush* and *Artful*, are meant to be in active service. *Audacious* was expected to be in commission already but has been delayed to 2018; *Anton* in 2020; *Agamemnon* in 2022; and *Ajax* in 2024.[32] According to a *Sunday Times* report, the fleet could shrink from seven boats to six.[33]

The cost overruns in the construction programme for *Astute* class have been disgraceful and are fairly described by the Royal Navy submarine service's most sympathetic historians, Peter Hennessey and James Jinks, in their book *The Silent Deep*. They note that there were problems from the start of the programme, with the MOD deciding it could lower costs by introducing more competition and outsourcing roles that had traditionally been carried out in house, including design authority. Issues then arose over coordination and cooperation between the MOD and the contractors. Ultimately, they say, 'the MOD also lost its "ability to be an informed and intelligent customer"'.[34] The scandal continues. It was reported in early 2017 that the entire existing fleet of attack submarines has been out of action. The four old *Trafalgar*-class submarines cannot continue in service much longer and, together with two of the new three

Astute-class submarines, are due for either extensive repairs or refits. Indeed, one of the *Astute*-class vessels still needed repairs after crashing into a tanker near Gibraltar in 2016.[35] There was just one *Astute*-class at sea, but only on trials following maintenance and not then ready for missions. Yet for global power we need an SSN fleet. It is hard for a Royal Navy still dominated by surface ships to accept that these vessels, now monitored by satellites, are not as useful as they were.

Credible blue water diplomacy will require surface ships, but not in the numbers which the navy wants. Unfortunately too, scandals within the MOD extend to the UK's frigate building programme. Construction of eight Type 26 frigates to replace the ageing Type 23 frigates is due to start in 2017. Initially part of an announced thirteen-ship build, one can only hope their engines will be far less noisy than those of the Type 45, which the *Sunday Times* claimed can be heard by Russian submarines 100 miles away.[36] That same newspaper made the even more serious claim that the Type 26 is starting to be built without the MOD's £178 billion ten-year equipment plan naming any type of existing missile for the ship or allocating any money for their manufacture. This is in spite of Defence Secretary Michael Fallon saying that they will be able to fire weapons, including the US-built MK 41 Tomahawk Cruise missile and anti-ship missiles. This is developing into an unacceptable budgetary sleight of hand, for Parliament must be given all the necessary information it needs, including the full costs of all major weapon systems, when authorising ships to be built in the annual naval estimates. The intention is to build twenty-four missile silos opening onto the deck of the new Type 26 frigates without fitting or carrying any missiles in the silos until a later unspecified date, which could be well after the ship is due to enter service.

There is another serious complication: the MOD is developing an anti-ship missile system with France that will not be ready until 2030,[37] some years after the initial Type 26s enter their service date. We know little about this Anglo-French naval system and its costings. We know, however, much more about the cost implications of using the US Tomahawk ship-launched missiles carrying conventional warheads which were used in Iraq by the US Navy, and as recently as 2014 on Syrian territory against ISIS. It is also used by thirteen other navies. At the very least, these costings should be put into the total cost of building the Type 26 and evaluated against postponing the programme as part of the £10 billion equipment savings currently being sought by MOD and assuming a reasonable SSN build rate.

As already mentioned, we need to contemplate dual use as an economy measure, along with a possible deployment of supersonic Cruise missiles in a vertical-launch mode with a conventional weapon in our four nuclear-armed ballistic missile submarines. We know there is likely to be room in the hull for silos that would not replace silos carrying ballistic missiles. At present, the dedicated nature of their mission precludes dual use; but can we afford to have these very costly weapon systems single use? They will never be able – as currently designed – to help out in a far-flung crisis where nuclear weapons would not be even contemplated, and there are no surface naval vessels or submarines within, say, two weeks' sailing time.

A major boost to our capacity to engage in blue water diplomacy will be the return of aircraft carriers to the fleet. By 2020, after a gap of some ten years, the Royal Navy should be fully operating HMS *Elizabeth* with the HMS *Prince of Wales* to follow into service soon after. One carrier should be available at all times.

The story of how the Royal Navy lost and won the fight to retain naval air power is well told in *The Age of Invincible* by Nick Childs.[38] In February 1966 with Denis Healey in the Chair, the Admiralty Board cancelled the aircraft carrier programme on the grounds of cost. By January 1970, the Chancellor of the Exchequer had agreed to three aircraft carriers, and the first of class *Invincible* being built against the loss of twelve or so frigates. In 1982 HMS *Invincible* was due to be sold when, with the unexpected outbreak of the Falklands War in 1982, it was desperately needed. It was continuously at sea for 166 days, then the record for an aircraft carrier. At one stage, it was operating ten Sea Harriers. Few have dared challenge the need for Royal Navy air power since the Falklands, a view reinforced when not having one available off the Libyan coast during that military engagement. In January 2006, a formal agreement was signed to give France access to detailed information about the British design of its next generation of *Queen Elizabeth*-class aircraft carriers, and hopefully France will build a new carrier which can operate with the Royal Navy.

Some dismissed these two much larger aircraft carriers as 'Cold War relics'. The new carriers will be 920ft long and are planned to have the capacity for forty aircraft. They are the largest warships ever constructed for the Royal Navy. Both carriers will fly short take-off and vertical landing (STOVL) Lockheed Martin F-35Bs, which effectively will replace both the Harrier, retired in 2010, and the Tornado, due to be retired in 2019. The F-35 fleet is intended to be the UK's primary strike attack aircraft for the next three decades. On 29 September 2016, Air Chief Marshal Sir Stephen Hillier confirmed that the UK would be making a full purchase of 138 F-35 fighter jets.[39] Yet they are emerging into a world where, besides the US and Russia, both China and India are building, developing and deploying much larger aircraft carriers.[40] The big attack on these two British aircraft carriers came in 2010 when Chief of the Defence Staff General David Richards wrote in his autobiography: 'I could not bring myself to accept that we needed to build two, vast new ships ... I couldn't see the justification either from a cost point of view or in terms of extra capability the new ships would offer.'[41] He wanted, not unreasonably, to build two more of the smaller *Invincible* class. It was, however, judged too late to axe the first *Queen Elizabeth*. The Secretary of State for Defence, Liam Fox, for good reasons wanted the two carriers to be fitted with catapults and arrester wires so that they would be capable of handling the larger US planes when operating with the US Navy. This was sensible and initially agreed upon. But later this vital equipment was cancelled by the Conservative–Liberal Democrat coalition, to some extent destroying the justification for such large ships. It was also announced that one might be sold, an extraordinary proposition and fortunately a position that was later reversed in 2014. This is a sorry tale and exactly how not to make an important and expensive procurement decision. But there is no sign that it will not happen again in the MOD, since to stop it the Chief of the Defence Staff (CDS) needs powers that he is not equipped to exercise. Unless and until that procurement policy is owned by a properly staffed CDS structural pillar with a permanent staff in the MOD, and the individual service chiefs have a far more limited locus, these procurement fiascos will continue. As part of the post-Brexit realism, the NSC should be empowered to look at strengthening the position of the CDS inside the MOD. Meanwhile, we have to live with the present and we are fortunate in having a very able CDS, Air Chief Marshal Sir Stuart Peach, who has the capacity to handle the rethink that is vital over many aspects of defence policy.

The F-35 JSF is yet another procurement development programme beset with delays and design flaws, making the Lockheed F-35 JSF the most expensive military weapons system in history. It has been criticised inside and outside government, both within the US and amongst its partner countries. While the US is the major contributor to the development programme, other NATO countries and US close allies contribute to the programme with the UK being the sole 'level one' partner contributing the most; UK industry will be responsible for manufacturing 15 per cent by value of each aircraft.[42] The programme includes the F-35A (conventional take-off and landing, CTOL) and F-35B (short take-off and vertical landing, STOVL). President Trump has already publicly said in February 2017 that the programme cost has jumped in the US from $233 billion in 2001 to around $379 billion, and he has asked his Defense Secretary, General James Mattis, to review the situation. This review includes looking at buying an alternative, the Boeing-made F-18 Super Hornet, which Australia too considered buying in the face of F-35 delays.

A RAPID REACTION FORCE

What to do with the two British carriers? They are, fortunately, designed to operate worldwide. They will be capable of operating against most navies, but will be vulnerable in the Baltic and North Sea, as well as in the Gulf and the South China Sea. They cannot operate the most sophisticated US aircraft because they do not have necessary equipment on their flight decks. They can, however, be quickly adapted for humanitarian missions. We need to assess with close Commonwealth allies the case for a Royal Naval carrier being the lead vessel in a Rapid Reaction Force in support of UN Security Council decisions. This has already been discussed in Chapter One. These carriers' flexibility over their operational missions will stem from the design of the ships, which are capable of taking ten medium helicopters and have the capacity to house 250 troops. They can operate short take-off and vertical landing (STOVL) aircraft such as the CH-47 Chinook heavy-lift helicopter, as well as the V-22 Osprey tiltrotor and Merlin HM.2 helicopter, for anti-submarine work and for airborne early warning. The UK should start a formal process of consultation over such a Rapid Reaction Force with the UN, NATO and individual navies. If the decision is favourable, the MOD can then make a final judgement about fixed-wing aircraft, the flexible relationship between planes operating from airfields and carriers, and whether or when they are operated by light-blue or dark-blue aviators (RAF or Royal Navy pilots).

It is likely that the British aircraft carriers will have a foreign base in Oman at the port of Duqm, which is being developed 'as a strategic port for the Middle East on the Indian Ocean'.[43] It is expected they would spend much of their time at sea around Cape Horn and in the Indian Ocean and the Far East. They could be deployed in the Mediterranean, but should not expect to be. This would be a new global deployment, one that fits in well with the new strategic thinking that a post-Brexit UK foreign and security policy must develop imaginatively and credibly to support UN peacekeeping as well as our new commercial and political orientation.

In looking at our naval presence, we need to adopt an unconventional approach in regards to the deployment of this additional aircraft carrier resource. There should firstly be a new emphasis on working closely with other Commonwealth navies. Priorities will need to be set jointly if some of these navies are from time to time to help provide sufficient escort vessels, refuelling tankers and supply vessels. The Royal Navy will operate occasionally with the US Navy around the world but, for reasons we have touched on in Chapter One and will go into in more detail in Chapter Seven, their prime area of activity should not be the South China Sea and this needs to be made clear to the US Navy from the outset. There is no military imperative to put our one operational aircraft carrier at any time into the controversy over the disputed islands in the South China Seas. Some may resist this limitation, but it is a strategic political economic and political military choice of the same kind as the UK made over Vietnam in 1964.

In returning to the Far East, the UK has a very different role to that of the US. They have longstanding military and political interests which we can neither match nor sustain. Our presence with our one operational aircraft carrier committed to an RRF capability will be helpful to the US, but is marginal in relation to any confrontation with China in the region and we should not pretend that it can be more than that. We are in the fortunate position that, of the five countries that have the deepest intelligence-sharing arrangement, four are in the Commonwealth: Canada, Australia, New Zealand and ourselves; and within this forum with the US, it should be very easy to establish priorities of mutual benefit. The reason for stating these limitations at the outset is to ensure that there is no misunderstanding between us and the US. We have no wish to repeat what happened over Vietnam, starting with the Gulf of Tonkin incident in 1964 when President Johnson misled Congress into giving him blanket authority to wage war in South East Asia. We began insidiously thereafter to pass through many of the thresholds of military escalation relatively unchecked, until the moment when the British Prime Minister came under sustained pressure from President Johnson to become involved in the Vietnam War. To his credit, Harold Wilson managed to hold to the distinction of not opposing US policy while avoiding the involvement of British forces. Without clarity from the outset about the purpose and limitation of our naval deployments in 2017, we can see a repeat of all the tensions of that period between the US and UK return. We would also risk not carrying public opinion in Britain with this new and necessary deployment of aircraft carriers in the Far East in support of our strategic and commercial interests.

A question for the UK that is bubbling in the background in 2017 is whether we should revisit our policy towards the Pacific. With the relentless eastward shift in the centre of gravity of global economic activity, our answer is an emphatic 'Yes'. The UK now has an opportunity of placing a renewed focus on the Far East, with the Royal Navy partnering with the escort vessels of Australia, New Zealand and, hopefully, India as well. It is a challenge but also a huge opportunity in conflict prevention, and one with a commercial payback. France is seen as 're-energising its maritime empire', particularly in the Pacific'.[44] As mentioned in Chapter One, under the United Nations Convention on the Law of the Sea, every qualifying island can claim up to a 200-nautical-mile exclusive economic zone (EEZ). French Pacific territories are extensive, including New Caledonia (which was promised a referendum on independence by 2018 under the 1998 Noumea Accord) and French Polynesia (more than a hundred islands and atolls including Tahiti and Bora Bora and which has an EEZ of 4.8 million miles^2). In total, France has the second largest EEZ in the world.

What of Britain? In 2006 we closed High Commissions in Vanuatu, the Kingdom of Tonga and Kiribati, which has an EEZ the size of India. Does this make sense as China extends its presence in the South Pacific? Indeed, the UK has specific constitutional and legal responsibilities for the Pitcairn Islands (officially the Pitcairn, Henderson, Ducie and Oeno Islands), one of our fourteen overseas territories. These are a group of four volcanic islands in the Southern Pacific to the east of French Polynesia. They cover a land area of about 47 km^2 or 18 miles^2. Only Pitcairn is inhabited. Most inhabitants are descendants of the Bounty mutineers and are Seventh Day Adventists. Pitcairn measures approximately 3.6 km and 2.2 km from east to west. Nevertheless, it has a Governor, an Administrator and a Mayor in Adamstown, and is the last British territory in the Pacific. The UN Committee on Decolonisation includes the Pitcairn Islands on the UN list of Non-Self-Governing Territories. A new global Britain should do more with Canberra and Wellington in the Pacific Island Forum where France, through having New Caledonia and French Polynesia as recent members, now has an influence. A global Britain should not ignore the Pacific.

THE DEFENCE BUDGET

Ultimately, no foreign policy can be divorced from defence policy; the two go together. To be ready to undertake credible military operations demands from us all financial sacrifice to protect, as best we can, the lives and continued health of the service personnel that we put on the frontline. We have tried to have a UK foreign and defence policy on the cheap, with disastrous consequences since the fall of the Berlin Wall. The cuts have taken time to bite and reveal their true nature. Now, we must rediscover the will as a country to match commitments to budgets, and to ensure that procurement under those budgets is significantly more efficient than it has been in the past. The failure to choose over the MOD budget has been a failing, above all, not of senior politicians (with the possible exception of nuclear deterrence) but of the senior military that keep sponsoring projects knowing that they are not financially fully covered. That has to stop. We cannot continue the pretence of being able to afford all that might be desirable. Yet even our more limited ambitions justify a higher percentage spending on defence, but not with the waste, inefficiency and overruns that is, it appears, part of the present MOD. In 1968 the whole Polaris project was delivered on time and to cost.

Today the government has committed only that the UK will increase defence spending by at least 0.5 per cent above inflation every year to 2022 and meet NATO's target of spending 2 per cent of GDP on defence. We believe that the UK must demonstrate a readiness to increase defence spending to 2.5 per cent of GDP by 2022. Whether this is done by 0.1 per cent each year for five years or in larger steps later is for the Chancellor of the Exchequer to plan for. It is, however, vital to make this commitment now because of the announcement of German forward-defence expenditure in 2016, which showed that the richest European NATO country will only reach 2.0 per cent of GDP spending on defence after five more years. On this issue, a post-Brexit UK must take the lead amongst the larger European members of NATO and, in so doing, we will be making a decisive contribution to holding the US firmly in NATO. Roger Bootle, one of the economists most regularly having their assessments confirmed by events, has never been one to urge increased expenditure frequently on his readers. In the *Sunday Telegraph*, Bootle made an exception when he wrote in April 2017 he was convinced that the defence expenditure budget would have to be increased.[45]

Once this message of increased UK defence spending on NATO by 2022 registers within the Trump administration, there will be substance, not just rhetoric, in our relationship with the US. Unless NATO is seen to be a UK priority, no UK security policy will be credible in Washington, Moscow, Berlin or Warsaw – the four capitals where it is most important that NATO is quickly recognised to be on a new transformative track. It is as simple as that. Money talks on this issue like nothing else.

The time for a new UK foreign and security policy to start to register in Beijing, Brussels, Ottawa, Canberra and Wellington can wait a little longer. As we shall come on to in Chapter Four, the National Security Council (NSC) is the forum in which extra resources can and must be found for increased defence and foreign policy spending. The priorities need to be set there in the NSC and then put before the full Cabinet, and the nation as a whole.

To put the UK's commitment to meeting the NATO guideline of spending at least 2.0 per cent of GDP on defence in context, NATO data for 2016 released in March 2017[46] estimated the US spent $664 billion on defence (3.6 per cent of GDP), compared with the UK's $57 billion equivalent (representing almost 2.2 per cent of GDP on the basis of NATO's calculation). Germany spends a smaller share of GDP than many EU states. The trouble with comparing European force numbers is the amount of double-counting that goes on, and this is one of the main arguments against the European Union defence arrangements, where double-counting is the norm. EU Defence will soon be duplicating the current single NATO HQ. EU Defence may become a fact of life for the remaining EU members, but it must not become so for the UK; we must remain focused on NATO. The arguments against EU Defence are very strong and have been made by every US Secretary for Defense, Democrat or Republican. They have also been made by the British military leadership. As former Chief of the Defence Staff, Lord Guthrie, said in an interview in 2016:

> To get twenty-eight people sitting round a table being decisive is very, very difficult. If you have a European Army, you will find that lots of those taking part will see it as a way of getting a seat at the top table as cheaply as they possibly can. Then they can actually do less, and the equipment programmes and the size of the forces suffer. When it comes to leading, you want a very clear chain of command, capable of making quick decisions.[47]

The UK should aim to have as little as possible to do with EU Defence and guard against going along with it as a sweetener to Brexit negotiations. The UK task is to focus resources on hard, front-line NATO defence, as well as stabilisation and conflict in the very poorest states. In the defence context, we can leave soft power, whatever that term really means, and any continued peacekeeping in Europe largely to the EU. For example, they have the Delegation of the European Union to Bosnia and Herzegovina which operates under the overall leadership of the High Representative of the Union for the Common Foreign and Security Policy/Vice President of the Commission, and whose head is also the EU Special Representative who reports to the Council of the European Union. An EU led force, EUFOR Althea, has the main peace stabilisation role under the military aspects of the Dayton Peace Agreement, having taken over from NATO. We should not exclude undertaking security tasks in the Balkans, but our priority is the Baltic states.

An independent Britain, able to take clear and fast decisions, will remain a valuable, and indeed indispensable, contributor to many aspects of European security. We will build a special relationship with the vice president of the Commission responsible for foreign policy and security issues. Our Permanent Representative to NATO stationed in Brussels should be authorised to speak directly to this individual and be part of the cooperation building structures pursuant to Article 8. After Brexit we should put in place such arrangements as already mentioned above and in Chapter One, in relation to our multilateral diplomacy, and in Chapter Four, in relation to the role of the National Security Adviser and the NSC itself.

We will also build strong bilateral defence arrangements with our allies in Europe, and there are already precedents for agreements outside the EU context. In December 2010, President Sarkozy and Prime Minister Cameron issued the Downing Street Declaration about the Lancaster House Treaties between the UK and France, for defence and security cooperation. Significantly, neither used the EU's Common Security and Defence Policy, nor the Lisbon Treaty's Permanent Structured Cooperation Facility nor involved the European Defence Agency. These bilateral treaties should be picked up by the two countries when the time is ripe. An early area for bilateral discussions is French interest in being involved in a Rapid Reaction Force. The new Macron government will need to see how it wishes to rethink French foreign policy in an EU without the UK. For example, do they want formally to be the single voice of the EU in the UN Security Council, reserve that policy forum for themselves, or try to bestraddle the interests of France and the EU as at present? Bilateral talks are also underway between the German Defence Minister, Ursula von der Leyen, and the British Defence Secretary. Let us see how these bilateral relations work before committing to any EU machinery on foreign and security policy. For us in the UK, the principal forum for security is and will remain NATO – clear and simple.

A post-Brexit foreign policy has as its most immediate priority increased resources for and commitments to NATO. We understand why Angela Merkel said that the EU could no longer 'complete-ly depend' on the US and the UK following the election of Donald Trump as President and the UK's Brexit vote, but we believe it is up to the European members of NATO to demonstrate to the American people a renewed relationship to NATO and thereby ensure that Merkel's fears will be proven wrong. When, after the G7 meeting in Taormina in Italy, Merkel described the meeting as 'deeply unsatis-factory', she reinforced isolationist sentiment in the US by saying, 'We Europeans have to take our destiny in our own hands.' The response from the UK should be that our destinies in NATO have been linked since 1949 and that should remain for decades to come.

The German Chancellor should remember how President Reagan did not use that sort of critical language about Germany during the 1983 Euro-missile crisis, when it looked as if the US deployment of Pershing missiles to Europe would be rejected in debates in the then capital Bonn. Fortunately President Mitterrand went to the Bundestag in person to urge the missile deployment be accepted. It was President Obama who first labelled the Europeans as 'free loaders' on defence. Europe is in no position to lecture or to denigrate the best interna-tional military command and control organisation the world has ever known. Jean-Claude Juncker, the President of the European Commis-sion, is wrong to say of NATO and EU Defence that 'we complement each other'. The EU contribution to NATO is dwarfed by that of the US, as it double counts its contribution to both organisations and de-ludes itself about the dangers to NATO of duplication and separation.

CHAPTER 3

BUILDING A PROSPEROUS FUTURE

Shaped by its geography and history, the UK has long been both a leading proponent of free trade and a global trading nation. Having voted to leave the EU, the UK has the opportunity to build on this heritage and reinforce its position as one of the world's leading exporters. In this chapter, we will examine the challenges the UK faces in achieving this and will look at how it might overcome them, to the benefit of its own citizens and the wider world.

The past decades have seen a remarkable growth in global wealth, with hundreds of millions of people – notably in China and India but also in a range of other economies around the globe – lifted from poverty. Unfortunately, at the other end of the spectrum, we have witnessed a significant growth in the number of failed or failing states. The deprivations and sufferings of the citizens of these states have often triggered significant migrations, and have also created a fertile breeding ground for ills which risk destabilising the wider economy, such as disease and terrorism. The socio-economic landscape has been further complicated since the financial crisis by growing populist anti-globalisation sentiment, particularly in Europe and the US where it has focused on the transfer of manufacturing jobs to countries with lower cost producers. This has given rise to increasingly protectionist rhetoric, not least in the US, where the administration has highlighted the intention to renegotiate the North American Free Trade Agreement and 'make it a fair deal, not just a free-trade deal',[1] a 'NAFFTA'.

Like beauty, fairness is often in the eye of the beholder; and, while there is clearly a role for measures such as anti-dumping regulations to prevent unfair competition, it will be critical to ensure that fair really does mean fair for all, and that we do not see economic growth stifled by a regression to protectionism. On a positive note, during a visit to London in April 2017 Paul Ryan, the Republican Speaker of the House of Representatives, said: 'The United States stands ready to forge a new trade agreement with Great Britain as soon as possible so that we may further tap into the great potential between our two people.'

Navigating these troubled waters and contributing to the continuance of an open global trading system, which is focused on growing overall wealth in an inclusive and sustainable way rather than simply securing a greater slice of pie (which should also be an objective for the UK), will require a concerted partnership effort between government and the private sector to achieve success. As International Trade Secretary Liam Fox noted in his September 2016 speech on free trade, the UK's starting position could be better:

>...the UK has experienced a deteriorating trade performance since 2011, with our exports growing more slowly than some of our G7 counterparts including United States, Germany and France. Despite a stellar performance by our best exporters it is a sad fact that only 11 per cent of British companies export anything beyond our borders and the value of our exports is well below that of our European neighbours. We know from the performance of our best that we could do much better overall. In gross terms, our export to GDP ratio is only 27.3 per cent compared to the EU average, excluding the UK, of 47.3 per cent.[2]

Rhetoric, whether exhorting businesses simply to go out and export more, or calling for free trade, is not enough. Both need to be backed by concrete actions, both domestically and internationally. In its 'Plan for Britain'[3] which sets out its strategy for managing departure from the EU, the government highlights three areas related to trade and economic development which will contribute to building 'a global Britain that is outward-looking and embraces the world'. We will examine each of these elements, which are to:

- get on with the job of delivering Brexit, striking the right deal for Britain abroad and forging a new partnership with Europe that gives us control of our borders and our laws;
- help us trade beyond Europe and make Britain a leading advocate for free trade across the world, as we build on our relationships with old friends and new allies;
- continue to meet our commitments by supporting developing countries to help them improve their economies and support their people.

As we have highlighted earlier in relation to other foreign and security policy issues, building a cross-government approach will also be essential in driving a coherent agenda in this area, and the signs are generally positive. The National Security Strategy is very clear on the importance of promoting prosperity, with National Security Objective three being:

> to promote our prosperity – seizing opportunities, harnessing innovation to strengthen our national security, and working with industry to ensure we have the capabilities and equipment that we need. Our economic and national security go hand-in-hand. Our strong economy provides the foundation to invest in our security and global influence, which in turn provides more opportunities at home and overseas for us to increase our prosperity. A growing global economy helps to reduce poverty and build security for all.[4]

This now flows through into the objectives of key departments involved.

The government signalled its intent to provide a focal point for its efforts by setting up the Department for International Trade (DIT) in July 2016, shortly after the Brexit vote. This department has:

> overall responsibility for promoting British trade across the world. It will develop, coordinate and deliver a new trade policy for the UK, including preparing for and then negotiating Free Trade Agreements and market access deals with non-EU countries. The new department will be a specialised body with significant new trade negotiating capacity. It will take on the responsibilities of UK Trade and Investment, the relevant trade functions of the former Department for Business, Innovation and Skills; and take on responsibility for UK Export Finance.[5]

Given the numerous changes in leadership and the reorganisations of UK Trade and Investment over the recent past, it is important that the new department brings stability and consistency to its support for the UK's exporters.

DIT will work with other departments across Whitehall – notably the Treasury, the Department for Exiting the EU, the FCO and the Department for International Development (DFID) – to achieve its aims, with the latter two playing key international roles. The FCO, often criticised in the past for neglecting commercial business, has seen a major shift in terms of the way it now operates, with one of its three strategic objectives being to 'build the UK's prosperity by increasing exports and investment, opening markets, ensuring access to resources and promoting sustainable global growth'.[6] While many would argue that DFID has not progressed as far as the FCO in embracing the role of the market and private sector businesses in its work, under Secretary of State Priti Patel the department has also indicated its clear intent to focus on market driven development in its Economic Development Strategy:

> DFID's ambition will be at the heart of the Government's emerging

agenda on international trade and investment, led by the Department for International Trade. We will work across Government to agree trade and investment deals that bring the benefits of trade to every corner of the world. And we will use our voice in the World Trade Organization to promote free trade as one of the bedrocks of global prosperity and stability. We are focusing investment in job creation across manufacturing, infrastructure and commercial agriculture to provide strong foundations for inclusive growth in the developing world.[7]

There are clearly very different issues that arise when dealing with our trading arrangements, with advanced economies and stimulating economic growth in fragile or failed states. As indicated in the government's action plan and generally acknowledged in the discussion around the practicalities of Brexit, securing a favourable deal with the EU is a top priority. The Prime Minister made this clear in her 17 January speech setting out the government's objectives for leaving the EU:

> So as a priority, we will pursue a bold and ambitious free trade agreement with the European Union. This agreement should allow for the freest possible trade in goods and services between Britain and the EU's member states. It should give British companies the maximum freedom to trade with and operate within European markets – and let European businesses do the same in Britain.[8]

Securing such a deal would be a major boost for UK exporters, who, over the years of EU membership, have developed an understanding of the market and customers which gives them confidence to do business and integrate into wider supply chains. Simply put, the smoother the transition to a new trading regime, the better. Such relationships are not replaced in new markets overnight. We will examine the dynamics associated with achieving this with our former partners in more detail in Chapter Eight.

The Prime Minister went on to say:

...it is clear that the UK needs to increase significantly its trade with the fastest growing export markets in the world ... We want to get out into the wider world, to trade and do business all around the globe. Countries including China, Brazil, and the Gulf States have already expressed their interest in striking trade deals with us. We have started discussions on future trade ties with countries like Australia, New Zealand and India. And President-Elect Trump has said Britain is not 'at the back of the queue' for a trade deal with the United States, the world's biggest economy, but front of the line.

At a macro level, securing FTAs is a significant element of this; although, as indicated in that quote, we do not have an agreement in place with the US, which is already the biggest single market for the UK, with exports of £46 billion in 2016 and average annual growth rate of 4 per cent since 2009.[9] Similarly, there is no agreement in place with China, where exports were over £20 billion in 2016 (we will focus more on the commercial relationship with China in Chapter Seven). That said, the UK's exports to South Korea doubled following the implementation of the EU–South Korea FTA in 2011. The EU has trade agreements in place with around fifty partners. A key question for the UK will be whether these agreements can be 'grandfathered' or whether they will have to be renegotiated, either partially or in their entirety. Freed from the constraints of having to meet the interests of all EU members with differing sector priorities, there will be benefits in reviewing terms. In particular, there has been concern expressed about the Economic Partnership Agreements which the EU has in place with many developing countries, highlighted in the House of Commons International Trade Committee's report on trade options beyond 2019.[10] The removal of non-tariff barriers, such as licensing standards and procurement regulations, has a major part to play in stimulating trade growth, and is an area of focus of particular relevance to the UK, which has a high proportion of exporters in the service sectors, where barriers are more often the result of regulation rather than tariffs. Furthermore, as was seen during the Prime Minister's visit to India in November 2016, the negotiation of FTAs may also be dependent on other issues, where there are conflicting priorities – in this case, with visas and migration issues. One action which is likely to gain the UK credit with the high-growth markets is continuing to push for reform in key multilateral organisations where they are under-represented, such as the IMF, where we will be represented in our own right and can take a position independent of EU positions.

Aside from a longer-term focus on putting FTAs in place, which, while it needs to be prioritised, will inevitably be constrained by the limited experienced staff available to DIT, the government, through DIT and the UK's extensive network of overseas posts, has significant potential to build on the practical support it offers to exporters, particularly where it is encouraging entrance into newer or less developed markets. While larger companies, and multinationals based in the UK, have the management and financial capacity to explore new markets, this is less the case for medium size companies who have the potential to make major contributions to increasing exports. For them, focusing on the domestic market or growing in established export markets that are near to hand or easily accessible may well make the best business sense, and they will require enticement to look further afield. Indeed, many larger public companies follow the same strategy, given the challenges of doing business in emerging markets. Such risks include uncertainty over getting paid, lack of understanding of legal and regulatory frameworks and corruption, let alone political risks (as an example, Russia was seen as a high priority market by UKTI prior to the Ukraine situation erupting), and are frequently seen as outweighing the potential benefits offered by the higher growth rates in these markets. The UK government must not ignore the commercial potential of Russia, particularly for the City of London, which remains an important source of finance for Russian businesses. We traded with the Soviet Union throughout those far more difficult times. Now, with Russia part of the world economy, it would be absurd to ignore its markets. Furthermore, while large swathes of Russian business undoubtedly remain under government control or influence, there are independent, entrepreneurial companies whose growth and development we should be supporting and encouraging. It is in the interests of long term stability to see Russia more closely integrated into the global economy.

In its 'Manifesto for Exporters',[11] the British Exporters Association (BExA) highlights a number of practical areas in which the government can take action to help UK companies meet their potential in export markets. These include reinforcing the need for a whole of government approach, and the importance of providing 'information, encouragement and incentives' to exporters. DIT should continue to focus on exploiting technology to raise the profile of what the UK can offer, as it has done through the GREAT Britain campaign of coordinated marketing, which has already secured confirmed economic returns of £2.7 billion for the UK,[12] and link potential exporters to opportunities in international markets. But it must also not overlook or underestimate the importance exporters attach to having access to well-informed staff, both in the country and in London (where many businesspeople regret the passing of the dedicated country teams which UKTI used to maintain). A frequent criticism from the business community is that the focus is on providing support to the larger businesses that are, or should be, capable of shouldering much of the burden themselves, as staff see that as an easier route to get recognition.

DIT is right to set itself priorities in terms of markets and sectors, which were highlighted in a press release in January 2017.[13] However, these are extensive, and it is critical that adequate resources, including staff with the appropriate commercial skills and experience, are in place to deliver. In terms of sectors, these cover: advanced manufacturing; aerospace; automotive; bio-economy; consumer goods and retail; creative industries; defence and security; education; energy; financial services; food and drink; healthcare; infrastructure; life sciences; oil and gas; nuclear; professional services; sports economy; and technology. As mentioned above, it will be critical that access to expert support will be provided to a broad range of companies active in these sectors, and not just the largest. The list of markets being targeted outside of the EU is diverse, covering both well developed and emerging markets and shows the breadth of ambition:

Africa	China	Iraq	Mexico	Singapore	Tunisia
Australia	The Gulf	Japan	Mongolia	South Africa	Turkey
Azerbaijan	Hong Kong	Kazakhstan	New Zealand	South Korea	USA
Brazil	India	Kuwait	Oman	Switzerland	Ukraine
Canada	Indonesia	Lithuania	Philippines	Taiwan	
Chile	Iran	Malaysia	Qatar	Thailand	

The list includes key markets such as India and China, where good progress has been made in growing exports and attracting inward investment. The Middle East is another region which rightly remains a high priority for the UK, and has witnessed a number of senior level visits by ministers since the Brexit vote, as well as significant continuing inward investment (though it should be noted that much of this is in the real estate sector). This is a region which, for historical and cultural reasons, many British companies are comfortable to operate in. However, the list also includes a number of more challenging markets, where it has to be recognised that additional resources will be required, and it will take time to get results. Securing business in Lagos is a lot more challenging than in Los Angeles, and it is also harder to attract and retain staff who have the understanding and connections to make a real impact. In both developed and developing markets, DIT will benefit from drawing in more staff on either a permanent or a secondment basis, who have experience of the private sector and understand how best to position UK companies in a competitive landscape.

The above list noticeably includes Iraq, which is in a state of post-conflict reconstruction, and Africa, which encompasses countries across the spectrum from failed states upwards, with many transitioning from low to middle income and facing the various challenges that brings. In many of these markets, the UK is also playing a much broader role through its provision of aid under the auspices of DFID. DFID was established in 1997 as a separate entity from the Foreign and Commonwealth Office, where some of its new responsibilities had been housed to 'refocus [the UK's] international development efforts on the elimination of poverty and encouragement of economic growth which benefits the poor'.[14] This was based on the rationale that 'It is our duty to care about other people, in particular those less well off than ourselves. We all have a moral duty to reach out to the poor and needy'.[15]

As indicated earlier, DFID's role is increasingly focused on building the foundations for sustainable long term economic growth as well as dealing with near term crises. Given the threats which failed and fragile states pose to global stability (estimated to be some forty to sixty countries by Claire Lockhart and former Afghan finance minister, now President, Ashraf Ghani, and co-founder of the Institute for State Effectiveness),[16] as well as the suffering incurred by their populations, addressing their needs must be a central part of any policy designed to make the world a safer and wealthier place. This is recognised by the government which sees that poverty in the developing world is a direct threat to the UK's interests, even in the face of fiscal austerity.[17] DFID is committed to spending at least 50 per cent of its annual budget in fragile states and regions for each year up to 2020.[18] As Ghani and Lockhart argue, these states need to be rebuilt in an inclusive way and governance structures put in place which work for all of society, not just a small entrenched minority. In March 2017, former Prime Minister David Cameron reiterated the argument for the continuing UK effort to help fragile states at a time when there is an ongoing debate about spending on overseas aid at a time of cutbacks domestically. He also highlighted the need for good governance:

There are so many countries where the governments lack legitimacy or authority, and where corruption, conflict and violence are rife. These governments are frequently unable to provide the most basic services, such as healthcare, education, security or infrastructure.

The building blocks of democracy, such as a fair judiciary and the rule of law, are often completely absent. Crucially, there is no prospect of the creation of an effective private sector – and, with it, jobs. These are, in the development lingo, 'fragile states'.[19]

We share the view that the UK should continue to focus on these efforts. The UK is held in high esteem around the globe for its commitment to achieving the Sustainable Development Goals adopted at the United Nations Sustainable Development Summit on 25 September 2015,[20] and for its efforts in providing emergency relief. This was seen in the rapid response to the humanitarian crisis in East Africa in early 2017, where the UK provided food, water and emergency healthcare supplies. The UK has also been at the forefront in supporting humanitarian efforts in Syria. Public attention is focused on refugees coming out of Syria. It is not so easy to focus attention on where the aid effort is so crucial – inside Syria. It may still be necessary to consider again the case for safe havens inside Syria backed by security from neighbouring countries, Jordan and Turkey, who are already taking on huge responsibilities. In April 2017, the Prime Minister announced a further major package of support for education, skills and jobs for Syrian refugees and their host countries. Such rapid and generous responses are a credit to the UK and we should ensure that a significant proportion of our aid budget can be flexibly deployed to meet such demands.[21]

In 2015, the UK was one of a relatively small group of countries that met the UN's target of devoting 0.7 per cent of their GNI to official development assistance (ODA) as defined by the OECD,[22] spending approximately £12.24 billion or 0.71 per cent of GNI* and hitting the aid target for the third year. Only five other countries topped this,

---

*   Gross National Income (GNI) is a measure of output which values goods and services produced by the residents of a country. It differs from GDP, which is the most widely used measure of output, because it includes income such as dividend and interest payments received from other countries, less similar payments made abroad. GDP measures output within a country's territorial borders whereas GNI measures output produced by residents of a country, regardless of whether they are produced in the country or not. When the target was first adopted, it measured in terms of GDP. Figures for aid and GNI for 2015 may both be revised.

according to figures from the OECD: Sweden 1.4 per cent; Norway 1.05 per cent; Luxembourg 0.95 per cent; Denmark 0.85 per cent; and the Netherlands 0.75 per cent. The largest assistance by volume in aid budgets came from the US, UK, Germany, Japan and France. In absolute terms, the UK's aid spending in 2015 was second only to the United States.[23] This spending is disbursed both bilaterally and through multilateral bodies, including a significant portion through the EU's aid budget, as well as through other agencies including UN bodies and a range of World Bank trust funds. While control over the funds distributed through the EU will return to the UK as announced by the Chancellor in 2017, it is critical that transparency is enhanced over the disbursements made through other agencies, and this has been flagged in Parliament and elsewhere.

The House of Commons Committee of Public Accounts, in their Thirty-Fifth Report of Session 2015–16 on 'Department for International Development: Responding to Crises',[24] reported on the United Nations and other multilateral organisations. The following are selected extracts.

UN organisations received around half of the Department's £1,288 million spending on humanitarian activities in 2014–15. The UK is one of the largest donors to some of the UN's main humanitarian agencies. UN agencies told the National Audit Office that the Department was a well-regarded but demanding donor.

The non-governmental organisations we took evidence from were critical of the performance of UN organisations and of the Department's oversight of the funding it gave multilateral organisations. Médecins Sans Frontières told us that some of the defined mandates of UN bodies overlap, leading to turf wars, impeding effectiveness and slowing down the humanitarian system. It said it looked to the Department to streamline and improve UN agencies' performance. The British Red Cross said that quite a lot of money is channelled through multilateral organisations because it is simple and easier to do, rather than build capacity at a local level which can be 'complex, long-term work'. Save the Children suggested that the value for money of non-governmental organisations for the British taxpayer was scrutinised more than the funding given to multilateral organisations.

The value for money for the UK taxpayer of the Department's funding of UN agencies is undermined by the overlapping remits of the agencies and inflexibility in their systems. UN organisations received around half of the Department's £1,288 million spending on humanitarian activities in 2014–15. Despite being a major and well regarded donor, the Department has found it difficult to influence the UN to adapt its structure and the practices of individual UN bodies to improve their effectiveness. The Department has now identified three priorities for UN agencies – encouraging them to: work together more effectively; improve the quality of their data; and extend the period over which they commit to fund the partners they engage to deliver services. The Department sees the World Humanitarian Summit in May 2016 as an opportunity for it to influence the wider humanitarian system, of which UN agencies are a major part.

The government published its response from the Summit to the House of Commons Public Accounts Committee report in July 2016:

The World Humanitarian Summit took place from 23–24 May 2016 in Istanbul. It was the first global summit on humanitarian issues and was truly global, bringing together participants from governments, the private sector, civil society and non-governmental organisations. Leaders welcomed the United Nations (UN) Secretary General's Agenda for Humanity as well as his five priority areas: global leadership to prevent and end conflicts; upholding the norms that safeguard humanity; leaving no one behind, moving from delivering aid to ending need; and investing in humanity.

The UK led the way to secure agreement to a 'Grand Bargain' on more efficient humanitarian financing. This will change the way donors and agencies do business, and included commitments to:

- improve joint and impartial needs assessments, as well as more systematic use of shared analysis and planning;
- enhance transparency of data;
- harmonise and simplify reporting requirements;
- increase multi-year, collaborative and flexible planning and multi-year funding instruments;
- increase the use of cash-based approaches in crisis situations;
- increase support and funding tools for local and national responders, including adopting common standards to put affected people at the centre of the response;
- reduce duplication and management costs with periodic functional reviews;
- reduce the earmarking of donor contributions;
- enhance engagement between humanitarian and development actors.

The UK, alongside other partners, will continue to drive this reform agenda in the months and years ahead, including establishing a monitoring mechanism to track progress against the 'Grand Bargain' commitments. The monitoring mechanism is expected to be launched in autumn 2016.[25]

The government answer to the Select Committee's main report went on to say:

> For many of its crisis interventions, the Department does not have a full understanding of how much of the taxpayer's pound is spent by which bodies and on what. The Department's partners incur a range of costs in delivering assistance. For example, on staff, food and supplies, and on the transport and security necessary to get these items to beneficiaries. For many of its interventions, the Department does not have a good understanding of the size of the different cost components, making it difficult to establish

benchmarks and make better informed decisions on the selection and management of partners. Furthermore, in complex projects the Department does not always know the range of organisations its first-tier partners are funding, making it difficult for the Department to manage risks. The Department accepts that it ought to be able track who is receiving and spending UK taxpayers' money.

The Select Committee recommendation is that: As a matter of routine, the Department should identify all the bodies involved in providing assistance, the funding each receives and the main costs incurred. It should use this information to help manage risk and identify cost-effective partners and practices.

It is vital that the cost-effectiveness of aid spending channelled through third parties continues to be closely monitored, and that new grants are cut to any international agencies that the internal DFID review found wanting. There is too much blandness in DFID's many responses and not enough action to meet justified criticism. This will only serve to fuel the controversy which undoubtedly remains over whether the UK should be spending these amounts on aid, and DFID needs to demonstrate consistently to tax payers that their money is well spent. At a time when key areas of domestic spending are under pressure, many have questioned the expansion in the aid budget, which has grown significantly as the economy has recovered. There was a steep increase in 2013 when the UK government first met the 0.7 per cent of GNI target for ODA.[26] In 2015 a Private Members' Bill, sponsored by former Liberal Democrat MP Michael Moore, was passed into law with the support of the then coalition government. The International Development (Official Development Assistance Target) Act[27] made the UN's 0.7 per cent aid target legally binding for governments to meet it each year, which will lead to further increases in line with economic growth. Against this backdrop, there has been a steady stream of criticism of DFID projects which have attracted negative publicity in both Parliament and the press. While many of these cases cover areas not under the control of DFID, with spending from large UN agencies or NGOs funded centrally by DFID, that is not always the case.

At one end of the spectrum, recent examples include the comments of Meg Hillier, Chair of the Public Accounts Committee, on an airport project in St Helena:

> The Government has an obligation to support St Helena but a £285m white elephant serves neither its people nor the taxpayers footing the bill. The failure to undertake robust due diligence on this project is truly appalling. I also have serious concerns about the airport's business case, which was marginal at best.[28]

At the other, we see headlines such as 'Britain scraps £9million foreign aid for Ethiopia's Spice Girls after Mail revealed "blood boiling" waste of taxpayers' money'.[29] In this regard, the House of Commons International Development Committee noted in March 2017 that, 'While there has been some improvement, we still do not believe that DFID is robust in its communications and managing reputational risk'.[30] If it is to win the argument that spending these sums of money is in the British interest, DFID must improve the ways it communicates, both in the UK and in the markets in which it is deploying the funding. Too often there appears to be a reticence to promote the UK's involvement in providing support.

The controversy and debate over whether to continue to spend as much on development aid has been rumbling for some years, and has now reached crisis point. This was summarised in a House of Commons Library Briefing of 20 June 2016. In a March 2012 report on the Economic Impact and Effectiveness of Development Aid, the House of Lords Economics Affairs Committee stated that: 'we do not accept that meeting by 2013 the UN target of spending 0.7 per cent (£12bn) of Gross National Income on aid should now be a plank, let alone the central plank, of British aid policy'.

The Committee gave the following reasons for their recommendation that the government abandon the target:

(a) it wrongly prioritises the amount spent rather than the result achieved;

(b) it makes the achievement of the spending target more important than the overall effectiveness of the programme;

(c) the speed of the planned increase risks reducing the quality, value for money and accountability of the aid programme;

   [One witness told the House of Lords Committee that the target encouraged officials 'to turn a blind eye to flagrant abuse in the pressure to get the money out of the door'.]

(d) reaching the target increases the risk ... that aid will have a corrosive effect on local political systems

   [Professor Adrian Wood of Oxford University told the House of Lords Committee: 'If you give a country too much aid for too long you damage its basic governance structure because the politicians pay more attention to the donors than they do to their citizens'].

The House of Lords Economics Affairs Committee concluded that 'the core of aid policy should be choosing and funding the best ways of promoting international development and stability, rather than finding new ways to spend ever-increasing resources'.

The 0.7 per cent aid target is always likely to have its opponents in the national press and amongst some MPs in Parliament, but the level of criticism has now reached unprecedented heights. We cannot continue with present policies unchanged, as there is merit in the criticisms. In March 2016, John Wellington of the *Mail on Sunday* sponsored a petition calling on the government to 'stop spending a fixed 0.7 per cent of our national wealth on Foreign Aid'. After the petition passed the 100,000-signature threshold, thereby qualifying it for consideration for debate by the Petitions Committee, the Committee scheduled a Westminster Hall Debate for 13 June 2016. This was a good example of open debate and admission that all is not working well in the allocation of aid, but accompanied by a strongly expressed belief that we can and must improve the allocation but not the amount.

However, simply reducing the aid budget and opting out from 0.7 per cent target will not be supported in the House of Commons, because of a strong cross-party feeling that there should be no post-Brexit reduction which would be depicted as inward-looking and run counter to the new global outlook. Nor would it be morally right, and it would not send the correct message of a more global post-Brexit UK determined to do business worldwide. The commitment was reinforced in the conclusions of the International Development Committee's report referred to above which states:

> We agree with our predecessor committee in supporting the 0.7 per cent commitment. We acknowledge and understand concern that aid spending is protected whilst domestic spending is not. We have already set out that we think that aid spending is in the national interest. It is right that every penny of the 0.7 per cent is spent as effectively as possible, to tackle the harshest examples of poverty, humanitarian need, and causes of instability, and we regard it as our primary function as a Committee to scrutinise spending to ensure it achieves maximum benefit for its beneficiaries and the UK taxpayer. The examples we have seen of less effective spending do not represent a considerable portion of, nor are they an inevitable consequence of, the 0.7 per cent target.

DFID must seek to demonstrate that every area of aid spending brings a return in alleviating poverty or creating an environment which allows economic growth strategies to succeed.

But – and it is a big but – DFID cannot simply continue with past policies. Our approach to aid delivery has to adapt to the changing environment. Poverty reduction has been a major success in many countries, and the focus needs to be much more on private sector development. Part of this will be DFID contributing to the UK's overall efforts to boost our exports. This is well recognised by its current Secretary for State for International Development, Priti Patel, but it will be crucial to see concrete results.

An area in which we differ in view with the International Development Committee is on the subject of tied aid, where the Committee's view is that:

it is important that UK aid spending continues to be completely untied, whether explicitly or implicitly. While it remains to be seen how it works in practice, language surrounding leveraging aid for trade and creating opportunities for UK companies and the City of London needs to be used cautiously, so as not to create an impression that aid is being given conditionally.

It goes on to 'ask that DFID provides us with a full assessment of the current risk of UK aid becoming implicitly tied, and how it is mitigating those risks'. The fact that UK aid continues to be untied, in marked contrast to the aid programmes of other large contributors, must be challenged. Why are other countries supporting the tying of much of their aid? Indeed, OECD data[31] shows that in 2015, the share of US ODA reported as untied was only 55.5 per cent, down from 62.5 per cent in 2014. Why do some believe that in doing so it helps their business community gain a foothold in countries where they are not established? It is time to seek further and much firmer evidence on which to base decisions. BExA calls for:

DFID to increase promotion of UK export capability in relation to its aid projects. Other OECD countries assign a portion of their aid budget as 'tied-aid' to the benefit of their exporters – a review of the UK's position on 'tied-aid' could provide a real incentive for UK exporters to access new export markets.[32]

There are undoubtedly some issues around tying aid, but these could be addressed. What is needed right now is for a well-structured programme of tying a proportion of our aid spending to UK companies which can offer appropriate solutions in a cost-effective way (through, for example, a value for money assessment), and which meet objectives such as growing local employment and providing training. The proportion of spending deployed in this way should be carefully evaluated to ensure a win-win for both the UK and the recipient country. As well as the direct benefits of the project, it would also act to promote what the UK has to offer more generally in the market, and be well received by businesses and tax payers at home. This could be trialled in a meaningfully-sized controlled pilot programme.

In addition, even without directly tying aid as BExA points out, there is a sense amongst business that more could be done by DFID to encourage bids for its projects by UK contractors and promote UK products.[33] While there are many good examples of DFID working well with innovative UK companies, as profiled in the 2017 Economic Development Strategy, they should continue to focus on doing more in this area, and not be reticent about supporting British business.

Whether the separation of DFID from the FCO twenty years ago was wise is open to question. Fortunately, the creation of the NSC, as discussed in detail in Chapter Four, makes it possible to put that departmental question in 2017 to one side, since the NSC can play the role of the FCO in the past towards advocating aid but with a new much broader based framework for assessing government activity and priorities. The International Development Committee is clear in its view:

> We do not believe that abolishing DFID as an independent department would lead to any improvement in the quality of UK aid spending. The effect of merging DFID into another department would be to dilute its expertise as a specialist development department. The only outcome of such a move would be to diminish the focus placed on poverty reduction and development in UK aid spending, as the majority of ODA would become subject to more complex objectives in another department.

One area in which a more innovative approach has been taken is with the announcement in November 2015 of the establishment of the

Prosperity Fund under the remit of the NSC, with a budget of £1.3 billion over the next five years. Its priorities include improving the business climate, competitiveness and operation of markets, energy and financial sector reform, and increasing the ability of governments to tackle corruption.[34] These reforms are intended to drive sustainable development in developing countries and create opportunities for international business, including UK companies. Supporting countries in their efforts to develop their economies and to grow through trade is seen as a key element in meeting Sustainable Development Goals. The OECD, in its report 'Aid for Trade and the Sustainable Development Agenda',[35] has highlighted that 'too many developing country firms are still priced out of international markets because of high trade cost caused by obsolete or ill-adapted infrastructure, limited access to trade finance, cumbersome and time-consuming border procedures, and the need to meet an ever-broader array of standards'.

These are all areas in which the UK's government and private sector can make significant contributions. In particular, as highlighted by the OECD, when it comes to many growth markets, there are real challenges in getting access to trade finance, and the government needs to look at addressing these as it encourages UK exporters to venture into new markets. There are a variety of reasons for this, including banks deleveraging after the financial crisis and the impact of increased regulation, which has resulted banks reducing their risk profiles. They are now being more selective on their client base and reducing the number of correspondent banking relationships, essential for the smooth running of global trade. An article in the *Financial Times* in July 2016, drawing on a speech by IMF Chief Christine Lagarde, focuses on this issue, noting how regulation is 'eating into banks' cost-benefit rationale for servicing countries such as small island states, war-torn nations or other developing frontiers'. It goes on to say that 'the decline of correspondent banking is stirring the forces of deglobalisation'.[36] An IMF paper of the same year argues that 'coordinated efforts by the public and private sectors are called for to mitigate the risk of financial exclusion and the potential negative impact on financial stability'.[37] If UK exporters are to fulfil the expectations placed upon them and new markets are to be successfully opened up, these issues need to be resolved.

The challenge faced in doing business with Iran, where the UK government is encouraging 'UK businesses to take advantage of the commercial opportunities arising from the lifting of sanctions', is a case in point. Major banks have been holding off transacting business for fear of infringing current or indeed potential future reimposition of sanctions, feeling the risks are too high to justify it. Indeed, this is flagged in the UK government's own advice on doing business in Iran:

> On the whole, banks in the UK remain cautious of facilitating Iran-related transactions, due to remaining sanctions on Iran and the cost of fulfilling compliance requirements. As a result, many European banks including those in the UK may judge that re-engaging with Iranian entities falls outside of their risk appetite, except in a few cases for existing customers.
>
> This presents a challenge for UK business seeking banking services to facilitate trade with Iran. This could include services such as processing transactions, trade finance, and lending facilities.[38]

It is vital and urgent for those concerned about the legitimacy of spending aid money on prosperity outside DFID to define what aid flows count as ODA. Prosperity Fund disbursements also have to meet ODA eligibility requirements and the legal requirements of the International Development Act. As described in the House of Commons Library Briefing Paper of 20 June 2016,[39] aid flows count as ODA if they:

- go to countries and territories on the OECD's Development Assistance Committee's List of ODA Recipients[40] (which covers most low and middle income countries, and all Least Developed Countries) or to multilateral institutions, such as the World Bank;

- are provided by official agencies, including state and local governments, or by their executive agencies;
- are administered with the promotion of the economic development
  and welfare of developing countries as its main objective;
- are either grants or loans that have a substantial benefit to the bor-
  rower compared to a loan at market rate.

In the context of the activity of the Prosperity Fund, the list of countries eligible is an important one, as it covers a much wider range than
are priorities for DFID. Not only that, many of the countries are at a
relatively advanced stage of development, which will require significantly different approaches to traditional aid projects. How activities
are managed in those countries will be a critical issue, with initial projects, including on education, healthcare, energy and anti-corruption
already being rolled out in Brazil, Chile, China, Colombia, Indonesia,
Malaysia, Mexico, Nigeria, Peru, Philippines, South Africa, Turkey
and Vietnam. The International Development Committee in the
report cited has expressed its concern 'about the focus and capacity
of other government departments spending ODA, and are looking in
depth at these issues in our inquiry into UK aid'. The Committee goes
on to state that:

> DFID's administrative capacity appears to have fallen below what
> is required to manage its increasing budget optimally. The result of
> this has been that DFID has become more reliant on larger external
> organisations, including big multilaterals and private contractors,
> to the exclusion of smaller organisations and DFID being able to
> properly oversee its own spending.

This gives cause for concern over how effectively these funds will be
managed, and we shall return to this aspect later.

Although increasing numbers of developing countries are able to
finance more of their own development, many still face considerable
challenges, such as rapid urbanisation, climate change, and high and

persistent inequality, which can lower long-term growth prospects, including in middle-income countries where more than 70 per cent of the world's poor live. The Prosperity Fund focus in supporting the broad-based, inclusive and sustainable growth in these markets represents a step-change in deployment of ODA resources. The Fund aims to provide expertise and technical assistance in areas of UK strength to:

- promote economic reforms and remove barriers to trade;
- strengthen policy capacity and build strong institutions;
- develop sectors which support growth such as infrastructure, energy, finance, education and healthcare.

The latter in particular is an area in which there is significant potential to make a real difference, by deploying aid in new ways. In particular, many economies which are transitioning to more market based financing solutions encounter significant issues in raising finance for infrastructure, including social infrastructure, which do not generate sufficient economic returns to satisfy external investors. In these areas, other countries have been ready to provide concessional funding which can make such projects viable. Again this is an area in which many UK companies would like to see the government do more, and while it is important to ensure that such funding does not lead to market distortions, safeguards can be put in place, particularly around the nature of projects which would qualify. DFID and UKEF have explored the possibility of putting in place a concessional export finance facility, which would complement the long-term commercial funding that UKEF already offers. Yet such a facility is still not available to support UK exporters, and this leaves them at a competitive disadvantage in many markets. Even where commercial funding is available, one of the challenges in many developing markets is finding projects which have been developed to a stage at which they are bankable, and given the high risks involved, private sector companies are increasingly unwilling, or indeed unable to bear these early-stage costs. We recommend providing funding now, which would enable more projects to move from the planning phase to commercial reality.

All proposed Prosperity Fund programmes and projects are to be assessed against:

- impact: how the programme supports the economic development and welfare of developing countries (ODA projects only) and how it creates opportunities for business, including UK business;
- strategic fit: does it meet the needs and priorities of the partner country and the steer from the ministerial board?
- value for money.

The ministerial board has asked UK government departments to consider multi-year work in sectors including: financial services; insurance; business services; infrastructure; energy (to include extractives, renewable, low carbon and climate); environmental industries; healthcare; education; and other potential high-impact sectors. Work will also be developed on the 'golden thread' of robust institutions, good governance and reduced corruption. It will include work with a range of existing partners in the UK and in-country, including business, NGOs and international organisations, such as the World Bank, WTO and OECD, and new partners where this will help harness specialist expertise, extend reach and attract complementary financing. Non-ODA activity will support projects with the greatest impact and value for money for the UK.

This pre- and post-Brexit policy represents continuity, which is a strength, but the added urgency of a post-Brexit global position should help ensure that UK business and institutions are informed and ready to compete for new opportunities.

In November 2016, the Independent Commission for Aid Impact produced an 'Approach Paper on a Rapid Review of the Prosperity Fund'[41] designed to address:

- Effectiveness: Are the systems and procedures of the Prosperity

Fund adequate to ensure effective programming and good value for money?

- Learning: Has the design of the Prosperity Fund been informed by learning from other cross-government aid funds and instruments?

The approach included a rapid review of all bids made into the Fund, key informant interviews to explore strategy and governance arrangements, and a more detailed review of selected issues arising from the rapid review. In addition, it undertook an initial assessment of effectiveness by reviewing key Prosperity Fund documents covering governance and management arrangements, strategy and objectives, the funding approach at portfolio and programme levels and results management. To avoid duplication and overlap, it drew upon the infrastructure Project Authority's September 2016 review, which followed up on its March 2016 review.[42] This represents a very serious attempt to chart out a new approach on evidence based research. It is a welcome development and should give business confidence in the government's post-Brexit priorities.

In its report published on 7 February 2017,[43] the ICAI warned of 'serious risks' about the effectiveness of a £1.3 billion project to help developing countries. It described the Fund as 'fragmented' and lacking transparency. The report concluded that outline bids for money – known as concept notes – contained 'limited detail' as to how objectives will be achieved and 'given the speed at which participating departments are expected to move from concept notes through to full business cases and implementation at scale, the lack of delivery capacity in key departments and diplomatic posts presents some serious risks.

ICAI's chief commissioner Alison Evans said the Prosperity Fund was a 'complex and ambitious initiative', adding that it has made 'significant progress' in a short space of time but 'to deliver on its aims it must continue to improve its systems and processes, particularly given the risks associated with its current speed of delivery'.

The government claimed it was already implementing the vast majority of ICAI's early recommendations, including transparency.[44]

> Sustained economic growth is the only long term solution to poverty and the Prosperity Fund supports the vital economic development needed to help middle-income countries – home to around 70 per cent of the world's poor – to reduce poverty and become our prosperity partners of the future.

These are fine sentiments, but where is the drive to achieve results? We need to see a real urgency on the part of the government in implementing this programme, and an underlying resolve to improve performance.

Going forward, the UK will need to watch its aid policy very carefully and ensure it is adapting to meet the most critical needs in terms of both poverty reduction and providing the conditions for economic growth, especially in the poorest and most fragile countries of the world. There needs to be an open debate on where our funding is spent, given the acknowledgement of the need to address the challenges of failed and fragile states. In the *Guardian* article cited earlier, former Prime Minister David Cameron, in describing the plans for the new Commission on State Fragility, Growth and Development which he was then chairing, said:

> We want to generate the most cutting-edge recommendations that governments, donors and NGOs can put into practice. This may destroy some long-held shibboleths. It may show that, when it comes to aid, there should be more investment in security. It may show that the building blocks of democracy – critically, the rule of law – are more important than the act of simply holding elections.

Such fundamental examination of the issues should be welcomed. There is no doubt that such proposals will spark controversy, but, given the huge expense of dealing with the consequences of failed states militarily, devoting a portion of aid budgets to enhancing security should be seen as a logical and justifiable approach, not a way of shifting funding from the aid budget to defence. The NSC should ensure that in meeting our commitment to meet the 0.7 per cent target, spending will cover all aspects of the overall prosperity strategy, and include projects led by other departments: notably the MOD and FCO, as well as DFID. How such cross-government coordination is implemented is the subject of the next chapter.

CHAPTER 4

COORDINATING AND IMPLEMENTING POLICY

Tony Blair and David Cameron, as Prime Ministers from 2001 to 2007 and 2010 to 2016 respectively, operated a system whereby the Cabinet and the Cabinet Office were diminished and the politicians in No. 10 and No. 11 exercised considerable and relatively unchecked power. A welcome exception to this was foreign and security policy, with the creation of the NSC in 2010 whose workings are described in some detail in this chapter.

Theresa May's claim to have restored Cabinet government was initially taken at face value. But when she announced a general election in 2017 – after repeatedly saying she would not do so – and proceeded to campaign as if she and she alone was making policy with constant use of phrases such as 'my government' and 'my manifesto', people began to sense that all was not as it seemed. Then the fiasco over the so called 'dementia tax' being hastily revised made clear that only those in her immediate circle had been involved and the Cabinet had been ignored. A campaign that started off with predictions of a massive Conservative majority ended with a 'hung' Parliament and the government dependent on ten MPs from Northern Ireland. Theresa May now appears likely to join the ranks of four other Prime Ministers – Lloyd George, Neville Chamberlain, Margaret Thatcher and Tony Blair – who, having acquired a personality trait described as 'hubris syndrome', were eventually removed from office before leading their parties into another general election by a revolt of MPs.

The exceptional circumstance which will define what happens is the need to complete the UK's exit from the EU by March 2019. Returning to the tried and tested mechanism of a democratic Cabinet and parliamentary democracy is relatively easy. But there are no parallels to the situation facing us post-Brexit of returning to UK laws when since 1973 we have increasingly come under EU law in many aspects of our lives. This is not a time for jingoism, pseudo patriotism or turning back the clock to when we did stand alone from May 1940 to December 1941.[1] This sixteen-month period was unique. We were not alone in 1914–18, nor were we alone from 1941–45. We relied in two world wars on allies in Europe, from the Commonwealth and across the Atlantic. We are not alone now over Brexit. There are many people and governments worldwide, not least in the US and Australia to name but two, who know what we are trying to achieve and identify with our British stance. We also know that many people in the EU are sympathetic to our stance and many show this in opinion polls and demonstrate this as voters, indicating that they would like to follow us in part or in whole. After the 'hung parliament' where the Conservatives lost their overall majority in June 2017 we must come together as a nation and make a success of Brexit on the basis of pride and confidence in British products, technology, design and culture.

What we need in 2017 is the maximum unity across the UK amongst our citizens, whether remainers or leavers in 2016, so that Cabinet can negotiate effectively on our behalf in complicated treaty negotiations with twenty-seven EU member states over our withdrawal from the EU and in doing so re-establish an independent British voice.

No discussion of foreign policy post-Brexit can ignore the fact that the very structure of foreign policy making in the UK has only relatively recently, since 2010, been changed in a major way, and there are understandable teething problems. The National Security Council was introduced by the coalition government under Prime Minister David Cameron, soon after he had taken office in 2010, having never before held any ministerial position. Fortunately, Dame Pauline Neville-Jones, a former Chairman of the Joint Intelligence Committee, had been made a member of the House of Lords and acted as the Prime Minister's adviser as Minister of State for Security and Counter Terrorism in the Home Office. She had in mind three main considerations for reform that she disclosed in a House of Lords debate on 12 July 2016. The first was the need, for which the then Cabinet committee system did not adequately provide, to bring foreign policy and domestic security together in one place for decision and to increase the government's ability to operate across the piece. Secondly, in an era of the increasing importance of intelligence to policy making, she felt it made sense to create a forum for direct discussion between the agency heads and senior ministers. Her third and overriding consideration was to try to prevent 'sofa government' (the term used to describe Tony Blair's unstructured informal government style in the report of the Inquiry into Intelligence on Weapons of Mass Destruction, chaired by the former Cabinet Secretary Lord Butler), which had led to the UK's greatest foreign and security policy failure over Iraq.

The terms of reference of the NSC are: 'to consider matters relating to national security, foreign policy, defence, international relations and development, resilience, energy and resource security'. The NSC was designed to provide regular and inescapable time for consideration of the complex threats and challenges to the security of this country that the weekly Cabinet meeting agenda did not, in reality, provide.

There is, perhaps surprisingly in view of the experience in Iraq, no legislative provision for the NSC. Perhaps a specific legal basis could prevent Cabinet procedures being short-changed by a Prime Minister intent on governing on their own, but legislation can easily be too restrictive and rigid to fit in with operational timetables. We therefore suggest that the Cabinet Secretary be given a formal responsibility from now on to notify relevant permanent under secretaries of any changes in NSC procedures. Already as accounting officers, they are obliged to let the Public Accounts Committee know if there are specified concerns. The Cabinet Secretary should also be required to notify the new joint Committee of the House of Commons and House of Lords on National Security Strategy if previous NSC procedure or practice is being changed, whether it is being improved, bypassed or side-lined. Then those bodies will have a duty to report to Parliament and hold the Prime Minister to account in the way that best suits the circumstances of the time, whether in peace or war.

The full members of the NSC are: the Prime Minister; the Chancellor of the Exchequer; the Home Secretary; the Foreign Secretary; the Secretary of State for Defence; the Secretary of State for Business; the Energy and Industrial Strategy; the Secretary of State for International Development; and the Attorney General. Others in attendance on a routine basis include: the CDS; the Director of GCHQ; the Director of the Security Service (MI5); the Chief of the Secret Intelligence Service (SIS/MI6); the chairman of the Joint Intelligence Committee; and the National Security Adviser. During the time of the coalition government under David Cameron, Nick Clegg as Deputy Prime Minister and Leader of the Liberal Democrats also attended, along with Danny Alexander as Chief Secretary to the Treasury, and two senior Conservative figures, Ken Clarke when Minister of Justice and Oliver Letwin in his capacity as Minister of State for Policy. Behind David Cameron sat his Chief of Staff, Ed Llewellyn. However, the routine attendance by the Prime Minister's Chief of Staff is not necessary.

The NSC's operation is vividly described by its first Chief of the Defence Staff, Sir David Richards, in his book.

> I am a great supporter of the NSC in principle. It was important to reset the practice of government after the distortion of the Blair years and no other body that met regularly covered the remit set out for the NSC. My frustration with it, which was evident throughout our discussions on Afghanistan and the conduct of the war in Libya, was that it tended to focus on the near-term and the tactical as opposed to the big foreign policy and grand strategic issues. The redeployment of 120 men in a war in Afghanistan controlled by NATO, for example, should not have been a decision taken by the NSC or the Prime Minister, a point I once welcomed being made by Nick Clegg at an NSC meeting.[2]

Richards felt that some confusion had arisen about the respective roles of the NSC secretariat, chaired by the National Security Adviser (NSA), and the Chiefs of Staff Committee, chaired by the Chief of the Defence Staff. He believed the NSC secretariat did not have the experience, processes or skill needed to run a war, even if it involved a major cross-government effort, and this is surely correct.

A new committee known as the 'Super Chiefs' – or NSC (Officials), NSC(O) – emerged initiated by Richards consisting of the traditional armed forces Chiefs of Staff Committee plus the NSA, the heads of MI6, GCHQ, the FCO and DFID, as well as the Chairman of the Joint Intelligence Committee. It developed as an attempt to reflect the realities of creating and implementing a military strategy and conducting a military campaign in which civilian agencies play a key role in most military operations. In times of a full scale war, aspects of the present NSC machinery may need to be modified with a much smaller War Cabinet perhaps introduced along with other changes.

On the subject of Whitehall mandarins, Richards encouragingly writes:

> Individually and collectively I soon began to realise what an impressive bunch they are. Successive governments, and indeed the country, should be much more grateful to them for their intelligence, integrity and commitment than sometimes appears to be the case. I also learnt that it's much easier to criticise those in government, politicians and mandarins, than to actually do it. Something I would ruefully compare with how easy running complex military operations clearly appears from the comfort of editors' offices and academics' studies, especially with the benefit of hindsight.[3]

Whatever the criticism of the NSC which arises from time to time in this book, we believe it is a very worthwhile new mechanism for bringing coherence into foreign and security policy in its widest sense for the future and our criticisms are meant to be constructive. Where we do believe there is need for urgent reform is in increasing the powers and back up for the Chief of the Defence Staff. As set out in Chapter Two, we recommend the NSC as a body consider this question and make recommendations through the Prime Minister to the Cabinet.

The National Security Secretariat is based in the Cabinet Office,[4] which serves the Prime Minister, the Cabinet and the NSC, with a view to making sure that ministerial decisions are well prepared and properly followed through. Its creation was entirely an administrative act, with prerogative powers exercised by ministers.* The Prime Minister needs to be careful not to monopolise the time of the National Security Adviser. Taking them on foreign visits can be an inefficient use of their time when they can be briefed on the visit by the Prime Minister's own staff. The NSC must not become an extension of the Prime Minister's Office. It is fundamental that it strengthens Cabinet government by ensuring Cabinet has broad based and well informed advice coming to it on key issues. While many decisions can, and must, be made purely within the NSC, it is the major, principled issues which must still be brought to Cabinet.

During the last parliament, there were two ministerial sub-committees of the Council: NSC (THRC) to consider Threats, Hazards, Resilience and Contingencies, and NSC (N) to consider Nuclear Deterrence and Security; both chaired by the Prime Minister. Theresa May also created an additional sub-committee NSC (C) to deal with Cyber programmes chaired by Philip Hammond. The Review Implementation sub-committee originally chaired by Oliver Letwin is now chaired by the Home Secretary, Amber Rudd.

The first two tasks of the new NSC coordinated by the National Security Adviser were to oversee the publication of the 2010 National Security Strategy (NSS), and Strategic Defence and Security Review

---

* Prerogative powers are those powers that a British government has historically been able to exercise without any recourse to parliamentary scrutiny or approval. Originally prerogative powers would have been exercised by the reigning monarch. However, over time a distinction has emerged between the monarch acting on his or her own capacity, and the powers possessed by the monarch as head of state. In modern times, government ministers exercise the majority of the prerogative powers either in their own right or through the advice they provide to the Queen, which she is bound constitutionally to follow. Prerogative powers were changed by legislation as recently as 2010.

(SDSR). They set out the new coalition's approach to national security issues. As Prime Minister, Cameron, and the Chancellor, Osborne, used this SDSR process to centralise power and decision-making in the NSC structure. This was strongly resisted by the MOD, and the Defence Secretary, Fox, regularly spoke out against the burden they were being asked to bear. He was angry that the protected areas – health, schools, and international development – escaped free whereas the MOD faced cuts of some 8 per cent in real terms. Cameron felt the MOD was too big, too inefficient and spending too much money. The strategy, he argued, must shift away from military intervention towards conflict prevention, with a new focus on unconventional threats. The army was reduced by 7,000 to a front-line strength of around 95,000, the Royal Navy by 5,000 to 30,000, and the RAF by 5,000 to 33,000 by 2015. The 2010 SDSR generated 'enduring bad blood, less from the Foreign Office and intelligence communities than from the MOD, especially from Fox and chief of the general staff, David Richards'.[5] No. 10 was furious at the briefings from the MOD to sympathetic journalists and to backbench Tories with service backgrounds, but the spending review did achieve its desired end of savings, even though it created bitterness that spilled over in later years and was 'widely criticised for being rushed and insufficiently strategic'.[6] In fairness, there was a deep global economic crisis at the time and that has not entirely gone away, but, as we argued in Chapter Two, there is a new strategic concern following the annexation of the Crimea and the security of our country demands an increase in our 2 per cent GDP commitment to defence spending.

In January 2011, the Prime Minister and the Cabinet Secretary asked the National Security Adviser and the Chairman of the Joint Intelligence Committee to review how the central national security and intelligence machinery and structures could best support the NSC, building on the Butler Report of 2004. The key recommendations from the review are:

- The NSC's priorities should be the lead driver of the JIC agenda.

- The needs of the NSC are best supported by the JIC meeting in two formats, at a Principals and a sub-Principals level.
- The JIC should produce a wider range of tailored intelligence products. The number of full JIC papers should be reduced, and replaced by more current briefs and summaries.
- The wider assessment capability, including Defence Intelligence (DI) and the Joint Terrorism Analysis Centre (JTAC), should be put more directly at the disposal of the NSC where appropriate.
- The leadership of the Joint Intelligence Organisation should be charged with ensuring that the collective business plans of the government's assessment bodies align with the NSC's priorities.
- In supporting the NSC, the policy implications of analytical judgements should be identified in significant assessments given to ministers.
- The Joint Intelligence Organisation should also implement the recommendations of its open source audit.
- Clearer processes should be established to ensure that ministers receive timely, well-chosen and auditable intelligence reports consistent with the principles set out in Lord Butler's report of 2004.

To these we would suggest adding post-Brexit an additional ninth point: that the National Security Adviser should maintain the closest contact with key governments within the EU as a contribution to the Article 8 partnership (referred to in Chapters One and Two).

The NSC, as discussed, does not have a separate legal or operational existence in terms of decision-making from the government as a whole. Formally speaking, its major decisions are reported to the Cabinet by either the Prime Minister or another relevant minister, and Cabinet makes the final decisions. These will, however, be based on major policy discussions that have taken place within the NSC and the recommendations made in that context, which the UK government as a whole then considers. Of course, in practice, given that many of the most senior ministers overlap, it will be very rare for the Cabinet to ignore or contradict recommendations emanating from the NSC. Where the NSC is different from the previous Cabinet sub-committee, Defence and Overseas Policy Committee (DOP), which dealt with defence and foreign security issues for many years, is the size and the involvement of officials as specialists, not ministers. But this practice of mixed participation is not new. It was followed on a special Cabinet sub-committee established by James Callaghan for dealing with nuclear weapons and the NPT in 1977. It was also followed in the seminar format he created for discussing monetary policy with the Prime Minister in the chair, the Chancellor, the Treasury Secretary, the Governor and Deputy Governor of the Bank of England, and Treasury officials.

In the event of a declaration of war or the commitment of British forces to military action, constitutional convention still requires that authorisation is given by the Prime Minister on behalf of the Crown. An attempt by then-Prime Minister Gordon Brown to change this was abandoned because of the difficulty of legislating for every circumstance, some very urgent; in effect war is still authorised by the Prime Minister following discussion in the Cabinet as in 1914 and in 1939. This will continue but with professional advice from the NSC including the Chief of the Defence Staff. Yet after 2003, when the decision to invade Iraq was agreed in a cross-party vote in Parliament, Prime Ministers will be rightly expected to try to bring any declaration of war, if they have time, to Parliament.

The National Security Secretariat, led by the National Security Adviser, has formal responsibility for agreeing the agenda for meetings of the NSC. However, it will only do so following consultations with the Prime Minister, ministers and government departments, so in practice the Prime Minister will have the final say. As a Cabinet committee, information about its proceedings is not formally disclosed, but briefings from No. 10 have been frequent and there have been many unofficial leaks.

As part of the planning for the implementation of the 2015 National Security Strategy and SDSR, the government considered how it could further strengthen strategic direction and oversight and learn from 2010, which was not without faults. The results were published on 23 November 2015 and some changes were announced.

One of those changes was the establishment of a new committee of the NSC – chaired by the then Chancellor of the Duchy of Lancaster, Oliver Letwin, now chaired by the Home Secretary, Amber Rudd – to oversee implementation of the strategy, review how the NSC and the Cabinet Office Briefing Rooms (COBR) are supported during crises, and evaluate the structure for strategic assessment within central government.

A number of new issue-focused cross-government teams aimed at removing duplication, consolidating national security expertise and making the most efficient use of it across government have also been created under NSC auspices.[7] They are:

- A Euro-Atlantic Security Policy Unit, hosted by the Foreign and Commonwealth Office (FCO).
- An International Counter-Terrorism Strategy Unit, hosted by the Home Office.
- An Arms Control and Counter-Proliferation Centre, hosted by the Ministry of Defence (MOD).
- An Export Controls Unit, originally hosted by the Department for Business, Innovation and Skills (BIS).
- A Gulf Strategy Unit, hosted by the Cabinet Office.
- A UN Peacekeeping Unit, hosted by the FCO.
- A single provider of National Security Vetting Services.

We suggest a further point should be added:

- An Article 8 policy unit hosted by the FCO.

We believe that the NSC is the correct forum for keeping progress on Article 8 under review and for bringing any recommendations for further action to Cabinet.

'A "virtual National Security Academy" is being established, to act as a "hub" for sharing, developing and maintaining critical knowledge and skills across the national security community.' This mechanism may need supplementing with an actual National Security Academy, but that can evolve if need be over time. At present the NSC is new enough to need some stability, but not so old to become set in its ways or deaf to new thinking.

In addition to the Prosperity Fund discussed in the previous chapter, there are at least three other key budgetary pools which fall under the ambit of the NSC, and these demonstrate the benefits of taking a cross-governmental approach in an increasingly interlinked policy-making environment.

CONFLICT SECURITY AND STABILITY FUND (CSSF)

The CSSF became operational in April 2015. It is an enhanced version of the tri-departmental (FCO, MOD, DFID) Conflict Pool which started in 2001, originally as two separate funds: the African Conflict Prevention Pool and the Global Conflict Prevention Pool. Everything is now managed and controlled by the NSC, and it represents an attempt to fulfil the longstanding aspiration for a 'whole of government' approach to national security.

The CSSF is now the main means for the implementation of the 2011 Building Stability Overseas Strategy (BSOS), which was produced in order to act upon the conflict prevention agenda originally set out in the 2010 UK National Security Strategy.[8]

A key element of the UK's conflict prevention agenda will be a greater focus through UK overseas development assistance on fragile and conflict-affected states.[9] The Independent Commission on Aid Impact (ICAI) said in a critical report on DFID's work in fragile states published in February 2015 that a growing proportion of UK ODA effort is being spent today in high-risk countries, but that also applies to the MOD.[10]

A target was set to spend 30 per cent of UK ODA on such states by 2014–15. In 2013, this was achieved when 43 per cent of UK ODA was spent in fragile and conflict-affected states.[11] In a speech on 16

November 2015, David Cameron announced that in future at least half of DFID's budget would be spent on 'stabilising and supporting broken and fragile states'.[12] We cannot expect the MOD contribution to this effort continuing to fall on a defence budget designed for national defence without some offsetting financial contribution.

First announced in 2013 and funded from core departmental budgets, the CSSF was worth £1.033 billion in 2015/16 and £1.127 billion in 2016/17. The government said that the CSSF would be worth over £1.3 billion annually by 2019/20.[13] This contrasts with £683 million for the Conflict Pool in its final year 2014/15. The CSSF can be counted as ODA, or towards the pledge to spend 2 per cent of the national budget on defence – or both, if this is 'consistent with the classification guidelines'.[14] In 2016/17, £134 million of the CSSF's £1.127 billion budget counted towards both government targets.[15]

This is where we are at last starting to see a more rational distribution of ODA spending and, from now on, it must be the source of much of the increased defence spending we have argued for when it occurs in conflict-affected states, making it possible to reach spending targets set by the NSC with additional MOD and FCO spending. It has caused a lot of justified resentment that a substantially reduced defence budget has hitherto been expected to carry stabilisation costs in the poorest conflict areas, when, in all fairness, it could never be ascribed to what most people would consider defence spending. The NSC is an ideal forum for achieving a more rational distribution and that has been helped by some sensible changes in the OECD guidelines. However, these changes are relatively limited, and most military related spending is still excluded under the current OECD definitions:

- **Military aid**: No military equipment or services are reportable as ODA. Anti-terrorism activities are also excluded. However, the cost of using donors' armed forces to deliver humanitarian aid is eligible.
- **Peacekeeping**: Most peacekeeping expenditures are excluded in line with the exclusion of military costs. However, some closely

defined developmentally relevant activities within peacekeeping operations are included.[16]

Given the critical link between security and development, particularly in the most fragile states, we would argue that the UK should press for the scope to be widened further. We note that the Conservative manifesto for the 2017 election recognises the need for change:

> We do not believe that international definitions of development assistance always help in determining how money should be spent, on whom and for what purpose. So we will work with like-minded countries to change the rules so that they are updated and better reflect the breadth of our assistance around the world. If that does not work, we will change the law to allow us to use a better definition of development spending, while continuing to meet our 0.7 per cent target.[17]

This is undoubtedly a controversial issue, and there has been strong opposition in the past to including military expenditure under ODA budgets. However, if public support is to be retained for current levels of international aid, and as we have noted there are many who challenge the current commitment, this issue must be tackled. If the UK is to make a carrier-based Rapid Reaction Force available to the UN, to tackle security and/or humanitarian crises, it would not be unreasonable to see at least some of that financial commitment, as assessed for where and why it has been deployed, credited as expenditure of ODA funds. This issue is best handled openly and with as much transparency as possible. Apart from France and Canada, there are very few major countries ready and able to help stabilise the poorest countries in the world, and the incentives to do so from the OECD should be positive ones. It is impossible to forecast what percentage of the defence budget in 2020 (hopefully by then 2.5 per cent) would be made up of ODA if such changes could be agreed, but it is likely to be significant.

In other key areas of ODA spending there should also be transparency. The Joint Committee on the National Security Strategy (JCNSS) wrote in paragraph twenty-two of their 2017 Report: 'There is a risk that the CSSF is being used as a 'slush fund' for projects that may be worthy, but do not collectively meet the needs of UK national security.'[18] Hence their stress that the National Security Adviser should be the 'undisputed accounting officer'. The government has said that, under the departmental allocations from the Fund in 2015–16, the FCO will receive £738.8 million, the MOD £191.5 million, DFID £59.9 million and other departments and agencies £42.81 million.[19] The FCO's CSSF allocation appears to have been entirely transferred from DFID's budget.[20] This is sensible post-Brexit, and justifiable if DFID's budget is to be maintained.

The JCNSS was very critical, and complained that the government had failed to provide the Committee with the evidence that they needed to assess whether their activity was as coherent as it could be or was sufficiently linked to the UK's core strategic objectives. It went on to say that 'The objectives, operation and achievements of the CSSF are opaque.'[21] They refused to legitimise the CSSF by endorsing the Fund's operation. About half the CSSF budget of £1.127 billion is being ring-fenced and earmarked for predetermined activity and standing commitments in 2016/17. Opaqueness may have short term political advantage domestically, but it engenders suspicion. Overseas aid has to adapt to the changing international situation and there is a role for greater education around it.

JOINT SECURITY FUND

In the 2015 summer budget, the Chancellor of the Exchequer, George Osborne, announced the creation of a Joint Security Fund. This is another mechanism for reallocation to defence spending and in combination should go some way to meet necessary increases in the defence budget.

SINGLE INTELLIGENCE ACCOUNT

The Single Intelligence Account and the National Cyber Security Programme provide the funding for the UK security and intelligence agencies, MI5 and the Secret Intelligence Service (MI6), and for the GCHQ budget. They can all make bids to the Joint Security Fund to support 'key capabilities'. For example, additional funding of £6.4 billion was provided by the Joint Security Fund for the equipment programme.

The government must now take steps to integrate global NSC policies further and implement them. In Brussels, the UK Embassy to the EU with the UK Permanent Representation to NATO will be the two key day-to-day channels for building the Article 8 policy. The UK Mission to the UN in New York needs to be the main hub of foreign policy outside London. Currently it consists of around ninety staff, roughly equally split between UK- and locally-based. DFID has three to four people directly represented. It needs more staff in New York to get to grips with establishing greater accountability and transparency in UN agencies currently receiving extensive UK support. Some of these will come from DFID and the Treasury. The FCO political staff numbers also need to be increased to cope with the greater activity rate and resolutions now stemming from the General Assembly. A new focus on the fifty-one Commonwealth countries in the General Assembly needs to be undertaken quietly but seriously to both help and inform them about UN Security Council matters. The aim should be to provide the sort of sustained relationship that the UK has given to formal and informal EU consultations on a regular basis since 1973 in New York. The Commonwealth, with its Secretariat in London, is responsible for its overall development. It would make more sense to leave this arrangement intact under the new Commonwealth Secretary General, Baroness Scotland, and put the UK global emphasis through our Mission in New York, where exposure to all the different UN activities is concentrated.

Permanent membership of the Security Council is a privilege. One way of being seen to recognise this is to ensure UK representation, from either the FCO or DFID, in the capitals of virtually all member states of the UN, even if this can only be justified exceptionally by a one-person mission which may not always be kept open during holiday periods. The interchange between the FCO, DFID and other domestic ministries' personnel must be far greater than hitherto. The interchange with the private sector also needs to be more systematic, with more bilateral exchanges of meaningful length between companies – not always the large ones – and the FCO, as well as single transfers.

In opening up debate, the Select Committees on Foreign Policy and Defence Policy have proven their worth, especially since the chairs have been elected by the House of Commons as a whole since 2010. Another development of foreign and security policy has been the establishment of the House of Lords and House of Commons Joint Committee on the National Security Strategy, appointed to consider the NSS. It is currently chaired by a former Foreign Secretary, Margaret Beckett MP, and its First Report of Session 2016–17 was published on 10 July 2016.[22] The government's response was received on 15 September 2016. We largely share their conclusions about the need for greater cross-government coordination in and a realistic assessment of the financial implications of the policies being espoused. Their Report shows that there is a cross-party consensus developing in both Houses, and the UK needs to do much more in terms of expenditure and staffing levels to boost NATO's defence. It also demonstrates that there is considerable scepticism about the projected efficiency savings of £9.2 billion delivering a better defence for the UK and NATO. That is an important post-Brexit message that must be acted on by the government in 2017. They have it within their power from existing resources coming from DFID to ensure that extra money for defence is made available, drawing on existing departmental budgets within the parameters set internationally.

The government's refusal to support the Joint Parliamentary Committee's recommendation to have a new National Security Strategy and Strategic Defence and Security Review in the light of the Brexit vote has been a disappointment to some, but there are merits in this decision, provided it is just for a pause and if it is accompanied by what we called for in Chapter Two, a post-election SDSR, and a thorough NSC review of its own record. Admittedly, some findings of such a report may need to remain private, for commercial as well as security reasons, but as much as possible should be sent to the Joint Parliamentary Committee.

THE NSC'S TRACK RECORD

In responding to world events in the first six years of its existence, the NSC made, in our view, some mistakes in relation to Iraq and Afghanistan; in particular, in the case of the former, compounding some of the far bigger errors made over Baghdad during the immediate aftermath of the invasion in 2003. However, in reviewing how the NSC operated during this period and assessing the lessons to be learnt, we have focused on contemporary accounts of the two main new operations which the NSC were responsible for: Libya and Syria. The UN implications were discussed in Chapter One.

LIBYA

The controversy around the military intervention in Libya continues to this day, as the country has both collapsed into chaos and become a major trafficking hub for migrants seeking to cross to Europe. Once again, the lack of sufficient boots on the ground after initial destructive aerial bombing has raised questions about the continued use of this particular strategy of intervention confined to the use of air power. A new factor was a lack of enthusiasm from the US for the intervention in principle. The hesitation was understandable in view of the outcome. The Obama administration was bound to dictate the shape of a limited intervention in Libya, and without their initial attack on ground-to-air missile emplacements it would have been far more costly in terms of troops and equipment. What should, therefore, have been emphasised was the far greater role that diplomacy would need to play during and after the military action. The reluctance to involve Russia from the start in continuing discussions at the UN Security Council was an error. By abstaining in the Security Council vote, Russia and China had let the UN resolution approving action through, but they had been assured throughout that regime change was not the objective. Dmitry Medvedev, who was, at the time, the President of the Russian Federation, was helped in his decision not to use the veto by Obama saying publicly: 'Broadening our military mission to include regime change would be a mistake … If we tried to overthrow Gaddafi by force our coalition would splinter.' Whatever the rights or wrongs of handling Gaddafi, a large section of global opinion believes France and the UK in particular were intent on re-moving him, and much of what Sarkozy and Cameron said at the time fed that impression.

In the US, those who advocated a no-fly zone in February 2011 did so to correct the imbalance where only Gaddafi's forces had access to air power, according to the account by Mark Landler on which we have drawn.[23] Senator John Kerry on 3 March used a budget hearing in the Senate to press Hillary Clinton to support a no-fly zone saying: 'The global community cannot be on the side lines while airplanes are allowed to bomb and strafe.' On 6 March, Gaddafi sent in tanks and artillery against disorganised rebel forces that advanced swiftly along the Libyan coast towards Benghazi. On Monday 7 March, at a Cabinet meeting held in Derby, Cameron told ministers he did not regard UN support as a prerequisite for military intervention in Libya, rather something desirable but not essential; shades of Prime Minister Blair in 2003 over Iraq. On 11 March, EU leaders met at an emergency summit in Brussels over a dinner with fellow leaders, at which Sarkozy became so angry with the failure of other leaders to support the emerging Anglo-French initiative that he stormed out.

Cameron soothed Sarkozy enough to bring him back to the table, but their fellow EU leaders were still far from convinced of the need for a strong EU response. Angela Merkel felt let down and out of the loop, while Obama had an eleventh-hour change of heart, and began to favour a no-fly zone. The Italians were readier to act, as were some other EU countries, but as an entity, the EU was split.

The transforming decision came on 12 March 2011 when the Arab League called for the UN Security Council to impose a no-fly zone over Libya, attacking the Gaddafi government. In the US those in favour of UNSCR 1973 were Secretary of State Hillary Clinton, Vice President Joe Biden and UN Ambassador Susan Rice. In opposition were much of the State Department, Secretary of Defense Robert Gates and National Security Advisor Thomas Donilon. Obama, while his position remained unclear, did not take calls from Downing Street. In the White House late on 15 March President Obama rechristened the 'no-fly zone' as a 'no-drive zone' in relation to Gaddafi's tanks threatening Benghazi. Also, Susan Rice, then the US Ambassador to the UN, having exchanged harsh words with her French counterpart, Gérard Araud, saying: 'You're not going to drag us into your shitty war', to which he retorted France wasn't a 'subsidiary of the United States of America Inc', had to call back after Obama decided to seek UN authorisation for 'all necessary measures', telling the Frenchman, 'Ok, we're a go.' But the US position became characterised as 'leading from behind' and France and Britain, now that US power had delivered a situation where their planes could fly virtually anywhere risk-free, began to escalate the conflict. Merkel had decided Germany would not participate. This incidentally gives a flavour of how hard it has been to herd the other 26 EU members into collective action in a Common Foreign and Security Policy.

On 17 March, UNSCR 1973 was passed by ten votes to zero, with five abstentions (Russia, Germany, Brazil, China and India). The Gulf Co-operation Council (GCC) and Arab League ensured regional support from other Arab and Muslim states. On Friday 18 March, Cameron held an emergency Cabinet meeting and later made a statement to the House of Commons. The Libyan Army was now on the outskirts of Benghazi and the expectation was that the city might fall at any moment. Had Gaddafi pulled his forces back, UN Resolution 1973 would not have passed. On Saturday 19 March, Cameron travelled by train to Paris while the NSC met in Whitehall. As the train entered Gare du Nord, Cameron was on a mobile phone and took the decision to go to war.

Cameron and Sarkozy's goal soon became to capture Gaddafi dead or alive, allowing Putin, then Russian Prime Minister, to talk later of the Libyan operation as a medieval crusade by the West. President Medvedev deserved better from the US, UK and France. At the very least, they should have involved the Russian military through the NATO–Russia Council on the real problems of target selection, as Gaddafi continued to operate as the controlling force of the military. There should have been a discussion even if there might well have been no agreement. Thereafter, the Russians appeared determined never to let a UN Security Resolution pass over Syria that could be used to justify overthrowing President Assad, and this was a serious blow to solving the civil war that began to rage in that country.

President Obama, in an interview with the *Atlantic* magazine in 2016 quoted at the beginning of Chapter One, was also critical of the UK and France for failing to stop Libya becoming what he called a 'mess'. He singled out Cameron for allegedly becoming 'distracted by a range of other things'. Certainly, without US air power the Libyan ground-to-air missiles would never have been so comprehensively destroyed before French and British airplanes flew bombing sorties. This was the major contribution that the US Secretary of Defense, Robert Gates, made. While being opposed to the whole intervention, Gates made sure that at least in the early stages NATO, because of the US, had the means to create an effective no-fly zone. For Gates, implementing a no-fly zone is a declaration of war, not a half way house. Many still misread air power in Kosovo in 1999, which was never as effective as claimed. The reason air power did work in tilting the balance of a three-way fight in Bosnia and Herzegovina in 1995

– and would have done so in May 1993 to support the implementation of the Vance–Owen Peace Plan – was the Bosnian government and Croatian forces fighting on the ground had become much more effective against the Serbian forces and could exploit their relative weakness compared with 1992. What is needed is people in position on the ground trained to control air power. By 1995 there had been much more sophisticated training of Croat and Bosnian government forces to make them far more effective. In Libya, military from Qatar made an important contribution in this ground-to-air control, but it is still necessary to reappraise no-fly zones as an instrument of intervention. In Syria, particularly over Aleppo, though a no-fly zone was repeatedly examined, the fear was that it would strengthen undesirable elements and create a humanitarian disaster even worse than the one the citizens were facing at the time.

An important lesson for the NSC to learn from its first six years in operation is that the UN Security Council only works if there is an acceptance that it operates under the limitation of consensus in the formulation of resolutions. If countries, particularly those on the Council, play fast and loose with that concept between themselves, once a resolution has been passed, in the event the mechanism of co-operation stalls then the veto system becomes the default mechanism. Sustaining a resolution with dialogue and the sharing of information is an essential condition for keeping reluctant countries 'on board'.

The NSC needs too to formally examine its decision-making over Libya to help it to determine how France and the UK should or could have operated more consensually. President Sarkozy was not temperamentally well suited to building a consensus in NATO, but neither was Cameron. A humanitarian operation has built-in legal constraints which if ignored change the nature of an operation.

The judgement expressed in *Cameron at 10* was that after Libya, Cameron straightaway emerged as 'the dominant figure on foreign policy, eclipsing Foreign Secretary Hague, and even on defence, eclipsing Fox'.[24] Cameron took 'to the full the opportunities a Prime Minister possesses – trips, speeches, visits and PMQs – to achieve limelight to advance his agenda'. He made it clear he was not interested in maintaining relationships for the sake of relationships – a 'blasphemous concept to the Foreign Office' – nor was he interested in strategy for the sake of having a strategy, 'blasphemous to the MOD'. He established himself 'rapidly as *sans pareil* at establishing one-to-one relationships with overseas leaders'. Yet Cameron we are told respected Hague, and gave him and the FCO wide measures of freedom on defined areas, including the Middle East Peace Process and Russia. Relations between No. 10 and the Foreign Office did settle into a more harmonious rhythm, returning to style of the early 1990s when John Major replaced Margaret Thatcher as Prime Minister.

The NSC started meeting at least once a day over Libya, and there were sixty-nine meetings eventually of the full NSC or its Libya sub-committee. Fatally, one option was off the table: UK 'boots on the ground'. No one advocated it. An NSC meeting later in March revealed a widening split between John Sawers who, as head of SIS, argued that Libya was not a matter of national interest but acceptable for humanitarian reasons. Cameron replied, 'Yes, yes, but it is important that we do these things.' It is general answers like this, according to Anthony Seldon, that led many in the intelligence and defence community to worry that the whole situation was 'not clearly thought through'.[25]

As Chief of the Defence Staff, Richards was clear from the start that curtailing Gaddafi's air power alone through the imposition of a no-fly zone would be insufficient, and that it was essential to target and hit Gaddafi's tanks and artillery from the air in order to create what he called in military parlance a Ground Control Zone. Admiral Mullen agreed the UN Resolution's wording involving the vague 'right to protect' doctrine was sufficient authority to be able to hit targets on the ground, but that was where the strategic vision about how to handle the aftermath of enforcing a no-fly zone in Libya ended. We saw very soon what a misguided decision the coalition government had made to scrap the carrier-based Harrier jump jets. With no UK aircraft carrier available, UK Tornado pilots had to fly from the UK, conducting three mid-air refuelling operations on the way out and one more on the flight back home. Later, the RAF flew from southern Italy. Richards had no doubt a carrier would have made the task a lot easier. While Qatari trainers were present in Libya, and their chief-of-staff later acknowledged, 'the numbers of Qataris on the ground were hundreds in every region',[26] no mechanisms existed to enforce an overall strategy. Small, ill-disciplined rebel groupings began to spring up and there were no substantial bodies of British or French forces to control them. It is no use blaming the Americans for this, as they had made it clear from the start they would not be providing such forces.

In the NATO-led campaign, there were NATO lawyers who argued that some actions were inconsistent with the UN Security Council resolutions, and they ruled some out. This rational approach vital for maintaining a tenuous unity in the Security Council, as well as amongst some NATO countries, provoked Cameron to favour cutting loose from NATO and taking action unilaterally. *Cameron at 10* recalls that:

> Richards' complaints do not let up: he feels Cameron and the NSC are interfering with the military operation and being involved even down to the most tactical level. 'We had really frequent meetings where the Prime Minister felt that the system wasn't really committed or trying its hardest to make this work', recalls one official. 'He wanted to keep checking on all the details.'[27]

A BBC reporter asked General Richards about Gaddafi as he was leaving No. 10 after a meeting, and Richards said that he thought he was not a legal target. His more specific view was that under the UN resolution, Gaddafi could be targeted if he was in a military complex or another setting where he was helping to direct the war. Cameron's response was to tell Richards: 'You do the fighting, I'll do the talking.' It is very hard to decide in a humanitarian military operation whether one is entitled to pursue regime change by targeting a political head of government, when, as in the case of Gaddafi, he was clearly, at times, acting as a military commander. Attacking him in a military command position was judged acceptable; the question which remained was: is the headquarters or the head of government the real target? The same difficulty had not applied to Saddam Hussein for the US since Congress had authorised action.; In that instance too, the US/UK invasion was not a 'humanitarian operation', but one taken explicitly to remove the head of state because he was thought to be developing weapons of mass destruction. In Libya, the complicating factor was that the head of state had given up the nuclear weapons option and none were found when his government collapsed.

At no stage were the US, UK or France ready to talk strategy through with the Russians about how to deal with Gaddafi. The intervention became bogged down in what, to many, is now perceived as a military failure. With continued support from France, the UK and Qatar, including the intensification of air strikes, the rebels reached Tripoli and captured Gaddafi's compound. The fighting continued in other parts of the country and it was not until October that Gaddafi was captured and subsequently killed, following an attack on the convoy in which he was travelling. NATO operations ended on 31 October.

On 15 September Cameron and Sarkozy were eventually able to visit, and they were mobbed by the hysterical crowds in Benghazi. Shades of Blair in Kosovo. Cameron was cautiously optimistic – too optimistic, it turned out. 'Libya is not to be the success that the Falklands War was for Thatcher.'[28] Yet he invested much personal and political capital in Libya and made many of the same mistakes as Blair had done in Iraq. From 2013 the situation in the country gradually deteriorated before collapsing into increased factional violence in 2014, and it is still chaotic in 2017.

Libya, Richards claims, was a qualified success in that it showed well-directed proxy (Qatari) forces can be a powerful alternative to Western boots on the ground. The problem with that argument is that after the head of government has been toppled, you also need disciplined troops in large numbers on the ground to help restore order. That issue came up again in the context of Syria when Richards wanted a big training scheme for civilians fighting Assad. In Libya, the proxy option worked in one sense, as it stopped Gaddafi attacking his own people by inserting a limited number of trained special forces to help rebels fight back, but there were not enough troops to prevent chaos. Richards was never in any doubt that, as a general rule, a land component was essential for a successful military campaign. 'You will not win wars by air and sea alone. So if you are not prepared to put boots on the ground yourself, you have to find a substitute.'[29]

SYRIA – 2011 ONWARDS

In NSC discussions over Syria, General Richards advocated what he called a 'containment strategy' to prevent the war spreading outside Syria. It involved training up Syrian rebel forces for an eventual defeat of Assad. Yet he found the focus of UK politicians was more on day-to-day events inside Syria and, in particular, whether or not to support attempts to get rid of Assad using rebel forces linked to Islamic extremist groups. There was also the US rejection of the Turkish wish to establish a 'safe area' for refugees on Syrian territory near their border and from it to exercise control over a sector of Syria in a quasi-partition.

Richards wrote, 'While we – the West – dithered on the side lines, the conflict became ever more complex and fractured with Muslim extremists increasingly taking advantage.'[30] Richards' strategy from 2011 was 'Extract, Equip and Train'. It was a sensible, but insufficiently dramatic, plan to train a proxy Syrian Army that could provide the land component to be used decisively against the regime alongside air and maritime offensive action by Western powers in a few years' time. His ambitious idea was to extract tens of thousands of Syrian men and then equip and train them in bordering countries over a twelve-month period. It was never tried. Yet in the slow build up of forces in Iraq to take Mosul back, the Americans did take this much longer view and prepared and trained Iraqi forces, taking their time in planning to destroy ISIS in Mosul while limiting civilian casualties.

Had we from the start done the same in Syria, it might have worked. Patience is, however, not an attribute of most politicians when under pressure from public opinion to act. Whether the NSC ever fully supported the Syrian strategy is not clear, nor indeed is how much notice Cameron took of their views, but it never seemed the UK was ready to train on a significant scale and to implement it as a UK initiative. The UK appeared to be awaiting a US response but that too never went much further than lip service to the concept. David Petraeus, as Director of the Central Intelligence Agency (CIA), supported Richards, but President Obama had concerns about vetting and arming rebels of whom so little was known and who might have turned out to be Islamic extremists. But measures could have been put in place to help the trainers to minimise the risk of extremists not being discovered and dismissed in the process of training.

Richards believed, had his strategy been implemented in late 2011, the war could have ended by the autumn of 2012 and certainly in 2013. A better strategy would have been for the US to have accepted President Erdoğan's early wish for a large safe haven to be established in Syria across from the Turkish border. But the US saw it as an anti-Syrian Kurd device to stop them having a military presence along the entire Syria/Turkish border. This it probably was, but Turkey had the resources close by to make the designated area properly safe, unlike the situation in Bosnia from 1992 to 1995. It also would have had the merit of letting the Turkish government control an area which could have extended to include Aleppo. In 2017, after the sarin gas episode and President Trump's response, much has changed. But Erdoğan still continued to push his concept and was ready to bargain a different safe area with Aleppo excluded, but as always was reluctant to see the Syrian Kurds consolidating in their eastern enclave.

The truth is that everything changed in Syria in the summer of 2015 when Assad warned the Russians the road link between Damascus and the Mediterranean was in danger of being blocked militarily by rebel forces, and Putin responded swiftly and intelligently. In September 2015, the Russian naval base, which they had occupied since 1971, was quickly reinforced by adapting a nearby Syrian airfield, and Russia began flying their planes on a bombing campaign to tilt the balance back in favour of Assad, while claiming they were going in to attack ISIS. The Russians were obviously now going to control an area of Syria in the west like the Turks had wanted to do in the east (see also Chapter Five). President Obama should have acted at this stage very differently, for the threat to Damascus, to which Putin was responding, was real. Had Damascus been captured by rebels with ISIS already ensconced in the suburbs, it would have been devastating. Obama should have told Putin to focus on Damascus and the Mediterranean while the US would help protect Aleppo and create from the air a safe haven for refugees. That would diplomatically and militarily have forced a de facto partition, with Russia and the US distant, but influencing subsequent events. This would have been far more controllable. Neither Assad nor Erdoğan would have total control of any part of Syria and the Kurds might have been in control of an area.

Slowly and brutally, Assad's area of control increased from 2015 onwards, and he temporarily won a reluctant acceptance as the major power in Syria by January 2017. Yet the use of sarin gas in April 2017 changed all of this. This time, it was President Putin who should have acted very differently. It was an opportunity for the US and Russia to have again cooperated over Syria in the UN Security Council in much the same way as they did in August 2013. If Foreign Minister Lavrov had been authorised by Putin, on learning of the sarin gas attack, to say publicly that he was very disturbed to hear of the use of gas – having thought in good faith Assad had removed it all in 2013 – and then added that he was ready to agree to UN inspectors going back into Syria, Russia would have gained respect, and greater influence. It might have been difficult to have UN inspectors visiting the battlefield areas, but the ultimate breakdown of relations between Russia and the US might have been avoided. Fortunately, after a few months Russia appeared to be recognising that they needed the UN for a peace settlement and probably the goodwill at least of President Trump. By June 2017 it was not possible to predict where Syria would end up.

A partition strategy was advocated in articles in various international outlets, but a de facto partition of Syria never won favour in Washington, London or Paris.[31] Perhaps the Russians would not or could not have persuaded Assad to let the Turks become a major influence in Aleppo. We perhaps underestimate Assad's belief that with Iran's support he did not need Russia. Perhaps that explains his use of sarin gas? It certainly embarrassed the Russians, and may lead to their acceptance of the replacement of Assad with a more reliable Syrian leader.

The realpolitik of a Russian sphere of influence in Syria is from the Mediterranean to Damascus. This is their fixed objective which will not change, nor will they leave Syria. As a quid pro quo, a Turkish influence from their border, to include Aleppo, seemed at one stage acceptable to the Russians as a way of ending the fighting, not a permanent peace. Because of their readiness to fight ISIS, the Kurdish influence on Washington has become ever stronger. It is, and it was, an influence which the Turkish government resents. Turkey will never readily accept a Kurdish province in the east of Syria unless it is balanced by their having an influence in the west. The Kurdish wish to go to the Mediterranean is understandable, but not likely to be achieved. What they could end up with is being in control of Raqqa and a major part of the Rojava region of Syria with the full support of the US and the acquiescence of Russia. The impending referendum in the Kurdish part of Iraq will also present a great problem. Changing national boundaries by consent is always difficult. In the case of Iraq and Syria it will tax the cohesion of the Security Council and test the unity of the P5, who will at some stage have to guide the process or maintain existing borders.

Throughout the diplomatic world, there is a reluctance to grapple with partition as a technique for de-escalating conflict. It is feared, not unreasonably given past experience, that any sub-division, however much it may be presented as temporary, will become permanent. But this principled opposition frequently refuses to face up to the casualties and displacement of people on the ground. Such was the case over Syria. The tragedy of the Syrian civil war is that it has continued much longer because of a reluctance to accept temporarily a geographical division as a result of fighting on the ground and also to face up to the problem created by the 1919 settlement over Syria. In the negotiations over Bosnia and Herzegovina from 1992 to 1995, there was a somewhat similar optimistic view in many quarters that the only solution lay in creating a unified state within the regional boundaries of the former Yugoslav republic. It is arguable whether that has been achieved some twenty-two years following the Dayton Peace Agreement. The humanitarian price of waiting while conflicts continue and eventually burn themselves out is often intolerable. It is an old dilemma: short term horrors for long term peace.

An eventual evaluation of the Syrian war will have to make retrospective assessments of these issues. A good case can be made out that outside intervention in Syria following the Arab Spring from 2011 onwards made the internal situation worse, and that view has been forthrightly expressed by Peter Ford, former UK Ambassador to Syria from 1999 to 2003. 'The British Foreign Office to which I used to belong, I'm sorry to say has gotten Syria wrong every step of the way...' The UK, in his view, should either have 'put everything, including our own forces on to the battlefield or if in our judgement – as it would have been my judgement – that was not realistic, refrain from encouraging the opposition to mount a doomed campaign'.[32] On 7 April 2017, Ford went on to criticise the American attack on the Syrian airfield which the US had identified as the location from which planes carrying chemical weapons had flown on the attack on 4 April which affected civilians, many of them children, in the town of Khan Sheikhoun in Idlib province. Such a position risks undermining the Geneva Protocol signed by the UK in 1925, and which entered into force in 1928 with further treaties in 1972 and 1993 which covered the production, storage or transfer of chemical and biological weapons. This Protocol is universally regarded as international law, and rules out the use of gas in all warfare, in part because of the widespread revulsion to the use of gas in the 1914–18 World War. Realism is a

virtue in diplomacy but principle has its place too. It is not acceptable for diplomats or politicians to treat the use of weapons of mass
destruction as a fact of life which can be tolerated. That mistake was
made, as we have discussed earlier, in the Iraq–Iran War in the 1980s.
The UK and the US must not make that mistake again.

It is worth analysing in some depth what happened in 2013. It is
interesting to look back on how the House of Commons responded to
Assad's use of sarin gas and, in particular, to the question of whether
the British government should participate with the US on air missions
over Syria in support of President Obama's proposed response, limited in terms of a few days and targets. This was a complex debate and
there are risks in drawing simplistic conclusions.

On 21 August, reports came in of a chemical attack in the Ghouta
region east of the Syrian capital of Damascus. The effects of poison
gas were estimated by *Médecins San Frontières* to have affected some
3,600 Syrians who had to be treated for 'neurotoxic symptoms'.[33]
Later it was claimed 1,300 had been killed. The chemicals had been
delivered by rocket artillery of a type used by the Syrian government's
armed forces. The UN claimed the gas was probably sarin, a nerve
agent 'twenty times deadlier than cyanide'.

On 27 August, Prime Minister Cameron returned to London from
holiday to chair a meeting of the NSC, and later that day asked the
Speaker to recall Parliament. Cameron, Clegg and the leader of the
Labour Party, Ed Miliband, met. Initial agreement was followed by
Labour wanting the UN report on the gas incident to be published
before any debate; otherwise they would oppose any motion. Cameron pressed ahead for a vote on 29 August, which was claimed to be
only a vote on the principle, with a promise of a further vote to take
place after the UN inspectors' findings were known. A JIC finding was
published in the form of a letter. 'We also have a limited but growing
body of intelligence which supports the judgement that the regime
(Assad) was responsible for the attacks.' This use of gas clearly had
echoes of the 1980–88 Iran–Iraq war, a comparison Cameron did his
best to dispel. A Labour amendment was tabled with six conditions

that had to be fulfilled for Labour to support. Miliband, in his speech, noted that the 'UN is not some inconvenient sideshow' and spoke of wanting 'to adhere to the principles of international law.' In the vote the government motion was defeated by 285 votes to 272. Thirty Conservative and nine Liberal Democrats MPs rebelled against their coalition government. The Labour amendment was then also defeated by 322 votes to 220. Cameron correctly accepted defeat, saying: 'it is clear that Parliament does not want intervention.' A very detailed and fair account of what happened in the discussions between the parties appears in *The Imperial Premiership*.[34]

If President Obama had gone ahead with the sort of limited bombing campaign we now know he was planning against Assad in late August 2013, it might have temporarily weakened Assad, but would certainly not have toppled him. The reason for Obama's limited action over a few days, and with limited targets, was that the US feared toppling him without having sufficient moderate Syrian forces on the ground and leaders available who could replace Assad. So US action would have been demonstrative and not decisive, leaving the different and often opposing forces to fight on. Also, most importantly, sarin gas would still be in the country in substantial quantities with the fear of widespread release if bombed accidently in air strikes. What was being proposed to Obama was very similar to what had been undertaken previously by President Clinton against Saddam Hussein; a few days of Cruise missile attacks and little more. That sort of limited intervention – prepared to destroy, but not to defeat – has a long history of not working, going right back in history. War is an all-out affair; graduated attacks, as the US saw in Vietnam, do not succeed. A limited intervention would also have been blamed, however unfairly it might have been, for the later success of ISIS forces. For it was only in June 2014 that ISIS made world news headlines by taking Mosul in Iraq and capturing large amounts of US weaponry given to the Iraqi forces in Mosul, but their emergence was already known to Western intelligence. Having consolidated their position even further in Iraq, ISIS then extended their territory in Syria, taking Palmyra in 2015.

They were still holding out in Mosul in late May 2017. Meanwhile, ISIS had spread their forces to Sinai, Libya, and other parts of northern Africa. Even when the caliphate's large land holding is taken away from them in Syria and Iraq, as will happen, they will almost certainly fight on through terrorist attacks and develop a 'cyber caliphate'.

For all these and other reasons, it was not foolish for the House of Commons to make the distinction between the military action in Iraq, where UK support in tackling ISIS forces had been requested by the UN-recognised government, and what it was being asked to approve in Syria, where it had not. More importantly it was another gesture intervention from the air, not a ground-based intervention. The proposal to bomb Syria based on retaliation against Assad for his use of chemical weapons, but not remove the gas, was demonstrative but ignored diplomacy which offered a far better course, which some were arguing for – namely for chemical weapons to be negotiated out of Syria. That diplomatic activity which depended on being able to bully, not bomb, Assad was begun within days of the House of Commons vote under an initial Russian/American agreement. Why had the UK government not called for negotiations to remove all sarin gas from Syria to be led by Russia and the US before the debate on 20 August 2013?[35] That, rather than a wish to support US military action, and in a minor way to participate in it, should have been the immediate response of both the UK and the US. It was also, until 2017, successful in terms of the use of sarin gas. Deplorably, while not as lethal as sarin gas, Assad was still using chlorine thereafter and ignoring protests from experts who had verified its use. The UK, US and Russia should have gone to the UN Security Council and called Assad to account for this as soon as it was verified. Perhaps the fact that we did not do so is in part an explanation why Assad would contemplate the use of sarin gas again in April 2017. Another explanation that has been discussed is that Assad was becoming overconfident of outright victory and listening more to Iranian generals on the ground with troops than Russian advisers.

Before the UN takes all the blame for the failure of Western diplomacy, Lakhdar Brahimi's analysis that it was not the UN that failed over Syria is worth studying and very persuasive.[36] An Algerian diplomat, he served as the UN and Arab League special envoy to Syria from 2012 to 2014. 'A deeper understanding is needed', he argues, 'of why the UN fails when it fails, and why the UN succeeds when it succeeds.' What failed in Syria was essentially the inability of the Russian Federation and the US, France and the UK to work together in the Security Council. It has been a tragic conflict in which, according to some estimates, as many as 470,000 people may have died, while there are five million refugees and thirteen and a half million people in desperate need of humanitarian assistance. In this deadlock between Russia and the US, it was a pity that France and the UK felt unable to promote a different strategy that might have been based on a temporary partition. The superficial, distorted analysis that almost every country made in 2011 of the likely balance of any fighting in Syria was wrong. The regime did not disintegrate and was not likely to collapse politically. We need to understand what assessments were made at the time by our intelligence community. Russia's analysis that Assad's regime was stronger than Western governments believed was correct. Politicians seemed to forget that the Assad family, father and son, had good longstanding relations with revolutionary Iran who throughout supplied money, food, weapons and militia to Syria. The UN from top to bottom warned from day one that there was no military solution to the conflict. It took nearly three years before this even began to be recognised. The UK and France were too dismissive of this.

Having supported military interventions in Iraq, Afghanistan and Libya, all of which failed, many MPs were not ready to support another failure over Syria in 2013. The House of Commons on a cross-party basis made the correct decision and when President Obama, within days, put the same question to the US Congress they also backed off endorsing military action. This rather important fact is glossed over by those in the UK who want to pretend that there was a party political issue behind the divide. What many sensed, in the US as well as the UK, was the complete absence of a strategic policy to settle the Syrian conflict. The problem for the Obama administration was that the President had used the words 'red line' in relation to any use of gas in Syria, and now faced a dilemma. If the US attacked Syria, Russia would not lift a finger to force Assad to remove sarin gas; but US bombing would not remove the gas threat, since targeting any storage site would risk the gas leaking out and killing civilians. That dilemma was never faced up to honestly and openly. The debate was a political response to the cry to do something militarily when the wiser course was diplomacy.

The terrorist attacks by ISIS in Paris in November 2015 made a much stronger case for judging the threat from ISIS in Syria and justifying UK military action in self-defence under Article 51 of the UN Charter. The French-drafted UN Resolution, as amended by Russia, was unanimously agreed on 20 November 2015, and the way was cleared for Parliament, with a large cross-party majority, to agree the UK should bomb ISIS in Syria. That was the correct response.

The traditional right of the UK Prime Minister with the power to take military action will never be the same again after 2013. It has become, in effect, after Iraq in 2003 and Syria in 2013, a qualified power. There is now a political imperative, rightly, to involve Parliament wherever possible. There will, therefore, in future be democratic debate in Parliament with a vote if necessary before the UK goes to war, except for the most urgent and dire circumstances. That is a major curtailment of Prime Ministerial power, but wisely it was not enshrined in law – as Prime Minister Gordon Brown had attempted – because, as already argued, it is impossible to frame a law that covers every eventuality. So declarations of war remain, but now mainly in theory, a decision only for the Prime Minister and the Cabinet to make.

The 'blame game' between politicians in Washington and London ever since 2013 has been, on the face of it, deeply divisive; but an interesting gloss on what happened over the sarin gas removal came in John Kerry's farewell press conference as US Secretary of State, on 5 January 2017. He spoke out in the terms of the *Guardian* headline in which he linked Britain to the derailing of Obama's plan for intervention in Syria.

> The President of the United States of America, Barack Obama, did decide to use force and he announced his decision publicly, and he said we're going to act, we're going to do what we need to do to respond to this blatant violation of international law and of warnings and of the red line he had chosen.

Kerry continued:

> Now we were marching toward that time when, lo and behold ... Prime Minister Cameron went to the Parliament ... and he sought a vote for approval for him to join in the action that we were going to engage in. And guess what the Parliament voted no, they shot him down ... Then the question became, 'Do I need to go to Congress to get that permission? ... we felt that we'd quickly get Congress's approval because this was such a blatant violation ... the President decided that he needed to go to Congress because of what had happened in Great Britain and because he needed the approval.

Kerry then recalled that, in a press conference in London at the time in 2013, he was asked if there was anything that Assad could do to avoid being bombed, and he replied, 'Yes, he could agree to get rid of his chemical weapons'. Within an hour and a half, Kerry said he was telephoned by his Russian counterpart, Sergei Lavrov, suggesting that they cooperate on such a deal, something that Obama and Putin had previously discussed. Kerry said:

> All of a sudden Lavrov and I were thrown together by our Presidents in an effort to try and achieve that and guess what, we did achieve it, before Congress voted. The President never said 'I won't drop a bomb.' What happened was people interpreted it. The

perception was that he was trying to find a different road. And I will acknowledge to you, absolutely, I heard it all over the place. The perception hurt, yes.

Kerry added: 'The perception came about despite the fact that we actually got a far better result of getting all of the weapons of mass destruction out of Syria without dropping a bomb. If we had dropped a bomb, there is no guarantee we would have got any of them out.'[37] Vast quantities of lethal poisons were removed and, in June 2014, the Organization for the Prohibition of Chemical Weapons certified that all declared weapons had been removed. However, in February 2016 James R. Clapper Jr, the US National Intelligence Director, told Congress that 'we assess that Syria has not declared all the elements of its chemical weapons programme'. This, along with the use of chlorine bombs, should have been taken to the Security Council and Russia asked to investigate.

That description, while a little self-serving in its bid to protect the reputation of the Obama administration and criticise the UK, focuses attention on the real issues behind the House of Commons vote in 2013. The UK decision not to intervene by bombing Assad's forces in Syria brought about the right international response: namely to force Russia to move in and remove very large quantities of deadly nerve gas using UN inspectors. It was an independent British decision taken on a cross-party basis and it had important ramifications on US decision-making. The subsequent party political blame game, with many different interpretations, continues regrettably to this day. That we should have blithely followed the US lead demeans the importance of being a self-governing nation. UK forces were not needed in any military sense. The US could and should, if they really wanted, have bombed on their own as President Clinton did in Iraq in the 1990s and as President Trump did in April 2017. 'Me-too-ism' is not a serious basis for a British military strategy pre- or post-Brexit.

The UK Parliament in 2013, perhaps in a somewhat confused or even opportunistic way, helped to develop a foreign policy stance

different from, and wiser than, the one the US President was embarked on. It helped create a pause in the bombing to uphold a 'red
line' that Britain, a proven democratic friend of the US, should not for
one moment be ashamed of doing. It provides a benchmark for UK
foreign policy post-Brexit of considerable importance. The Conservative MPs who rebelled did their own government a good service. The
government's promise of a second vote before military action – since
we now know they were unsure when Obama intended to attack –
would we now know have been impossible to fulfil, with Parliament
recessing afterwards for its interrupted holiday. If the US timetable
had been within days, as some believed, there would have been even
more disillusionment in Parliament later about being misled.

The use of gas in Syria in April 2017 reinforced for some their criticism of the lack of action taken by Obama in 2013. But there is value
in due process when dealing with these serious issues. In 2017 the
Americans felt they had good evidence that there were not, in this
case, agent provocateurs using gas on their own people after sensing
Assad was winning. The main reason for President Trump's military
action was the lack of any prior response from Russia to support the
UN Resolution calling for credible on the ground inspection. This
was the massive mistake made by President Putin. It was the moment
when the former Lavrov/Kerry response should have been mirrored
by a Lavrov/Tillerson response. Quick proportionate action taken by
President Trump was therefore appropriate to support the Convention against all forms of gas being used in war.

In 2017 peace talks orchestrated by Russia, Iran and Turkey took
place in Astana, Kazakhstan, without a UN presence. Whether they
can succeed where the UN Geneva talks appear to have failed is not
certain. But it is probable that both sets of talks can run in parallel to
some advantage and may eventually be merged together.

The NSC should – as part of the internal review we have called
for of NSC policy in the first seven years of its existence – question
their decision-making process in August 2013 very closely. Did any
of their professional advisers point out that it was essentially a decision

for a US President to make and execute? That there was no military need for the UK to be involved? This rush for military action championed by the press needs to be challenged, otherwise politicians will have no counter to such pressures. The US timetable was set by Obama with, not unreasonably, no consideration for the fact that the UK Parliament was in the summer recess. It was political opportunism to announce the dubious prospect that there would be an opportunity for another vote before US planes bombed. It was held out to wavering MPs with little certainty that it could be honoured. The FCO should be asked whether the alternative strategy of negotiating all sarin gas out of Syria was considered by the Foreign Secretary and why did the Defence Secretary not raise military questions within the NSC? The UK government had the expertise within it to demonstrate to the politicians that diplomacy was the only feasible way of removing the gas. This episode makes it very clear that the NSC machinery was not sufficiently focused on ensuring alternative strategies were kept open. Ultimately a mixed group of this kind cannot decide to bomb or not to bomb, but its creation was designed to make sure the Prime Minister and senior politicians were aware of all the options. Were they? Let us not wait for decades to pass before we know the answers.

In the other models that the UK has used, such as the War Cabinet in 1940–45 and the Defence and Overseas Policy Committee of the Cabinet (DOP), there have usually been a few senior ministers who are not part of the security team who over decades past did challenge the conventional wisdom. Robin Cook over Iraq is the most recent example, but there was dissent in the Cabinet over Suez in 1956. Figures in the Cabinet because of their standing in the party are in a position to ask, why the rush? Why does the Prime Minister feel the need to be involved so personally? In the NSC, the Chancellor of the Exchequer or Home Secretary ought to feel they have the independence of mind that can sometimes better see the 'wood from the trees' than colleagues close to the issue. Indeed, a greater readiness to express controversial positions should, in the light of Libya and Syria, be encouraged amongst all participants. We know that on occasions the CDS and MI6 did, in fairness, speak out. The NSC should be wary of a group-think mentality developing. Given the implications for our armed forces of many wrong decisions being taken over Afghanistan and Iraq – by senior military figures, not just politicians – it is essential that the NSC is a forum of equals without deference. Its decisions should be collective. Its advice should go to ministers for decision in a Cabinet committee or Cabinet itself. There should be no reluctance therefore to speak out in the NSC. If there are serious differences it is for the Prime Minister to take those differences away as advice and not claim it as an NSC decision, but go to Cabinet for a political decision.

Before the NSC machinery was established Admiral Sir Michael Boyce, now an Admiral of the Fleet, was near to retirement after a period of only two years as CDS. Yet, in 2003, he insisted on having a written statement from the Prime Minister that the invasion of Iraq was legal. He got it at the last moment from the office of the then Attorney General on the eve of war. General Sir David Richards, as mentioned earlier, risked – and got – a public remonstrance from the Prime Minister over his view on Libya, when he told a BBC reporter that in his view Gaddafi was not a legal target.

There has been little other appearance of dissent from the heads of the respective armed services over the past fifteen years, apart from some semi-public 'rumblings' from Generals Jackson and Dannatt mainly after they had left office. This is very different from the situation in the US, where senior military personnel have spoken out about their concerns, as highlighted in Chapter One with the example of General Shinseki's testimony to the Senate Armed Services Committee relating to inadequate troop levels in Iraq in 2003. Unlike in the UK, the US separation of powers allows for such frankness in congressional hearings. Traditionally, UK service leaders keep their advice to ministers private when appearing before select committees in Parliament. In the light of the detailed analysis contained in the Chilcot Report on the Iraq Inquiry[38], Parliament should assess whether it is time that military advice to ministers can be revealed in exceptional circumstances. That is against the prevailing wisdom, but it is worth analysing and Parliament should review this convention of silence where military opinion differs, even if only to establish clearer guidelines for the future. At present, dissent emerges through leaks and memoirs. The first can be embarrassing, the second self-congratulatory.

It is an inescapable fact that, with the UK marking Brexit by a significant shift in its foreign and security policy, we have to be ready to strengthen the NSC and learn from its performance. Only by routinely retrospectively and, in part, privately examining the handling of past events can the NSC establish a learning curve. In addition to the cases cited above, there are lessons to be learnt from a range of other events. Fortunately and most seriously, now that we are leaving the EU, there is no longer much point in spending too much time studying the development of the EU–Ukraine Association Agreement; however, the response to the annexation of Crimea and the hesitancy to invoke the Belgrade Memorandum does deserve retrospective examination. There are other complex military and political decisions over economising on equipment with risks to service personnel that need to be reviewed, not just leaving to rest on press criticism. Furthermore, in analysing what has gone before, the NSC should also focus on addressing another area in which it has been criticised, which is the need for it to devote more of its time to consider longer-term strategic planning. It needs to draw on past lessons to develop new thinking as to how to address the root causes of current foreign and security problems, and prepare contingency plans for the next set of crises. Notwithstanding these criticisms, the NSC in our view is an important and worthwhile innovation.

PART 2

NEAR TERM
CHALLENGES &
OPPORTUNITIES

A statesman's test is whether he can discern from the swirl of tactical decisions the true long-term interests of his country and devise an appropriate strategy for achieving them.

Henry Kissinger, *Diplomacy*[1]

CHAPTER 5

RUSSIA AND STABILITY
IN WIDER EUROPE

A quarter of a century after the collapse of the Soviet Union and the emergence of Russia as the successor state, the euphoria and high expectations for stability and prosperity in the region have been replaced by levels of tension, fear and paranoia which some would say have not been seen since the Brezhnev years of the Cold War. Before turning to the situation today, it is perhaps worth briefly reviewing his place in Russian history, which established the immediate backdrop to the events which led to the situation we face today.

Leonid Brezhnev lived from 1906 to 1982. He was grounded in industry, agriculture, the Communist Party and the army. His first job was in the foundry where his father worked. He was a Russian who had arrived in Kamenskoye on the River Dnepr in the Ukrainian part of Imperial Russia. Nikita Khruschev arrived in Ukraine as General Secretary of the Party in 1938, and recalled in 1963 that he had appointed the young Brezhnev as provincial secretary at Dnepropetrovsk. When the Great Patriotic War, as it is still referred to by Russians, started with Hitler's surprise attack on 22 June 1941, the Germans made rapid progress and the Ukrainian capital, Kiev, fell on 16 September. Khrushchev escaped to Moscow. Brezhnev stayed evacuating heavy machinery and skilled workers and getting in the all important harvests. He then became a political commissar in the Soviet 18th Army, ending the war as a Major-General. Brezhnev was at the victory parade in Moscow on 8 May 1945 and more significantly thereafter at Stalin's victory banquet. After the war, he returned to Ukraine, subsequently holding posts in Moldova and Kazakhstan.

In the power struggle following Stalin's death in 1953, Khrushchev emerged as his successor, and in February 1956, delivered in secret his now famous four-hour speech, which denounced almost every action of Stalin's rule and presaged a less harsh era in the Soviet Union. This was a speech Mikhail Gorbachev later recalled as a huge political risk. Brezhnev was brought back to Moscow by Khrushchev to be Deputy Chairman of the Central Committee of the CPSU. For the next twenty-five years, he was never again away from the centre of power. In October 1964 Brezhnev emerged seamlessly as the new leader after the ousting of Khrushchev. Domestically, his period in office saw the era of economic stagnation, which Gorbachev's reforms were aimed at ending, and a reversal of the liberalisation seen under Khrushchev. In the international arena, it is for 'the Brezhnev Doctrine' that he is remembered in the West.

This Doctrine originated during the Prague Spring in 1968, when the Czech leadership sought to introduce political reforms, only to see the Soviet Union intervene militarily. Brezhnev's position was that:

> Each Communist Party is free to apply the principles of Marxism-Leninism and socialism in its own country, but it is not free to deviate from these principles if it is to remain a Communist Party … The weakening of any of the links in the world system of socialism directly affects all socialist countries, and they cannot look indifferently upon this.[2]

The crushing of the Prague Spring sent a clear message to others as to what the Doctrine meant in practice.

The invasion of Afghanistan was unwisely undertaken in part in defence of that Doctrine, and it started the collapse of the Soviet Union. On 24 December 1979, Soviet forces were sent to the Bagram airbase outside Kabul and installed a pro-Soviet government. The actual decision to invade was taken two weeks earlier at a meeting of the Politburo with Brezhnev, by then a sick man, in the chair. He died in 1982. Three years later the Soviet Union suffered a humiliating defeat and, with Mikhail Gorbachev in power, began its pull back from Afghanistan. The final withdrawal came four years later, closely followed by the fall of the Berlin Wall.

At the start of 2017, the 'Doomsday Clock', already at the highest level it had been since that period of the mid-1980s, was moved forward by half a minute, to two and a half minutes to midnight. One of the contributing factors to the move was that:

> The United States and Russia – which together possess more than 90 percent of the world's nuclear weapons – remained at odds in a variety of theaters, from Syria to Ukraine to the borders of NATO; both countries continued wide-ranging modernizations of their nuclear forces, and serious arms control negotiations were nowhere to be seen.

While the situation is indeed far from stable, it is important to keep a realistic perspective and, as mentioned in Chapter Two, note that under President Putin we are dealing with a very different country than the USSR at the height of the Cold War. It is also important to note that despite his long tenor in office and relatively young age, the time will come when Russia has a new leader. We must bear in mind the need to engage and build relationships with a broad spectrum of Russian society, remaining aware of the potential long term impact of short term measures.

Nevertheless, there are increasing, and understandable, fears of Russian intentions, particularly the possibility of incursions onto the territory of NATO members following its annexation of the Crimea region in Ukraine and support for separatists in the east of that country. These fears have been exacerbated by wider Russian actions,

---

* A symbol which represents the likelihood of a human-caused global catastrophe. Maintained since 1947 by the members of The Bulletin of the Atomic Scientists' Science and Security Board, http://thebulletin.org/timeline.

including allegations of extensive cyber warfare and interference in elections in a number of countries, not least the US. NATO members have been warning of an increasingly aggressive Russian stance and Russian efforts to destabilise the situation in neighbouring states. As mentioned earlier, recent Russian activity in Syria in support of President Assad has also been met with widespread criticism. In written evidence to the Foreign Affairs Committee in December 2016,[3] the FCO noted that 'Russia has become more aggressive, authoritarian and nationalist. Internationally and domestically it is increasingly defining itself in opposition to the West. Russia uses a range of powers to pursue its policies – including propaganda, espionage, cyber and subversion. It continues with assertive and provocative military activity.' NATO has deployed increased forces in response. The Russians, for their part, continue to portray NATO expansion as a threat, and have stepped up deployments and large scale exercises in its border regions. How did we reach this situation? Should it have come as such a surprise? And, most importantly, what can be done, particularly by the UK, to counter this dangerous downward spiral? In particular, is the current situation symptomatic of Russia returning to type and reverting to the tactics honed during the years of the Cold War; or can we look forward to a new relationship between Russia and its neighbours in Europe? Can we see Russia putting its differences with the rest of Europe behind it in the way that France and Germany so successfully put their history of confrontation behind them in the years following the Second World War through the initial establishment of the European Coal and Steel Community and what is now the EU (as discussed in detail in Chapter Eight)?

At the root of many of the tensions is the evolution of Western attitudes to Russia's role in the post-communist world and Russia's reaction to it. To many in the West, the end of the Cold War marked a comprehensive victory which left Moscow as merely a bit-player in the new world order – albeit one with nuclear weapons – whose views counted for little. There was also the widely held expectation that Russia would speedily and fully embrace the Western politico-economic model, which sowed the seeds for future disappointment. Initially the messages from Western leaders were ones of support for the changes being brought about. President Bush, in his address to the nation on reducing United States and Soviet nuclear weapons in September 1991,[4] spoke of the 'peoples of the Soviet Union ... [facing] the daunting challenge of building fresh political structures, based on human rights, democratic principles, and market economies. Their task is far from easy and far from over. They will need our help, and they will get it.' However, following the dissolution of the USSR and the collapse in the Russian economy as the 1990s progressed, there was a greater triumphalism over the demise of the Soviet Union and the West's part in bringing about its downfall, and an increasing readiness to dismiss Russia as a serious power.

Whether this was an active policy decision in some quarters or an inadvertent lack of attention can be debated, but the end result was the same – a growing feeling of humiliation and resentment in Russia, and a harkening for a return to the glory days, as Robert Skidelsky highlights in an article entitled 'Another Reset with Russia?':[5]

> ...Robert Gates, who headed the CIA in the early 1990s, later conceded that the West, and particularly the US, 'badly underestimated the magnitude of Russian humiliation in losing the Cold War'. The spectacle of 'American government officials, academicians, businessmen, and politicians' arrogantly 'telling the Russians how to conduct their [...] affairs' inevitably 'led to deep and long-term resentment and bitterness'.

In this regard, one of the fundamental lessons of twentieth-century history – the failure of the post-First World War settlement – appears to have been overlooked, with dangerous results. While it is understandable that many who suffered as a result of the actions of the USSR feel that Russia should be made to pay and is not to be trusted as a partner in today's Europe, it is critical that a patient, dispassionate approach is taken if we are to see stability return.

This is not to say that the Russians themselves did not make many mistakes and miscalculations along the way, not least in the management of their economy. Furthermore, the perception of being shut out from the developments on Russia's western borders encouraged them to revert to counter-productive tactics designed to demonstrate their capacity to disrupt and destabilise, tactics which have only served to reinforce the arguments of those who see Russia as a leopard which cannot change its spots. However, in the enthusiasm to consolidate the roll-back of communism and secure the market-based, liberal democratic model, another fundamental diplomatic precept was not given the weight it warranted: that was the need to understand the point of view of the other side. Edmund Burke's warning that 'Nothing is so fatal to a nation as an extreme of self-partiality, and the total want of consideration of what others will naturally hope or fear'[6] can apply equally to a group of states. Failure to pay sufficient consideration to Russian views, whether fundamentally justified or not, played a major part in the current problems facing Europe and the US in their dealings with Moscow. This is not, by any means, an argument that Russia should have been accommodated at every juncture, or given any right of veto over developments outside its own borders then (or indeed in the future), but rather there should have been a greater willingness to recognise the validity of their holding a different point of view over both EU and NATO expansion. Nevertheless, it must be acknowledged that the countries which had formerly been part of the Soviet bloc had a legitimate right to develop their own economic and security relations with the West and define for themselves the form they wanted those relations to take. The challenges in squaring this circle of differing viewpoints were, and remain, significant. While an ambition on the part of Western governments to see them resolved quickly was understandable, in retrospect a more considered and patient approach might have avoided the situation in which we now find ourselves.

These risks had been flagged almost a decade earlier in an article in the *New York Times* in February 1997, where the veteran US diplomat and Soviet expert George Kennan had warned very clearly of the risks of NATO expansion:

> The view, bluntly stated, is that expanding NATO would be the most fateful error of American policy in the entire post-cold-war era. Such a decision may be expected to inflame the nationalistic, anti-Western and militaristic tendencies in Russian opinion; to have an adverse effect on the development of Russian democracy; to restore the atmosphere of the Cold War to East-West relations, and to impel Russian foreign policy in directions decidedly not to our liking.

Kennan returned to the charge in May 1998 in an interview with Thomas L. Friedman of the *New York Times* when he commented on the US Senate's agreement on NATO expansion:

> I think it is the beginning of a new Cold War. I think the Russians will gradually react quite adversely and it will affect their policies. I think it is a tragic mistake. There was no reason for this whatever. No one was threatening anybody else. This expansion would make the founding fathers of this country turn in their graves. We have signed up to protect a whole series of countries, even though we have neither the resources nor the intention to do so in any serious way. [NATO expansion] was simply a lighthearted action by a Senate that has no real interest in foreign affairs.
>
> I was particularly bothered by the references to Russia as a country dying to attack Western Europe. Don't people understand? Our differences in the Cold War were with the Soviet Communist regime. And now we are turning our backs on the very people who mounted the greatest bloodless revolution in history to remove that Soviet regime.[7]

Kennan's critical distinction between the communist Soviet Union and post-communist Russia, for all its shortcomings, has to be borne in mind in how we deal with Russia and its people today.

However, the path eastwards was embarked upon, by both NATO and the EU, and Kennan was shown to have been correct. This was highlighted in the conclusions of the House of Lords 2015 report on the crisis in Ukraine:[8]

> While we are clear that NATO is a defensive alliance, for the Russians NATO is seen as a hostile military threat, and successive rounds of NATO's eastern enlargement have, as the Russians see it, brought it threateningly close to the Russian border. EU enlargement, as it has become conflated with NATO enlargement, has also taken on the aspect of a security threat. These views are sincerely and widely held in Russia, and need to be factored into Member States' strategic analyses of Russian actions and policies.

Some would argue that the primary reason why such views are widely held is that the state dominated media relentlessly portray NATO as such for their own political reasons, and a change in the Russian official rhetoric would be a welcome first step in building a dialogue based on greater openness and trust.

The early signs of finding a common framework for cooperation and bringing the divided continent back together had been positive. German reunification took place in October 1990. In November of that year, the leaders of the Conference on Security and Co-operation in Europe (CSCE) met and issued the 'Charter of Paris for New Europe',[9] which reaffirmed the commitments of members under the UN Charter and the Helsinki Final Act. This noted that 'The era of confrontation and division of Europe has ended. We declare that henceforth our relations will be founded on respect and co-operation.' It went on to state that 'Now that a new era is dawning in Europe, we are determined to expand and strengthen friendly relations and co-operation among the States of Europe, the United States of America and Canada, and to promote friendship among our peoples.' This set the framework for a Euro-Atlantic dialogue, and echoed Gorbachev's earlier references to building a 'Common European Home'.

However, one of the key disputed issues from this period, which has influenced the subsequent chain of events, is the matter of what was said to the Russian leadership in 1989–90, particularly in securing their support for German reunification, and about the future role of NATO and its potential expansion. Again, there have been many analyses of the events undertaken, and while it is clear that there were no explicit, formal undertakings, there does appear to have been room for misunderstanding of comments made at the time. This perception that the West went back on its word has fuelled the stance of the current Russian leadership. Gorbachev, in an interview with *Der Spiegel*[10] in January 2015, expressed the view that:

> NATO's eastward expansion has destroyed the European security architecture as it was defined in the Helsinki Final Act in 1975. The eastern expansion was a 180-degree reversal, a departure from the decision of the Paris Charter in 1990 taken together by all the European states to put the Cold War behind us for good.

A major step forward on the security front was the signing of the Budapest Memorandum[11] in December 1994 by Russia, Ukraine, the UK and the US, which saw Ukraine's accession to the Non-Proliferation Treaty and its agreement to the removal of all nuclear weapons from its territory. In this memorandum, the signatories agreed to 'respect the independence and sovereignty and the existing borders of Ukraine' and reaffirmed 'their obligation to refrain from the threat or use of force against the territorial integrity or political independence of Ukraine'. As we discuss later, Russia's flagrant breach of these undertakings in 2014 brought about the subsequent nadir in the post-Cold War relationship.

The trajectory again appeared to be continuing in a positive direction with the signature of the Founding Act on Mutual Relations, Cooperation and Security between NATO and the Russian Federation[12] in May 1997. Under this agreement, NATO and Russia undertook to 'build together a lasting and inclusive peace in the Euro-Atlantic area on the principles of democracy and cooperative security'. This acknowledged the cooperation of Russia in support of UN and Organization for Security and Co-operation in Europe (OSCE) peacekeeping operations including in Bosnia and Herzegovina, where Russian cooperation in securing Serbian support for a settlement had been an important milestone. NATO and Russia undertook to 'seek the widest possible cooperation among participating States of the OSCE with the aim of creating in Europe a common space of security and stability, without dividing lines or spheres of influence limiting the sovereignty of any state', while observing their obligations under international law. It also set up a Permanent Joint Council to 'provide a mechanism for consultations, coordination and, to the maximum extent possible, where appropriate, for joint decisions and joint action with respect to security issues of common concern'. The agreement was flagged as a historic achievement at the NATO summit in Madrid in July of that year,[13] which spoke of a 'commitment to an undivided Europe' and of a new Europe emerging of 'greater integration and cooperation'. The summit also announced the invitation of the Czech Republic, Hungary and Poland to begin accession talks (which led to accession in 1999) and the signature of the Charter on a Distinctive Partnership between NATO and Ukraine,[14] which was designed to move NATO–Ukraine cooperation onto a more substantive level, offer new potential for strengthening our relationship, and enhance security in the region more widely. NATO's journey eastwards was now well underway.

One of the events that Russia has since claimed as evidence that NATO was not a purely defensive organisation was the intervention in Kosovo in 1999 without UN Security Council authorisation, which saw NATO forces mount a sustained bombing campaign against Russia's traditional ally, Serbia. Nevertheless, the dialogue continued against the backdrop of growing concerns over international terrorism in the wake of the 9/11 attacks, following which Putin had been at the forefront of offering support to President Bush. Putin was also to be very supportive of the US in the initial stages of its intervention in Afghanistan and had not raised major issues around the US's withdrawal from the 1972 Anti-Ballistic Missile Treaty in 2002 – actions which the Russians later felt had gone unrewarded.

A key step in deepening NATO–Russia ties was the establishment of the NATO–Russia Council at NATO's summit in Rome in 2002.[15] This built on the Founding Act and set out to provide 'a mechanism for consultation consensus-building, cooperation, joint decision and joint action on a wide spectrum of security issues in the Euro-Atlantic region'. President Putin, in his statement,[16] spoke of Russia having no alternative to developing its ties with NATO:

> For Russia, given its geopolitical position, the deepening of equal interaction with NATO is one instance of its multi-vector approach to which there is no alternative and to which we are firmly committed. We cannot imagine ourselves outside Europe, as we have told some of our colleagues just now. But we believe it is equally inconceivable to underestimate the role of the time-tested mechanisms of cooperation in the CIS and Asia. Only a harmonious combination of actions in all these areas opens broad opportunities for creating a common security space from Vancouver to Vladivostok.

It is critical that this forum should be able to weather the stresses and strains put upon it by the challenging nature of the relationship between NATO and Russia, and provide a mechanism for dialogue in bad times as well as good.

2002 saw seven more countries invited to join the alliance – Bulgaria, Estonia, Latvia, Lithuania, Romania, Slovakia and Slovenia. The intervening year had seen the second Gulf War, which had been strongly opposed by Russia, and Russia was feeling that it was getting little in return from the relationship with the West. It was now seeing not just NATO but also the EU expand into what it regarded as its traditional sphere of influence, with the seven countries mentioned above joining in 2004, followed by Romania and Bulgaria in 2007. From a Russian perspective, the model was not one of a new European order, but an extension of the existing political and military blocs over which Russia felt it had minimal influence.

With Ukraine and Georgia seeking closer ties with NATO, Russia made its increasing concerns about the direction of travel clear. But Russian action, such as President Putin's December 2007 suspension of Russia's implementation of the Conventional Armed Forces in Europe Treaty (CFE), a key element in the conventional arms control structures in Europe, was also causing concerns in NATO. As the Bucharest summit in April 2008 approached, there were significant disagreements within NATO about further expansion, with the US strongly advocating membership for Georgia and Ukraine, while Germany and France were opposed. In the end, while it was agreed at the Bucharest summit to begin accession talks with Albania and Croatia, the decision on applications for Membership Action Plans by Ukraine and Georgia was postponed, although the statement noted: 'We agreed today that these countries will become members of NATO.' Earlier that year in February, Kosovo had unilaterally declared independence from Serbia and had been recognised by the US, UK, France and Germany amongst others; the Russians rejected the declaration. This led to a change in Russian approach to the breakaway republics of Abkhazia and South Ossetia, with the State Duma calling on the government to establish diplomatic links with them (and the breakaway Moldovan region of Transnistria). Tensions increased, culminating in a military clash between Russian and Georgian forces in August. The Independent International Fact-Finding Mission on the Conflict in Georgia, established by the EU, came to two broad conclusions in its final report.[17] Firstly, that shelling by Georgian forces had triggered the wider conflict; and secondly, that the Russian response, while initially justified, had subsequently been disproportionate and a violation of international law. The situation in Georgia was one of the scenarios that critics of NATO expansion had feared could lead to a potential crisis in the organisation. In such circumstances, given the uncertainty in the initial phases, would NATO have stood by its Article 5 commitment to mutual defence? Given the circumstances, it seems unlikely that it would have done, but either way it would have been an extremely critical and dangerous test of NATO's role in the post-Cold War world.

2008 saw another attempt by a more assertive and confident Russia to broaden the context of the security dialogue in the form of the 'Medvedev Initiative' which, undoubtedly intentional in its timing, was launched following the Bucharest summit. In a speech in June in Germany, President Medvedev reiterated the point that Russia wanted to be seen as an equal partner in the new Europe, and in particular highlighted that Russia did not expect to be absorbed into the existing structures:

> The end of the Cold War made it possible to build up genuinely equal cooperation between Russia, the European Union and North America as three branches of European civilisation. It is my conviction that Atlanticism as a sole historical principle has already had its day. We need to talk today about unity between the whole Euro-Atlantic area from Vancouver to Vladivostok. Life itself dictates the need for this kind of cooperation. But looking at the future construction of relations between the countries of Europe, we see a worrying tendency to take a selective and politicised approach to our common history. It is highly symptomatic that current differences with Russia are interpreted by many in the West as a need to simply bring Russia's policies closer into line with those of the West. But we do not want to be 'embraced' in this way. We need to look for common solutions.[18]

Medvedev went on to develop these themes, approving a new 'Foreign Policy Concept of the Russian Federation'[19] in July 2008 and picking up on them in his address to the World Policy Conference in Evian in October 2008 (the themes were elaborated on in various fora in the subsequent years). However, the timing against the backdrop of the Georgian crisis led many to see it as a Russian attempt to split the Western allies, and lacking in real substance. In particular, there were

serious reservations, which continue to exist, over the divergence between the statements of principle made in the policy concept, and the
realities of Russian behaviour. These included undertakings to:

> influence global processes to ensure formation of a just and dem-
> ocratic world order, based on collectiveness in finding solutions to
> international problems and supremacy of international law, first of
> all provisions of the UN Charter, as well as relations of equal part-
> nership among States with a central and coordinating role of the
> UN as the key organization governing international relations and
> possessing a unique legitimacy.

and

> promote good neighbourly relations with bordering States, to assist
> in eliminating the existing hotbeds of tension and conflicts in the
> regions adjacent to the Russian Federation and other areas of the
> world and to prevent emergence of the new ones.

Such statements rang hollow in the light of events in Georgia and
elsewhere. Again, this was seen by many as Russia simply paying
lip-service to global norms while continuing a campaign of disruption and destabilisation in what it regarded as its sphere of influence,
with the ultimate aim of re-establishing its hegemony in part at least
of the former Soviet empire. Until Russia acknowledges that its days
of empire are behind it and it must adapt to a new role, in the way that
others, notably the UK, have done so, it will be difficult to counter the
argument that *revanchist* tendencies remain a major threat to peace in
the wider European region. Acknowledging such a change should not
be seen as a sign of weakness, but rather a sign of confidence in taking
a new approach to its role in the world.

The Russian action in Ukraine in 2014 (and indeed the nature of
their intervention in Syria, discussed in Chapter Six) served only to
reinforce this perception that the Russian approach was to make lofty

statements about adhering to international norms, while continuing to act in a manner that was in direct contravention of those norms; thereby leading to a crisis point in Russian relations with the West. However, it is critical that the sequence of events, and the way they were handled, is examined in context.

As noted in the House of Lords' report referred to above, 'the EU had not taken into account the exceptional nature of Ukraine and its unique position in the shared neighbourhood'. A number of factors contribute to the uniqueness of Ukraine in the Russian mind, from the historical ties going back to the ninth-century era of Kievan Rus to its critical location as the home for Russia's major naval base at Sevastopol in the Crimea, a region which had been ceded to Ukraine by Khrushchev as recently as 1954; not to mention the significant numbers of Russian speakers, particularly in the east of the country. Equally strongly held views on the Ukrainian side meant that this was a potentially highly volatile situation, but, despite all the warning signs, as the Lords' report observes, there was 'a strong element of "sleep walking" into the current crisis'. The report goes on to say that:

Collectively, the EU overestimated the intention of the Ukrainian leadership to sign an Association Agreement, appeared unaware of the public mood in Ukraine and, above all, underestimated the depth of Russian hostility towards the Association Agreement. While each of these factors was understood separately, Member States, the European External Action Service and the Commission did not connect the dots.

When Putin returned to the presidency in 2012, the backdrop had moved on since the Georgian conflict of 2008. The economy had recovered with a growth in commodity prices, and with it Russian confidence about its role in the world. The Russian leadership had learnt lessons from their intervention in 2008 and had set about re-forming and re-equipping their military to prepare them for more flexible engagement, lower level conflicts and 'hybrid' warfare, blending conventional and non-conventional techniques, including use of disinformation, cyber etc. The situation in Ukraine had also been developing, as its leadership tried to maintain a difficult balancing act between strengthening ties with the EU and retaining their traditional links with Russia. Putin had warned of these challenges in his statement following the EU–Russia Summit in January 2014:[20]

> My colleagues and I held a sincere exchange of views regarding the Eastern Partnership* initiative. We are concerned about the stability and prosperity of our common neighbouring nations. These states are striving to cooperate more actively with the European Union and simultaneously maintain close historical and cooperative ties with Russia. We must certainly help them do this, but it is unacceptable to create new, dividing lines. On the contrary, we need to work together on building a new, unified Europe.

Events came to a head when the Ukrainian president, Yanukovych, suspended the signature of the Association Agreement,[21] which had been negotiated with the EU. This agreement contained language on foreign and security policy areas which it should have been recognised were likely to be highly provocative to the Russians. Key examples include Article 7.1, which states:

> The Parties shall intensify their dialogue and cooperation and promote gradual convergence in the area of foreign and security policy, including the Common Security and Defence Policy (CSDP), and shall address in particular issues of conflict prevention and crisis management, regional stability, disarmament, non-proliferation, arms control and arms export control as well as enhanced mutually-beneficial dialogue in the field of space.

---

* The Eastern Partnership is a joint initiative involving the EU, its member states and six eastern European partners – Armenia, Azerbaijan, Belarus, Georgia, Moldova and Ukraine, https://eeas.europa.eu/topics/eastern-partnership_en

Article 10.3 went on to state: The Parties shall explore the potential of military-technological cooperation. Ukraine and the European Defence Agency (EDA) shall establish close contacts to discuss military capability improvement, including technological issues.

But their potential impact appeared to have been overlooked or ignored by politicians in EU capitals, including London. As the House of Lords' report indicates, this decision 'triggered the protests now referred to as 'the Maidan'. These protests took both the EU and Russia by surprise. Events had begun to take on a momentum of their own which neither side could predict or control.

These events saw President Yanukovych flee Kiev in February and the Ukrainian parliament taking steps which were seen as increasingly hostile by Russia. In particular, Russia feared that agreements on the Sevastopol naval base would be rescinded. Pro-Russian protests took place on the Crimean Peninsula, the local government announced a referendum, armed men took over key buildings and Russian forces took over strategic facilities. The hastily organised referendum was held in March 2014, with an overwhelming vote in favour of a return to Russia. The vote was widely condemned as illegal and illegitimate, including by the EU and US, who imposed sanctions on Russia. However, President Putin, who shortly after issued a decree, 'On the recognition of the Republic of Crimea', remained intransigent and drew a comparison to the earlier declaration of independence by Kosovo (which Russia had never accepted), saying:[22] 'We keep hearing from the United States and Western Europe that Kosovo is some special case. What makes it so special in the eyes of our colleagues?', going on to reinforce the message about how Russia saw itself in the world: 'Russia is an independent, active participant in international affairs; like other countries, it has its own national interests that need to be taken into account and respected.' This use of examples of Western actions, often controversial in their own right, to legitimise their own activity is an area in which the Russians have become adept, even though the rationale behind the examples they quote may be completely at variance with their own intentions. The situation in Ukraine deteriorated further with armed clashes in eastern Ukraine and the pro-Russian Donetsk and Luhansk regions declaring independence. Despite a second peace agreement ('Minsk II') being signed in Minsk in February 2015, the fighting continued and sanctions remained in place, with no final resolution in sight. The role of the EU and its member states, in managing the negotiations with Ukraine on the Association Agreement and ultimately in dealing with the subsequent crisis, has come in for much criticism. Richard Sakwa, in his article, 'The death of Europe? Continental fates after Ukraine', wrote:

> The Ukraine crisis exposed the flaws in Europe's post-Cold War development… In the Ukraine crisis the EU not only proved inadequate as a conflict regulator but itself became the source of conflict. The EU's ill prepared advance into what was always recognised to be a contested neighbourhood provoked the gravest international crisis of our era, but once the crisis started Europe was sidelined.[23]

The UK's role has also been specifically criticised. Despite its position as a signatory of the Budapest Memorandum, mentioned earlier in this chapter, the UK has not had a prominent role in trying to find a solution to the crisis, with Germany and France taking the lead in Europe. This limited engagement was noted by the House of Lords: 'As one of the four signatories of the Budapest Memorandum (1994), which pledged to respect Ukraine's territorial integrity, the UK had a particular responsibility when the crisis erupted. The government has not been as active or as visible on this issue as it could have been.' Playing a key role in reaching a resolution to this crisis and developing a new relationship with Russia must form a key plank in any UK foreign policy outside of the EU. It will be by no means easy.

Finding a common approach with Russia will require patience and there are likely to be disruptions on the way, as Russia continues to flex its muscles to demonstrate is capabilities. It is essential to recognise that in a European context, Russia certainly sees itself as a major player, and indeed the West made a number of moves to recognise this, such as the establishment of the NATO–Russia Council mentioned above, and bringing Yeltsin's Russia into the G8. Accepting Russia as a major player does not mean acquiescing to every Russian demand; however, it does require a much greater level of genuine engagement than has been the case in the recent past, and we acknowledge that it requires two willing parties to create such engagement. The need for the FCO to continue to rebuild its expertise in dealing with Russia is critical. In its March 2017 report, the Foreign Affairs Committee noted 'the FCO must once again invest in the analytical capacity to understand Russian decision-making in order to develop effective and informed foreign policy'.[24] It is acknowledged that this is underway, as evidenced by the FCO's submission to the Foreign Affairs Committee[25] in January 2017, which highlighted the strengthening of resources in this area, though more needs to be done. In an era of 'fake news' and 'alternative truth', disciplined, rigorous, well-informed diplomacy is required. Without a clear-headed analysis of the options, an understanding of others' perspectives (which does not require agreement with them) and a readiness to compromise where appropriate, we run the risk of repeating the mistakes of the recent past. And there is no doubt the risks of continuing to talk over or through each other remain high. There are fundamental differences of perception about the world order, and Russia's place in it, as can be seen in President Putin's speech to the seventieth UN General Assembly in September 2015:[26]

We are all different, and we should respect that. Nations shouldn't be forced to all conform to the same development model that somebody has declared the only appropriate one … It seems, however, that instead of learning from other people's mistakes, some prefer to repeat them and continue to export revolutions, only now these are 'democratic' revolutions.

The Russian view on the impact of NATO expansion was also reiterated, portraying Russia as the forward-looking state, in the face of an aggressive threat:

Sadly, some of our counterparts are still dominated by their Cold War-era bloc mentality and the ambition to conquer new geopolitical areas. First, they continued their policy of expanding NATO – one should wonder why, considering that the Warsaw Pact had ceased to exist and the Soviet Union had disintegrated … NATO has kept on expanding, together with its military infrastructure. Next, the post-Soviet states were forced to face a false choice between joining the West and carrying on with the East. Sooner or later, this logic of confrontation was bound to spark off a major geopolitical crisis. And that is exactly what happened in Ukraine.

The failure of the two sides to understand each other's fundamental positions has been flagged in many quarters. In its analysis of the development of the crisis, 'How the EU lost Russia over Ukraine',[27] Germany's *Der Spiegel* came to the conclusion that 'Russia and Europe talked past each other and misunderstood one another. It was a clash of two different foreign policy cultures: A Western approach that focused on treaties and the precise wording of the paragraphs therein; and the Eastern approach in which status and symbols are more important.' In more general terms, Robert Skidelsky had highlighted a similar issue of differences in perception or Russia's behaviour back in 2008:[28] 'The issue is complicated by the lack of a common language of international relations: what to Russians looks like encirclement to western politicians is simply spreading freedom, markets, and democracy.' Overcoming these differences, and in particular ensuring Russia lives up to the international obligations it subscribes to, will require a rebuilding of trust which has been swept away.

Rebuilding trust will be key if there is to be any resolution to the situation in Crimea. While Russia may see its continuing control of all Crimean territory as a fait accompli, the British position must remain that the annexation is an illegal act. This does not mean that there cannot ever be any discussion on the issue, but this has to be with the full engagement of Ukraine. Any final resolution which would result in changes to internationally recognised borders has to be the subject of negotiation in the region.

This may be the time to take a more ambitious path and seek to find a solution to the situation in Ukraine in the context of a wider agreement around the ongoing disputes over territory in Moldova and Georgia, which have been damaging to the wider relationship between Russia and the West. Changing boundaries on the map of the world is no minor matter; it must be negotiated. As mentioned earlier, this is best done in a framework involving the five permanent members of the Security Council and Germany, given its influence in the region and role to date, should also be involved. There would have to be incentives for all the parties to these disputes to engage fully in the discussions. In the case of Russia, as well as a path to sanctions removal, the terms of reference must spell out that one of the objectives of the initiative is an agreement on, and the mutual recognition of, the defined boundaries of all the parties involved, including the promoters of the settlement. For Ukraine, Moldova and Georgia, this would provide an opportunity to address and remove the major destabilising factor which undermines their sovereignty and holds back their wider development.

As well as disagreements with Russia on the international stage, the bilateral relationship was very negatively impacted by the killing of former KGB officer and critic of Putin, Alexander Litvinenko, in London in 2006 after he was administered a fatal dose of polonium. Russia refused a British request to extradite one of the suspects, another former KGB officer,

in 2007. That year, the UK expelled four Russian diplomats, which led to four British diplomats subsequently being expelled from Moscow. In the report of the public inquiry into the death of Litvinenko published in January 2016, the Chairman concluded: 'The FSB [Russian Federal Security Service] operation to kill Mr Litvinenko was probably approved by Mr Patrushev [head of the FSB at that time] and also by President Putin.' This conclusion clearly did not go down well in Moscow, and engaging with Russia against this backdrop has been problematical, to say the least. The last visit by a Foreign Secretary, prior to the announcement of a visit by Boris Johnson in April 2017 (subsequently postponed), was by William Hague in 2012. There is a growing recognition, as we discuss below, that it is critical to re-engage with Russia on the political front; we should not forget that in other areas, notably in the role City based institutions play in supporting Russian business globally, relations have remained good.

The continuing imposition of sanctions on Russia is a heavily debated topic. While sanctions do not yet appear to have had any real influence on Russia's policy and, in particular, its position on Crimea, they have sent a clear signal to Moscow. They should not, however, be seen as a long-term weapon, designed to bring Russia economically to its knees. That is in no one's interests. But their removal needs to take place in conjunction with Russian delivery on its obligations under the Minsk agreements, which may be easier to reach in the wider P5 format suggested. It is imperative that Russia is given the clear message that, while mistakes of the past have been acknowledged and its views and interests need to be taken in to account, it must live up to its obligations to abide by international law and respect the sovereignty of its neighbours. That does not mean to say that there cannot be changes to boundaries, but these must only take place in the framework of a negotiated settlement; as part of that, there could be a further referendum on the status of Crimea, though there would have to be international guarantees that this would be free and fair.

More broadly, as the Lords' report on Ukraine mentions, a solution has to be found to meet any genuine grievances of Russian ethnic minorities, so that these cannot provide 'a convenient pretext which could be used to justify further destabilizing actions in those states', suggesting an investigation in 'whether more steps could be taken to facilitate access to citizenship for ethnic Russians who have long-established residency in these states, but limited ability in the official language'. Again, such issues should also be addressed in some of the other areas of dispute, and form part of any new arrangements in Europe. Ensuring recognition of the need for tolerance by all parties involved should be a key part of the UK's diplomacy in this area, and it is well positioned to do so, given the respect in the region for its contribution to their re-integration into Europe.

Progress on this issue would allow the wider issues of a new model for European and, indeed, Euro-Atlantic cooperation to be tackled, and an attempt made to find common ground, not least in the genuine respect for obligations under the UN Charter. Given that the institutional structure is already in place, we would recommend reinvigorating the OSCE (which has been involved in the search for resolutions to many of these territorial disputes) as a framework for broader initiatives to bring all parties in the Euro-Atlantic area closer together, rather than establish a completely new framework where there would be significant risks of form taking precedence over substance. However, this is not without its own challenges. Russia's attitude to this body changed following the OSCE's 1999 Istanbul summit, where it called for a political settlement in Chechnya. Russia's current position, while acknowledging that the OSCE is 'one of the backbone organisations in the Euroatlantic region', is far from a ringing endorsement, going on to state:

> Today the OSCE is undergoing a long and systemic crisis. Now, almost twenty years after the collapse of the bipolar world, it is yet to determine its new destiny, however, it is struggling to uphold its primary function as a unique platform for discussion of security matters acting on the principles of equality and mutual respect. Many countries still use the Organisation instruments to realize their own goals, often to the prejudice of other partners' interests.[29]

At a time when the populations of many EU member states are looking for change, this may be the opportunity for some new thinking, and the UK, from its post-Brexit perspective, would be well placed to take a lead in this. The risk of not acting would be to open the door for a much wider regression into nationalism, heightened risks of tension and, indeed, confrontation.

All is not lost in restoring good relations with Russia. Russia today is a hugely better place for Russians and for EU citizens than the Soviet Union the West faced in the past, and which we saw invading Hungary in 1956, Czechoslovakia in 1968 and then Afghanistan in 1979. It has been too easily forgotten how President Gorbachev, President Yeltsin and, initially, President Putin all contributed to greatly improved relations over two decades. Relations have undoubtedly been very seriously set back over Ukraine and the annexation of Crimea, but we are a considerable way from returning to the Cold War. Patiently, persuasively and persistently the UK post-Brexit must help rebuild the relationship between Russia and the West and be prepared to face continued challenges along the way. Prime Minister May's comments in her speech to the Republican Party conference in January 2017 provide a good starting point for the rebuilding of the UK's relationship with Russia:

> There is nothing inevitable about conflict between Russia and the West. And nothing unavoidable about retreating to the days of the Cold War. But we should engage with Russia from a position of strength. And we should build the relationships, systems and processes that make co-operation more likely than conflict – and that, particularly after the illegal annexation of Crimea, give assurance to Russia's neighbouring states that their security is not in question.[30]

Rather than seeking a grandiose over-arching structure in the first instance, it will be important to look at practical steps for rebuilding confidence and trust, while encouraging Russia to look forward to a new and respected global role rather than harkening back to a past era of Russian hegemony which will not and should not return. The UK should recognise that its influence with Russia will not be of the magnitude of the US or Germany. There are a range of areas in which there is potential for cooperation, and where the UK, as a partner in the UN Security Council, has a good platform, not least in the combatting of ISIS and international terrorism more generally. However, as the Foreign Affairs Committee notes, this is not straightforward: 'It is difficult to envisage how to progress this shared interest considering the differences between the two countries' respective definitions and analyses of terrorism, and acceptable methods to defeat it. Any dialogue with Russia must be handled with the greatest care, but it is at least worth exploring.'[31]

The successful engagement of Russia in the P5+1 format to reach an agreement with Iran on its nuclear programme sets a good precedent, and continued engagement on nuclear non-proliferation, as outlined in Chapter Six, remains a key priority. Likewise, the UK should seek to reinvigorate discussions around both nuclear and conventional forces and ensure that NATO–Russia dialogue is not neglected. If and when sanctions are lifted, we should see substantial potential for an increase in UK–Russian trade, which can further positively reinforce our relationship, as will a return of major Russian companies to the London capital markets. But making progress in all these areas will require trust, and in that regard, especially given the era of 'fake news' in which we now live, we should follow the much-quoted approach of Ronald Reagan in his dealings with Mikhail Gorbachev – 'trust, but verify'.

CHAPTER 6

THE CHALLENGES OF
THE MIDDLE EAST

As the Middle East region can be defined in many ways, for the purposes of this chapter it is considered to include Egypt, Turkey, Israel, Palestine, Lebanon, Syria, Jordan, Iraq, the countries of the Arabian Peninsula and Iran. Middle Eastern politics have long been likened to a complex game used as a metaphor and as an explanation for recurring behaviour. The 'Rules of the Eastern Question Game' are characterised by Professor L. Carl Brown writings from Princeton University in 1984 as a kaleidoscope:

> shifting pattern of alliances – everything is related to something else – minor local issues and major international concerns – the most internationalised or penetrated diplomatic system – Great Power involvement and rivalries – rarely does a single political actor … have the ability to impose its will – politics of the limited fait accompli or quick grab – everything interrelated – reluctance to establish priorities – reactive politics or diplomatic counterpunching – preference for mediators and third parties, tactics zero sum political games.[1]

Navigating this complex landscape was once seen as a core skill of the British and, given our longstanding connections to the region, we can continue to draw on that experience – by no means always positive – and contribute to its future development.

2017 is the 100th anniversary of the British Foreign Secretary, Arthur Balfour, signing the famous – or infamous, depending on one's point of view – eponymous Declaration. It is fifty years since the Six Day Arab–Israeli War, the conflict which most threatened Israel's survival. Six years have passed since the start of fighting in Syria. This, from a British viewpoint, is the place to start an assessment of where our voice can usefully manifest itself from 2017 onwards. No policy on the Middle East conflict, after the passage of so many years, can be determined solely by what went before. It may ultimately not even rhyme with that history, but we in Britain cannot ignore it. The crucial second paragraph in Balfour's letter, set out below, strives to be balanced but it is changing the regional status quo and suffers from being insufficiently clear geographically.

Foreign Office
November 2nd, 2017

Dear Lord Rothschild,

I have much pleasure in conveying to you, on behalf of His Majesty's Government, the following declaration of sympathy with the Jewish Zionist aspirations which has been submitted to, and approved by, the Cabinet.

His Majesty's Government view with favour the establishment in Palestine of a national home for the Jewish people, and will use their best endeavours to facilitate the achievement of this object, it being clearly understood that nothing shall be done which may prejudice the civil and religious rights of existing non-Jewish communities in Palestine or the rights and political status enjoyed by Jews in any other country.

I should be grateful if you would bring this declaration to the knowledge of the Zionist Federation.

Yours,

Arthur James Balfour.

Understanding Britain's historical role in Palestine is an essential first step to comprehending the deep-seated nature of the strife between the Israelis and Palestinians. A fair-minded comprehension in the UK of this strife, with the aim of informing public opinion, has already been established by the Balfour Project.[2] It has produced a film *Britain in Palestine 1917–1948*[3] and published a *Companion Guide.*[4] The Project wants to mark the century that has passed since the Declaration with a reflective debate geared to finding a solution rather than being an occasion to celebrate, and to focus on unbiased and factual information. We should seek to mark the Declaration with as objective an assessment as is possible and a resolve to try to make progress towards a regional peace. Some will celebrate, while others denigrate the Declaration. Whatever their stance, few will deny that the Declaration had a profound historical effect after its signature on 2 November 1917.

Most unusually, Balfour had already been Conservative Prime Minister before becoming Foreign Secretary, resigning on 4 December 1905 to be succeeded as Prime Minister by Campbell-Bannerman, and this gave his tenure as Foreign Secretary an added authority. From 1916 to 1922 he was part of the Conservative-dominated coalition under the Liberal Prime Minister Lloyd George. Balfour went on to give his name to another document, the Balfour Definition, which emerged from the Imperial Conference of October 1926 when the Conservative Prime Minister, Stanley Baldwin, asked him to take charge of the crucial Inter-Imperial Relations Committee.

The Balfour Definition concerned the relationship amongst the self-governing states in what became, in fact as well as in practice, the British Commonwealth. 'They are autonomous Communities within the British Empire equal in status, in no way subordinate one to another in any aspect of their domestic or external affairs, though united by a common allegiance to the Crown, and freely associated as members of the British Commonwealth of Nations.'[5] As Britain determines how best to rebuild that relationship while leaving the EU, that definition is well worth bearing in mind.

Balfour's perceptive biographer, R. J. Q. Adams, analysed the character of the Foreign Secretary:

to Balfour anti-Semitism was a horror, and he accepted the profundity of the debt owed to the Jews by Christian civilisation – but he also believed that Jews shared a cultural identity beyond their religion which made it difficult for many to become British.[6]

The Prime Minister, Lloyd George – very typically for him – was in favour of 'the idea of reuniting the Jewish people with the land of their forefathers' but for many reasons saw strategic military significance in the 'Holy Land'. He agreed Balfour should meet with Lord Rothschild on 13 June 1917 and that Balfour be empowered to make a public statement which might help Britain win the war. The War Cabinet first discussed a draft on 3 September, but in the absence of Lloyd George and Balfour. It is very important historically to record that a number of senior Jewish politicians were opposed to the Declaration. Edwin Montagu, though not a member of the War Cabinet, was present at the first meeting. As India Secretary, he was passionately against what was proposed. He wrote Lloyd George an emotional letter, entreating that 'the country for which I have worked ever since I left the University – England – the country for which my family have fought, tells me that my national home ... is Palestine'. This was the man who also two years earlier had opposed Herbert Samuel's 1915 Zionist statement to the then Cabinet saying, 'I assert there is not a Jewish nation.'[7] Montagu was an assimilationist and he also argued, 'How would he negotiate with the peoples of India on behalf of His Majesty's Government if the world had been told that [Britain] regarded his national home as being in Turkish territory.'

On 5 October, the War Cabinet met for a second time with Lloyd George in the chair. Curzon, who knew the territory very well, was Lord President of the Council and a powerful figure in the War Cabinet. He always argued against Zionism and categorised it 'as sentimental idealism'. The meeting deferred a decision and it asked

Curzon to prepare a paper and also to find out the views of the US President, Woodrow Wilson. Curzon's memorandum was presented to the third Cabinet meeting on the 31st. It challenged the Cabinet to think about whether the arid territory of the region would be able to support the increased population. It also drew attention to the fact that the Jews were heavily outnumbered in Palestine by Arabs who had lived there for centuries, and questioned the likely reaction of Christians and Muslims to the Jews taking Jerusalem as their capital.

No one can say after Lord Curzon's intervention that the issues that would haunt the Balfour Declaration were not put firmly into the Cabinet discussion. The Declaration was no glibly constructed document. It was amended, discussed and fully debated. The Cabinet was told, according to the historian Schneer, that President Wilson had finally telegraphed an unambiguous message of support for Zionism. The Cabinet had also before them a powerful paper from Sir Mark Sykes, joint signatory to the Sykes–Picot Agreement of 1916. He claimed that 'with proper management Palestine eventually could accept a population five times its present size'. Given what he had heard from Sykes, that there would be no need for people to be dispossessed, Balfour told the Cabinet that while there were differences of opinion amongst the experts, he understood a much larger population was sustainable than had been under Ottoman rule.[8] In terms of the expansion of the territory, he has been proven right today. But tragically, many have been dispossessed. At the beginning of 2017 Israel's population was 8.6 million, of which 74.8 per cent were Jews and 20.8 per cent were Arabs. The most recent 2014 population figure for Palestinians is 4.4 million, with 1.7 million in the Gaza Strip and 2.7 million in the West Bank.

Curzon withdrew his opposition to the Declaration. Montagu was not present, though if he had been, he would have undoubtedly opposed it. Balfour asserted if the Cabinet 'could make a declaration favourable to such an idea we should be able to carry on extremely useful propaganda both in Russia and America'. Propaganda was a powerful word to invoke making it clear that his views were related to an assessment of Britain's war interests as was the view of the Prime

Minister. The Cabinet had taken their time, weighed the arguments and made a unanimous decision to support the Declaration.

On 2 December 1917, a month after Balfour had signed the document, the London Opera House was filled to capacity to celebrate the declaration of a national home for the Jews; but for some, the balancing promise in the Declaration that 'nothing should be done which may prejudice the civil and religious rights of existing non-Jewish communities in Palestine' was crucial. Many famous speakers, starting with Lord Rothschild, were all in favour speaking with confidence and optimism. One spokesman, Sheik Ismail Abdul al-Akki, evoked the biblical image of a land that would again flow with 'milk and honey' predicting that Jews and Arabs would share the land in harmony. Sadly, as we all know, those predictions have remained unfulfilled. Were the two balancing promises ever capable of being fulfilled? Ominously, on that very same day Lloyd George and members of his administration were:

> in secret manoeuvrings to detach the Ottoman Empire from the Central Powers. They were offering, among other inducements, that the Turkish flag could continue to fly over Palestine ... the lead up to the Balfour Declaration was anything but a simple triumphal progress. And since intrigue and double-dealing as much as bravery and vision were of its essence, the Balfour Declaration resulted not merely in celebration and congratulation but soon enough in disillusionment, distrust and resentment.[9]

In 1919 in Paris, President Wilson proposed a Commission which should visit Syria and Palestine for a six-week investigation of the views of the local population. Henry King and Charles Crane, two Americans, led the Commission and were against Britain and France being the supervisory foreign powers. This meant the French, British and Italian members of the Commission bowed out at the last moment, probably to avoid embarrassment. The Commission proposed that in the light of the people being consulted being strongly averse to the

Balfour Declaration and Zionism a united Arab kingdom under King Faisal should be established with the Americans as mandatories. The findings of the Commission were only made available in 1922 by which time much had happened and they were never implemented.

In 1920 at San Remo, France relinquished Palestine for Syria and what is now Lebanon. King Faisal was forced out of Syria by the French and the British left Syria. The League of Nations mandate for Britain in Palestine incorporated the Balfour Declaration so that the King–Crane Commission findings, that a Jewish state could not be achieved 'without the gravest trespass upon the civil and religious rights of existing non-Jewish communities in Palestine', had been ignored and their warning that the Zionist programme would have to be 'greatly modified'. Balfour, in his memorandum of August 1919, wrote that Britain did not propose to consult the wishes of the people like the American Commission since, 'The Four Great Powers are committed to Zionism. And Zionism, be it right or wrong, good or bad, is rooted in age-long traditions, in present needs, in future hopes, of far profounder import than the desires and prejudices of the 700,000 Arabs who now inhabit that ancient land.'

Churchill, visiting Palestine in March 1921 as Colonial Secretary, was met by an angry crowd in Gaza shouting 'Down with Balfour', yet he rejected all demands that the Declaration should be set on one side. In that same month after the Cairo Conference, Britain created the new Kingdom of Transjordan. In 1922 in the White Paper on Palestine, Churchill insisted Palestine was part of the excluded areas of Syria lying to the west of the District of Damascus. This was called into question in 1923 by the publication in the *Daily Mail* of the McMahon correspondence. Britain officially published the McMahon–Hussein correspondence in 1939. The Arab rebellion also ended in 1939 and a White Paper published that year on Palestine said:

> His Majesty's Government believe that the framers of the Mandate on which the Balfour Declaration was embodied could not have intended that Palestine should be converted into a Jewish state

against the will of the Arab population of the country ... His Majesty's Government therefore now declare unequivocally that it is not part of their policy that Palestine should become a Jewish state.

Once again, with the war imminent, British policy had been framed by a wish not to bring the Arabs and Muslims in the region into the war on the side of its enemies. Yet in the Second World War, a large number of Jews fought in the Allied forces. Immigration of Jewish people speeded up from Europe from the time the Nazis began to take power in the early 1930s. After the end of the Second World War Palestine was the instinctive place of refuge for Jewish people in Europe and Britain, trying to control the flow of Jewish refugees in the process, became widely criticised. It was seen, too, by many British people as a shameful period. On 1 February 1944 Menachem Begin, the leader of Irgun, the Zionist paramilitary group, had issued a declaration of revolt, and the armistice with the British was over.

At the Potsdam Conference in 1945, the British Foreign Secretary, Ernest Bevin, was passed a note from US President Truman (originally handed to Churchill while the British election, which had seen him lose in a Labour landslide, was still underway), which expressed the 'great interest' of the Americans in the Palestine problem and their passionate protest against the restrictions imposed on Jewish immigration by the British White Paper of 1939. When no obvious relaxation followed under the new Labour government, the stereotype of Bevin as the latest in a long line of persecutors of the Jews began to develop. Bevin's biographer writes after this: 'His relations with the Zionists became coloured with personal feeling (on both sides) and brought down on him the charge of anti-Semitism.'[10] 'He was not committed to opposing the Zionist programme', and, in 1940–41, there is evidence he was regarded by Zionists as a friend, in the War Cabinet.[11] By 1945 Zionism had been transformed. Weizmann's gradualism and diplomacy had been taken up by Rabbi Silver, who was pressing for the establishment of a Jewish state to provide a home for European Jews who had survived Hitler's Final Solution.

By February 1947 the British Foreign Secretary, Ernest Bevin, announced the handover of responsibility to the United Nations (the successor to the League of Nations) and all non-essential British personnel were evacuated. The United Nations Special Committee on Palestine (UNSCOP), which visited Palestine in mid-1947, recommended partition. UN Resolution 181 was passed by the General Assembly on 29 November 1947 proposing a Jewish state on 56 per cent of the land and an Arab state on 43 per cent of the land, with the UN retaining control of Jerusalem and Bethlehem. The British abstained. The General Assembly under Articles 10, 11 and 14 of the UN Charter had no power to impose such a Resolution but only to recommend it. The Arab countries rejected UNSCOP's partition.

The British mandate was due to end on 15 May 1948, but Britain refused to enforce partition with violence between the Jews and Arabs increasing. The so-called 'War of Independence' or, as the Arabs of Palestine choose to call it, Nakba (the Catastrophe), took place between 15 May and 7 January 1949, by which time 60 per cent of the area designated for the Arabs in the UN resolution was controlled by the newly declared state of Israel; Jordan had control of the West Bank and East Jerusalem.

For many Britons there was, and there should have been, a sense of guilt about the government's position. For those with the executive responsibility for Palestine it seemed, at the time, necessary to hold back the flow; many British people felt that their government had not changed its policy sufficiently to reflect the horrors of the Holocaust in Europe, but in Palestine it seemed unconnected. While Bevin 'could fairly claim that Truman's readiness to bend to Zionist pressure had made it impossible to take sufficient account of Arab feelings', as his biographer Bullock wrote, 'There had also been errors of judgement and timing as well as faults of temper on his part ... He could not even be sure in the summer of 1948 that the worst of all possible consequences, irreparable danger to the Anglo-US partnership had been averted.'[12] Bevin had even been ready to use the British veto against the imposition of sanctions which was supported by the US, France and the Soviet Union in the Security Council that May. He avoided doing so only because the resolution obtained less than the necessary seven votes, so the British abstained.

President Truman met with Marshall, his Secretary of State and former wartime Chief of the US Defense Staff, on 12 May 1948. Marshall told Truman that domestic considerations must not determine foreign policy; at stake was 'the great office of the President'. Reinforcing that assertion, Marshall said if in the elections in November he, Marshall – looking directly at Truman – were to vote and Truman had recognised Israel, he would 'vote against the President'. On 14 May, the day Israel, at midnight, was to be declared in Jerusalem a new state, Marshall, after being told by Robert Lovet, 'it was the President's choice', called the President to say he would not oppose recognition publicly. At 6 p.m. Washington announced recognition, becoming *de facto* the first to recognise, whereas the Soviet Union was the first to make the formal *de jure* recognition. Many US State Department officials, who had been up until the last moment with the British searching for alternatives, felt deeply hostile to Truman's decision and sympathetic to the British position.[13]

What all this shows is that the Balfour Declaration and the subsequent Arab–Israeli dispute has been the subject of both agreement and disagreement between the US and the UK. It was not a new phenomenon and the fractious relationship continued. While there was initially agreement in opposing Egyptian President Nasser's nationalisation of the Suez Canal, by October 1956 Prime Minister Anthony Eden had started to collude militarily with Israel and France. Their plan was for Israel to attack Egypt, and France and Britain would then put troops on the Suez Canal as peacekeepers to separate Israeli and Egyptian fighters. That military action ended on the night of 5 November with Eden being given an ultimatum by President Eisenhower, who was never told by them of the collusion, that the US would support economic sanctions against Britain unless British troops stopped fighting along the Suez Canal. Eden called a ceasefire against the wishes of France and Israel. Eden had, in effect, misled the Americans and went on to say an outright lie to the House of Commons: 'there was not foreknowledge that Israel would attack Egypt'.[14] There were some extenuating circumstances due to Eden's health, but it was a sorry tale and the worst British foreign policy mistake after Munich over the appeasement of Hitler.[15] It looks as if the invasion of Iraq in 2003 will prove to be an even worse error, but a crucial difference is that this was undertaken with the US, not against US policy.

There was a serious fissure in British relations with Israel during the Yom Kippur War of October 1973, when the Egyptian and Syrian armies caught the Israelis by surprise and, for a few days, the Israelis, facing an attack on two fronts, could have lost the war. On 25 September 1973 King Hussein of Jordan had warned Golda Meir that Syria was positioning for war. At 3.30 a.m. on 6 October Yom Kippur she was telephoned. The late President Nasser's son-in-law, then a confidant of President Sadat, had informed Israeli intelligence of an attack from Egypt and Syria at sundown. She dealt with the threat to Israel with great skill, mobilising the reserves even on this, the holiest of days, against the advice of her Minister of Defence, Moshe Dayan, who wished to wait for 'the first shot'. A few days later, Dayan cracked under great strain and offered to resign, saying: 'Golda, I was wrong about everything.' In truth, she probably saved Israel that day by mobilising reserves.[16]

It could be argued Yom Kippur was the first test of a European foreign policy, as Britain had joined the European Community on 1 January 1973. Edward Heath as Prime Minister and Douglas Home as Foreign Secretary and a former Prime Minister shamefully decided to withhold supplying arms to all sides. The British Ambassador called on US Secretary of State Henry Kissinger the day after the war commenced and was asked, 'And whose side are you on?' The Ambassador found the question offensive and urged the United States to avoid any overt intervention. Kissinger said to his officials, 'The Europeans behaved like jackals. They gave us no support when we needed it.' Inside the Cabinet, Hailsham told Douglas Home it was 'ignoble and immoral'. If you sell weapons, he maintained, 'you implicitly undertake to provide spare parts and ammunition … If you are not prepared to do this you should not sell weapons.'[17] Many, in all parts of the House of Commons, were not satisfied by Heath's explanation that it was an even-handed approach because the embargo affected the Arabs as well as the Israelis. Everyone involved knew that it would be the Israelis who were bound to be the most affected and, because of the surprise element, were the most endangered.

Kissinger, after the Israeli forces defeated the attackers, spent thirty-two days shuttling between Damascus and Jerusalem on a complex serious of disengagement exercises. On 24 October 1973 Leonid Brezhnev nearly sent a Soviet airborne force to the war zone and US forces were put on increased alert. Fortunately, the crisis passed, following a conference held in Geneva in December 1973, which was co-chaired by the US and the Soviet Union, though following the conference the Soviet Union's influence in the Middle East waned.

On 1 October 1977, a joint US–Soviet statement on the Middle East was made by US Secretary of State Vance and Soviet Foreign Minister Gromyko. There then followed vituperative attacks on the statement by the Israeli government, who were totally opposed to a reconvening of the Geneva Conference. This view was reinforced by the Jewish community in the US. President Sadat of Egypt had private doubts about yet further involvement of the Soviet Union, Egypt's main arms supplier, and was trying to back away from being seen as part of a Soviet sphere of influence. President Carter had also wisely sent Sadat a handwritten note towards the end of October appealing for a bold and statesmanlike move to help overcome the hurdles to the Geneva process.

On 13 November 1977, after some private diplomacy between Egypt and Israel, Menachem Begin invited Sadat to come to Israel, and on 18 November Sadat flew into Israel to propose a world summit in East Jerusalem to be attended by Syria, Jordan, Egypt and the PLO with the US, Soviet Union, China, France and the UK. That proposal was soon dropped in favour of the start of a dialogue between Sadat and Begin, but it had merit then and it could yet have merit forty years later. Sadat, a former air-force officer, had been a member of

Nasser's military committee that overthrew King Farouk. Begin, the longstanding right wing leader of the Likud Party, was now Prime Minister. They were devout leaders; one Muslim, the other Orthodox Jew. They needed a catalyst, however, and that quickly became President Carter, a devout Christian. The personal chemistry between all three led to the Camp David Agreement in 1978. Sadly, that historic opportunity never fully developed into a regional settlement of the Arab–Israeli conflict. But it did produce an Egyptian–Israeli Peace Treaty that still holds today.

Britain might have remained on the side-lines in 1977 along with the rest of Europe, but for an inspired request by Prime Minister James Callaghan for Begin to visit Britain before Sadat's visit. The FCO collective wisdom was horrified by even the thought of the man responsible for the 1946 bombing of the British administrative headquarters at the King David Hotel, which had left ninety-one dead, officially visiting London. The visit went well with no significant demonstrations or protest. During the visit Begin asked to see the Foreign Secretary's room where the Balfour Declaration had been signed. It was if he was visiting a sacred shrine and the Foreign Secretary, David Owen, took down from the bookshelves and presented to Begin a leather-bound volume of Hansard recording the House of Commons debates of 1973. Begin's family later said this was his most treasured gift and he showed it with pride to his visitors in the belief, with his failing eyesight, that this volume had been present on the day the Balfour Declaration had been signed. No one ever wanted to correct him and break its magic. With Sadat and Begin regularly flying through London on their way to Washington for the Camp David talks, it meant a level of engagement for the UK in the Palestine question which, though still modest, had not been seen since the UK held the Palestine Mandate. A few months later the Foreign Secretary made the first visit to Israel of anyone holding that office.

Begin made a huge step to stabilise the Middle East when he agreed to hand back every square hectare of Sinai to Egypt, but he was never ready to release territory to Arab Palestinians in what he called Samaria and Judea. Dayan, however, who had been Minister of Defence in the previous Labour government and who became Minister of Foreign Affairs in Begin's government from 1977, was disturbed when Begin changed his position after the signing of the peace treaty with Egypt. A new text was put forward and the sovereignty question over Judea, Samaria and the Gaza district was no longer, as in the earlier text, left open. Dayan was firmly opposed to the establishment of a Palestinian state, but he was in a minority in the Cabinet on this changed text and appropriating private Arab land. He resigned. Nevertheless, Dayan personally continued to talk to Arabs, since he was fluent in their language. In his book, he described his interpretation of Arab Palestinian views on the spectrum of left or right.

> The ties between the administered territories and Jordan were essential they said and the two could not be kept apart, because of the characteristics of their populations and their economies. There was hardly a family in Judea and Samaria and Gaza, rich or poor, urban resident or Bedouin that did not have a relative living in Jordan. And Jordan constituted the principal market.[18]

This relationship between a Palestinian state and Jordan has become side-lined over the last quarter-century, when three successive US Presidents have had their administrations deeply involved in drawing up the boundary lines for a two-state map. As the map became ever harder to agree, so the all-important nature of the relationship with Jordan, and indeed other countries in the region, was discussed less and less; in particular, especially since focus moved to the rise of al-Qaeda and then ISIS.

The signing of the Oslo Peace Process in 1993 had been a moment of optimism for Arab–Israeli relations, but the subsequent negotiations over maps defining two states, with the various moods of optimism and depression they engendered, has reached, not necessarily an end point, but a point where it is sensible to pause and think of a fresh approach. In retrospect, the peace settlement between Prime Minister

Rabin and Yasser Arafat did not create a change in mind-frame. A huge commitment of American Presidential time was given to making a success of this process. It followed a time when President Bush Sr and his Secretary of State, James Baker, were the only US leaders who seemed to be able to demonstrate a power relationship towards Israel that stemmed from real authority. This was demonstrated in the first Gulf War when they persuaded the most independent of all Israeli Prime Ministers, Shamir, to hold back from attacking Iraq as Scud missiles landed in Israel. By showing this constraint it helped those Arab countries that rallied to participate fully in the multinational force that ousted Saddam Hussein from Kuwait.

The administrations of Presidents Clinton, George W. Bush and Obama all spent, by contrast, a huge amount of time – twenty-four years in all – negotiating but never seemed politically capable of using sustained authority to force a compromise. The UN, Russia and the EU were for much of this time corralled into the so-called Quartet with the US, making it hard for the UK or France to take independent positions. Attempts were made to improve the economy of the Palestinian Arab areas by the appointment of special envoys as representatives of the Quartet. The first was the previous head of the World Bank, James Wolfensohn, who initially did well but stepped down after a year because of restrictions in dealing with Hamas and the withholding of money from the Palestinian Authority. Initial objections were made by Russia to the second envoy, Tony Blair, as to the scope of his authority. But Blair's views on potential military action against Iran in light of its nuclear programme – a matter totally outside his remit – helped neither the Palestinians' relations with him nor the British government, who did not agree with his views. Meanwhile, Israeli settlement building continued at an increased pace. Attacks from southern Lebanon, Gaza and the West Bank continued into Israeli territory. A high wall began to be built between the two states by Israel, highlighting the image of irreconcilability but leading to some diminution in attacks. During much of this time the Israeli government wanted the US to help them bomb Iran. Fortunately, the

Israeli military and intelligence community were opposed to any such military action. It is to the credit of President George W. Bush that he made it publicly clear in the transitional period of the incoming President Obama that he had refused the request of the then Prime Minister Olmert, making it easier for President Obama to also refuse Prime Minister Netanyahu.

In 2017, we all need to focus attention on the Middle East as a whole, and to do so we must involve Egypt and recognise their worries about ISIS in Sinai and ask them to help over Gaza. The instability in Iraq since the US and UK invasion in 2003 and the consequential break-down in Iraqi governance, combined with the humanitarian crisis in Syria that started with President Assad's military clampdown on the civil unrest which formed part of the Arab Spring of 2011, have had profound consequences regionally (which we have discussed earlier in the book). One of the most challenging has been the development by the end of 2016 of a new strategic reality, with a direct land bridge from Tehran through Iraq and Syria to Beirut. However, despite the potential threat this poses to Israel, there has been little trouble be-tween Syria and the Golan Heights which the Israeli government very wisely kept stable.

That said, the Israeli air force appears to have been active but in a clandestine way. It is widely believed to have carried out airstrikes on advanced weapons systems in Syria including Russian-supplied anti-aircraft missiles and Iranian-made missiles as well as Hezbollah positions, but Israel rarely confirms such operations. *The Guardian* on 18 March 2017 commented on an Israeli aircraft over Syria being shot at by Syrian anti-aircraft missiles and there was an accompanying assessment:

> Israel has largely avoided entanglement in the war in Syria, but the statement confirmed what has long been an open secret in Israel in recent years, that Israeli jets have been targeting weapons convoys linked to the transport of Iranian-supplied arms to the Lebanese group Hezbollah, which has been fighting on the side of Bashar

al-Assad's regime. Although Israel has operated with relative impunity in Syria, Russian-supplied anti-aircraft missile systems – including most recently S300 launchers – have long threatened to complicate Israel's freedom of action ... There has been growing concern in Israeli security circles at events turning the war in Syria in favour of the Assad regime, which is seen by some as benefiting Hezbollah in Lebanon, not least in its efforts to comprehensively rearm since the 2006 war.[19]

With the tide finally appearing to be turning in the fight against ISIS in Iraq and Syria (though it is no foregone conclusion), there may be an opening to seek a regional solution. New ideas often come from new people, and there is an opportunity in 2017. No country today, not even the US, can solve the Arab–Israeli conflict alone. We saw in 1991 a successful US-led regional response in reversing Saddam Hussein's invasion of Kuwait. A US initiative with Russia is well worth trying, but it will need a broader framework, stemming from a stronger regional base with a different approach. The past does not represent the 'only way'. In mobilising support for a different approach Britain, with our long historic friendships in the region, particularly with Jordan, must stress the regional security aspects of a Palestinian–Israeli settlement that have hitherto had insufficient attention.

Unfortunately, the Trump administration's engagement with the region did not get off to the smoothest of starts. In the last days of Obama's Presidency in December 2016, so late that the Presidential election result had already been confirmed by the Electoral College and Donald Trump had definitely beaten Hillary Clinton, President Obama and his Secretary of State, John Kerry, decided to abstain on a new UN Security Council Resolution about Israel. Their position was bitterly condemned by the Israeli Prime Minister, Benjamin Netanyahu, and disowned by the President-elect Trump. It was not a good precedent for the handling of future transitions between US administrations.

It had been rumoured for some time that President Obama was preparing to break with the practice of all previous US Presidents by not automatically vetoing all UN resolutions perceived to be hostile to the State of Israel, even those that dealt with continued Israeli settlements on land that was legally judged to be part of any separate Palestinian state. Obama was obviously wishing to protect Hillary Clinton while she was running as the Democratic nominee for President against the Republican nominee, Donald Trump. Only after Trump had formally won the election did Obama's officials indicate that an anticipated resolution on Israeli settlements was likely to be met with US abstention.

Egypt, who had been working with the Palestinians on a text, formally tabled a draft resolution. When the Israeli Prime Minister became aware that the Obama administration would not veto the resolution, he called in the President-elect's help, and Trump reportedly spoke directly to Egypt's President Sisi to urge him to withdraw it. On 22 December, President Sisi informed his UN mission to withdraw sponsorship of the resolution and to postpone the vote. However, it was reintroduced on Friday 23 December with new sponsors – New Zealand, Malaysia, Venezuela and Senegal – and UNSCR 2334 was passed by fourteen votes to none, with the four permanent members, China, Russia, the UK and France all voting for, and the US abstaining.

The choice for the UK in the circumstances of a transition between two US administrations was difficult; there was never any question of vetoing a resolution that in substance was UK policy. There was little doubt too that the wording was fully compatible with the EU's Common Foreign and Security Policy (CFSP). Yet France and the UK had defended their right to act independently in the Security Council and introduced wording into the Treaty of Lisbon (Article 34) which was designed to preserve their freedom. Here was the first opportunity, after the Brexit referendum result, for the UK to demonstrate an independent voice and not automatically follow the EU. It is not clear whether the vote was discussed in the NSC in London. On past precedent, the decision to vote for the resolution would likely to have been reported to Cabinet by the Foreign Secretary but the Foreign Secretary in any case has to be able to respond to last minute changes in wording and has a delegated responsibility, if decisions need to be made in the middle of the night because of the time difference between London and New York. The British Prime Minister interposed a cautionary note about Kerry's words on 28 December which said of Netanyahu 'his current coalition is the most right-wing in Israeli history'. Theresa May, it emerged, is a very committed supporter of Israel and one suspects, having voted for the UN Resolution, she wanted to indicate the UK was not turning against the Israeli government. Since then, she visited Saudi Arabia and Jordan in April 2017. She had dealings with Jordan when Home Secretary and it is clear from TV coverage of her most recent meeting with King Abdullah there is a good relationship.

There were some reasonable concerns in London about bouncing the Trump administration into a policy position just before taking office when the President-elect had made clear this was an area on which he expected to concentrate his attention, but the British position took sufficient account of this. At a Paris conference on Sunday 15 January called by the French Foreign Minister, with EU support, to follow up the UN vote, the UK only attended in an observer status and did not sign up to the communique. The UK position criticised the absence of both Palestinian and Israeli representation in Paris and the UK cited 'particular reservations' about an event 'taking place just days before the transition to a new American president when the US will be the ultimate guarantor of any settlement'.[20] Netanyahu said to his Cabinet 'This conference is among the last twitches of yesterday's world. Tomorrow's world will be different – and it is very near'. At the first real test of a post-Brexit UK foreign policy position on Israel, the UK's position turned out to be well judged. The Foreign Secretary knew a further conference was planned and by voting for the Resolution but not attending the conference, he was able personally to strike the correct balance.

There is no question that throughout his administration President Obama had been deeply committed to Israel and its security, and that commitment guided his pursuit of peace in the Middle East. This was despite the fact that in the run up to his re-election in 2012,

President Obama reinserted into the Democratic Party electoral platform the words 'Jerusalem as the capital of Israel'. This was, after four years in office, a significant decision knowing full well how much that would be criticised by Palestinian commentators. A credible explanation is that he was anticipating that he was going to have to include this commitment in any future settlement he might negotiate. It also serves to put President Trump's commitments on Jerusalem in perspective.

John Kerry, as Secretary of State, had made a huge commitment of personal time to the two-state solution, believing and stressing publicly that it was the only way to achieve a just and lasting peace between Israelis and Palestinians. Both Obama and Kerry believed a two-state solution was the only way to ensure Israel's future as a Jewish and democratic state, living in peace and security with its neighbours. Furthermore, that it was on the only way to ensure a future of freedom and dignity for the Palestinian people. But 'only way' is a very definite form of words to endorse in the changing world of diplomacy. The Syrian conflict has potentially opened up other options and other ways to approach the Arab–Israeli conflict. These need to be thought through in 2017 by all concerned, not least the new US administration and the UK government in a post-Brexit situation.

It was inevitable that Kerry, in a public speech of great impor- tance, after the US abstention, would draw attention to the attitudes of the Israeli government of Benjamin Netanyahu who had come to interpret, he said, US friendship as meaning the US 'must accept any policy, regardless of our own interests, our own positions, our own words, our own principles – even after urging again and again that the policy must change. Friends need to tell each other the hard truths, and friendships require mutual respect.' The UK Permanent Repre- sentative to the UN, who had been fully consulted on the draft resolu- tion, was correct in speaking about the UK's vote on Resolution 2334 as 'a sober recognition that the two-state solution is slipping away. By undermining the prospects for a contiguous Palestinian state, settle- ment construction is corroding the possibility of a two-state solution.'

Israel's Permanent Representative said of the US vote 'It was to be expected that Israel's greatest ally would act in accordance with the values that we share', and veto this resolution. Kerry later felt compelled to respond to this specific comment, asserting 'that the United States did, in fact, vote in accordance with our values, just as previous US administrations have done at the Security Council before us'.

Kerry claimed with justification that the United States had done more to support Israel than any other country. 'This friend,' he said, which had 'blocked countless efforts to delegitimise Israel, cannot be true to our own values – or even the stated democratic values of Israel – and we cannot properly defend and protect Israel if we allow a viable two-state solution to be destroyed before our own eyes.' He went on to say that the vote in the United Nations 'was about preserving the two-state solution. That's what we were standing up for: Israel's future as a Jewish and democratic state, living side by side in peace and security with its neighbors.' That may prove to be the case but that sentiment should not exclude a search for different solutions. Kerry, as Secretary of State, was leaving office while the British Prime Minister and Foreign Secretary were just starting to make their mark on the urgent need for a new intergovernmental search for peace in the Middle East.

Kerry's speech is a valuable source of information for approaching Arab–Israeli issues in 2017. He said:

Time and again we have demonstrated that we have Israel's back. We have strongly opposed boycotts, divestment campaigns, and sanctions targeting Israel in international fora, whenever and wherever its legitimacy was attacked, and we have fought for its inclusion across the UN system. In the midst of our own financial crisis and budget deficits, we repeatedly increased funding to support Israel. In fact, more than one-half of our entire global Foreign Military Financing goes to Israel. And this fall, we concluded an historic $38 billion memorandum of understanding that exceeds any military assistance package the United States has provided to any country, at any time, and that will invest in cutting-edge missile defense and sustain Israel's qualitative military edge for years to come. That's the measure of our support.'[21]

Continuing in the same speech, Kerry said:

Despite our best efforts over the years, the two-state solution is now in serious jeopardy. The truth is that trends on the ground – violence, terrorism, incitement, settlement expansion and the seemingly endless occupation – they are combining to destroy hopes for peace on both sides and increasingly cementing an irreversible one-state reality that most people do not actually want.

Kerry talked of a fundamental reality: 'if the choice is one state, Israel can either be Jewish or democratic – it cannot be both – and it won't ever really be at peace'. That is too definite a description of the complexities that a one-state solution would present. He also argued that:

if there is only one state, you would have millions of Palestinians permanently living in segregated enclaves in the middle of the West Bank, with no real political rights, separate legal, education, and transportation systems, vast income disparities, under a permanent military occupation that deprives them of the most basic freedoms. Separate and unequal is what you would have.

Again, that is too definite a prediction of the outcome. Kerry rightly pointed to the paradox where polls of Israelis and Palestinians show that there is still strong support for the two-state solution. But the status quo is leading towards one state and perpetual occupation. It is as if most of the Israeli public opinion and some Palestinian opinion either ignore that a two-state solution is becoming less and less likely or have given up hope that anything can be done to change the present situation. There appears to be a growing mood of resignation in Israel that nothing is going to achieve peace. They are destined to fight – that is too fatalistic. The problem, meanwhile, gets worse with the choices narrowing.

In the past Kerry, though he later withdrew his remark, has likened a single state option to apartheid; as has Boris Johnson more recently. This is a very emotive word associated in people's minds with colour and is not an apt description of what exists in Palestine and Israel. Apart from dramatising the problems of people of different races living together, it does not give enough credence to how well South Africa did under Mandela in terms of promoting reconciliation and moving towards uniting as one nation. There are, in truth, many different ways of solving these issues.

On the West Bank the number of settlers in the roughly 130 Israeli settlements east of the 1967 lines has steadily grown. The settler population, not including East Jerusalem, has increased by nearly 270,000 since Oslo, including 100,000 in the eight years of President Obama's two terms in office. These are not just in large settlement blocks. Nearly 90,000 settlers are living east of the separation barrier that was created by Israel itself in the middle of what, by any reasonable definition, would be the future Palestinian state. Also, the population of these distant settlements has grown by 20,000 just since 2009. In fact, just recently the Israeli government approved a significant new settlement well east of the barrier, closer to Jordan than to Israel. No one should pretend the settlements are the primary cause of the Arab–Israeli conflict. If the settlements were removed, peace would not follow automatically. But the destruction of Palestinian property in East Jerusalem at this time is rightly deplored.

Kerry was correct to make clear that in a final status agreement, certain settlements would become part of Israel to account for the changes that have taken place over the last forty-nine years and the new democratic demographic realities that exist on the ground. But as in most UN resolutions in post-war crises there is insufficient recognition of the realpolitik of international conflict. Gains made on the battlefield are very rarely totally reverted by negotiation and an almost irreversible relationship exists the longer a settlement is delayed; the more territory acquired by force, the less is returned. That is not a counsel of defeatism but of reality.

What Kerry identified in his 2016 speech as most troubling was the proliferation of settler outposts that are illegal under Israel's own laws, often located on private Palestinian land and strategically placed, designed to achieve a land,

> broken up into small parcels like a Swiss cheese that could never constitute a real state. The more outposts that are built, the more the settlements expand, the less possible it is to create a contiguous state. So in the end, a settlement is not just the land that it's on, it's also what the location does to the movement of people; what it does to the ability of a road to connect people, one community to another; what it does to the sense of statehood that is chipped away with each new construction. No one thinking seriously about peace can ignore the reality of what the settlements pose to that peace.

There are over one hundred of these outposts. Since 2011, nearly one third of these has been or is being legalised, despite pledges by past Israeli governments to dismantle many of them. There is an added problem in that the Israeli government wants to change the present situation and apply Israeli domestic law to the West Bank rather than military law. This law passed its first reading in the Israeli parliament, the Knesset, in late 2016, despite the present Israeli attorney general saying that the draft law is unconstitutional and a violation of international law. The Trump administration should try to use its new position at the negotiating table to delay all such actions while he proceeds with a new approach.

The most recent wave of Palestinian violence, Kerry, correctly and powerfully, asserted:

> has included hundreds of terrorist attacks in the past year, including stabbings, shootings, vehicular attacks and bombings, many by individuals who have been radicalised by social media. Yet the murderers of innocents are still glorified on Fatah websites, including showing attackers next to Palestinian leaders following attacks.

And despite statements by President Abbas and his party's leaders making clear their opposition to violence, too often they send a different message by failing to condemn specific terrorist attacks and naming public squares, streets and schools after terrorists.

Here there has to be more progress towards reconciliation and it can, as in other countries, precede progress on an overall peace settlement. It can be argued with justification that steps in these areas are the precursor to peace; progress has been made but it must be given a far higher priority, particularly in schools on the West Bank.

The situation in 2017 in the West Bank is very serious. Yet UN resolutions, on past precedents, hold out no hope of change. A mood is developing that only economic sanctions will change Israeli policy. This could be damaging for Israel because some of the people starting to use this argument have, it is claimed hitherto, not supported boycotts. Some appear to be, and this should worry Israel, the same people who argued for, and eventually got, economic sanctions against South Africa through world financial institutions. Britain is generally against trade boycotts and that means it is essential that the UK's voice is heard on Israel, not from the safe position of staying always within the European consensus but post-Brexit as a leader of new thinking that might lead to new initiatives.

Gaza presents very different issues to the West Bank and needs to be looked at separately. Gaza is now controlled by Hamas, and has become virtually self-governing with fewer and fewer links to the West Bank. Hamas continues to pursue an agenda which refuses to accept Israel's very right to exist, which Kerry described as:

a one-state vision of their own: all of the land is Palestine. Hamas and other radical factions are responsible for the most explicit forms of incitement to violence, and many of the images that they use are truly appalling. And they are willing to kill innocents in Israel and put the people of Gaza at risk in order to advance that agenda.

Kerry described the situation in Gaza, as 'dire' and that it was 'one of the world's densest concentrations of people enduring extreme hardships with few opportunities'. Some 1.3 million people out of Gaza's population of 1.8 million, Kerry claimed, are in need of daily assistance, food and shelter. Most have electricity less than half the time and only 5 per cent of the water is safe to drink. Past policies towards Gaza have been a miserable failure. Again, military confrontation threatens. New thinking is needed. That is why it is necessary to look at treating Gaza separately from the West Bank. To a great extent that is, in reality, already being done on the ground. Whether it can be formalised is a very much more difficult question. But it should not be ignored as a peace issue or merely dismissed as being impossible. The new Trump administration will have to try very hard not to prejudge or impose an outcome, but to instead provide a new basis for serious negotiations.

It is not beyond the realms of possibility that President Sisi would be ready to contemplate, what might, sometime after 1978, have been offered by Egypt as part of a regional settlement, namely the lease of a significant portion of Egyptian territory that abuts Gaza, without gas or oil rights. This would offer the opportunity to lift the suffocating overcrowding in Gaza and bring an opportunity for this enclave to breathe and prosper. Saudi Arabia, previously very generous to Gaza, but dispirited by finding its support destroyed by fighting, could be persuaded to help.

Were it possible for these two territories' future – Gaza and Golan – to be settled regionally, it would be possible to focus attention on the security situation that faces the West Bank in a very different context. A complicating factor for Egypt in contemplating such a move to help Gaza might be that two Red Sea islands owned by Egypt were due to be handed to Saudi Arabia in return for Saudi energy and financial assistance, but in January 2017, that arrangement was blocked by an Egyptian court. It had been previously signed up to by King Salman and President Sisi. The Saudis, who responded by cancelling the oil deal with Egypt, are hoping that the legal obstacles will be settled. The Egyptian Parliament subsequently approved the transfer in a vote in June

2017. If the deal goes through, hopefully public concern in Egypt over loss of sovereign territory will quieten, allowing President Sisi to consider an arrangement over Gaza. This would allow for a shared airfield and port with security arrangements agreed between Egypt and Israel.

The Trump administration is already trying to forge a better relationship with Egypt than the Obama administration, whose backing for the protest movement inside Egypt following the Arab Spring in 2011 had strained relations. The area where Egypt needs help is in Northern Sinai, where ISIS militants target their police and soldiers. In March 2017 seven Christians in Arish were killed. The US could and should help Egypt in Sinai, and in return Egypt should help a deal with Gaza and assist Israel.

There is a bargain to be struck here. Both Golan and Gaza raise very sensitive issues but they also have deep regional security implications that could be helpful to a resolution of the Arab–Israeli conflict. The chances of Syria taking back the Golan from Israel militarily or through negotiations are slimmer than perhaps ever before. Syria is going to need financial help to reconstruct their country and there are very few countries that will help. Israel may be the country with the greatest interest in reconstruction in Syria and its relationship with that country has been complex and secretive. Meanwhile, Golan provides a regional buttress of proven stability. It is not beyond the bounds of possibility that a long-term rental arrangement or even transfer of territory to Israel could possibly be part of a regional settlement. The present international map of Syria is not sacrosanct.

In 2002 Crown Prince Abdullah of Saudi Arabia made a break with the past and put forward a comprehensive Arab Peace Initiative offering fully normalised relations with Israel once it made peace. The Arab League now agree that the reference in the Arab Peace Initiative to the 1967 lines includes the concept of land swaps, and the Palestinians have acknowledged this as necessary to reflect practical realities on the ground, and mutually agreed equivalent swaps that will ensure that the agreement is fair to both sides. There is not, however, agreement over what would constitute secure and defensible borders, or how the territory of a Palestinian state could be made viable and contiguous. Here, too, there has to be new thinking and new concepts.

On security, Kerry said in his speech on 28 December that, 'there are many different ways without occupation for Israel and Palestine and Jordan and Egypt and the US and others to cooperate in providing that security'. We need from now on to discuss these military and political security issues and to define the measures, people, equipment, command and control arrangements and demonstrate how they could be implemented. Not enough appears to have been done and certainly, while secrecy has to be a factor, more needs to be shared publicly.

One of the biggest challenges for President Trump – after choosing to make his first ground-breaking visit abroad in May 2017 to Saudi Arabia – will be handling relations with Iran and influencing the way others deal with Iran. The reality is that Iran is far closer to establishing a land link to Israeli territory – through Iraq and Syria to the Golan and Lebanon – than ever before and there is, as yet, no abatement in the mutual distrust of each other. The first step would be for both countries to stop talking about military aggression against each other. The next step might be to encourage Saudi Arabia and Iran to talk together about the Yemen. In the background of all new thinking about the Middle East must be the fact that it is historically not inevitable that Iran and Saudi Arabia are doomed to have a bad relationship – there have been periods of better relations in the past. Nor is a Sunni/Shia fight inevitable: wise policies and persistence can restore better relations. In this regard, it is imperative that the UK politically or militarily does not line up with the anti-Shia forces and add to the split in the Muslim world. We need to take note of President Rouhani's impressive electoral victory in Iran in May 2017, and his public attacks, in tough language which he has not used before, on the extremists in and around the Republican Guard. For the UK, which has Shia and Sunni Muslims amongst its citizens and a long history of working well with Shia and Sunni dominated countries, to become militarily aligned against the Shia would be a grave mistake. We can, and must, reserve our right to criticise Shia countries or groupings in the course of trying to reduce tensions and provocation. But to contemplate engaging militarily on a sectarian basis in 2017 is not a British interest and very unlikely to ever become one.

It is noteworthy how, particularly since 2015, President Putin has kept in touch with all the Middle East leaders, particularly Prime Minister Netanyahu, who has been accorded equal status in visits to Moscow and diplomatic attention to that given to President Assad, President Erdoğan and leaders in Tehran, Baghdad and Riyadh. No one expects the Trump administration to embrace the Joint Comprehensive Plan of Action with Iran (JCPOA), but the US will not find it easy to unilaterally renegotiate this Plan of Action signed up to on 16 January 2016. The EU High Representative for Foreign and Security Policy, Federica Mogherini, was correct in saying that the JCPOA 'is not a bilateral agreement between the US and Iran. It is a multilateral agreement that we have negotiated.' The Plan is enshrined in UN Resolution 2231 unanimously adopted by the UN Security Council. Just a few days after the US Presidential elections were over the Council of the European Union went on record reiterating its view, to which the UK was fully supportive: 'its resolute commitment to the JCPOA … and the commitment to support its full and effective implementation, including by the lifting of nuclear related economic and financial sanctions.' There are times when the rhetoric out of Washington, as highlighted by Carlo Trezza, the former Italian Ambassador for Disarmament and Non-Proliferation, in a European Leadership Network (ELN) paper:

> will have to confront a situation in Tehran that has changed since the populist Ahmadinejad was in charge. A new more moderate, in some cases American-educated, leadership is part of the ruling establishment and played a key role in achieving last year's nuclear deal … There is no doubt that withdrawal or non-implementation of the JCPOA would help pave the way for the return of the extreme conservatives in Tehran.[22]

To abandon the JCPOA would undermine President Rouhani's recent victory. On this issue, the British position must be resolute, working with our other fellow signatories to the JCPOA – China, France, Germany and Russia. There is ample scope for the Trump administration to demand progress on other critical issues in relation to Iran, such as human rights, missiles programmes, regional responsibilities and their stance on Israel. But in relation to ISIS in Iraq and Syria, there is an ongoing involvement of Iran and increasingly of Israel, with the support of Russia, China, the UK and France. For the US to exclude themselves or to demand the exclusion of Iran would be unacceptable in the continuing struggle to check and then dismantle ISIS. President Trump is right to want a better dialogue with Russia in the Middle East and the push back from some elements in Washington against such a dialogue starting would be damaging if it was long postponed. President Putin has on the whole played a clever diplomatic role in the Middle East to accompany Russia's newfound military role, particularly in stopping the fall of Damascus in 2015. It would have done huge harm if ISIS had taken the city, so long a home for a wide range of religions. However, Putin's inaction over the sarin gas attack in April 2017, as discussed in Chapter Four, has called into question his support for the removal of sarin gas in 2013. Yet one has only to see the new Russian military airfield close to the Syrian city of Latakia, a very short flying time from Lebanon, to recognise that Russia is again a serious player in the Middle East. If Russia was checking Iran as part of an overall settlement, that would be far better than having it withdrawing from the region or supporting Iran overtly. The Trump administration has a great opportunity to reshape the whole negotiating strategy for the Middle East for the better. This is a transformational time. President Obama correctly made the secret direct negotiation with Iran through Oman a very high priority during his term in office. Progress was painfully slow, but having Russia involved with the UK, France and Germany made dealing with Iran much easier, particularly on such a very sensitive issue. We have to remember that they started to develop this capacity when they were threatened by Saddam

Hussein, who we know from the UN inspector's report of 1991 had developed a nuclear weapons programme. Now Iraq is not a threat, since it is controlled by the Shia majority in the country, the threat is seen to come from Saudi Arabia. Their fears are not without justification, in that there was a leaked report of the King of Saudi Arabia demanding that the US should bomb Iran, and Israel was pressing the US for the sophisticated conventional bombs that would destroy Iranian underground nuclear facilities. In light of all this, the fact that progress that was made with Tehran and agreements were reached was a considerable achievement.

The IAEA in its latest report asserted that Iran has continued to abide by the JCPOA. There is a real chance to build on the progress with Iran and take this forward into the framework of the NPT itself, as indicated in another ELN paper by the former US senior diplomat, Tom Pickering, and the former UK permanent representative to the UN, David Hannay, which could be an important reinforcement of any Trump/Putin discussion on nuclear weapons:

> the agreement between the P5+1 and Iran averted a crisis which could have brought the entire non-proliferation regime into jeopardy and the region into conflict. But it is time now to draw on that agreement to use its standards by applying them to all countries seeking to enrich uranium for any purpose or attempting to use plutonium for reactor fuel ... The Iran Agreement completes the work of the Non-Proliferation Treaty (NPT) for the first time by setting limits on enrichment and plutonium separation. Such limits will help by making it clear that enrichment for civil purposes is not in itself against the provisions of the NPT and by also blocking or making more prolonged any attempt to use civil facilities to 'breakout'.[23]

At present, in and around Iraq and Syria, the unifying feature is a determination to defeat ISIS and its pursuit of a caliphate. How long that unity lasts depends on how quickly ISIS is deprived of its geographical bases in Iraq and Syria. The danger is that when Mosul is back under control of the government and Raqqa taken out of the hands of ISIS there may be a coalescence of Sunni Islamic forces.

Russia is obviously hoping that Assad will be able to demonstrate a measure of control Syria-wide but this may not be easy to achieve. Despite taking Aleppo there are still small parts of the country that are resisting Assad's forces. Russia will be pushing for a return to full Assad control but this is unlikely to go without challenge, particularly from the Kurds across the region.

The Kurdish militia in Syria, the YPG, have formed an unofficial military alliance with the US Special Forces who are capable of calling in the support of the US air force. In addition, Russia has set up a base in the Afrin area close to the border with Turkey to train Kurdish forces. By establishing a point of direct contact like this, the Russians are reminding the Turks that they are not going to leave the YPG to be influenced only by the US. The Syrian Kurds have been given a licence to operate in a fairly large geographical area bordering on Turkey and Iraq. They will not easily give up this measure of independence for which they have fought. They dislike President Barzani who has been President of the Iraqi Kurdistan region of Iraq since 2005, but their main antagonist is Turkey who believes they are working with the PKK, which has been fighting the Turkish state since it was established in 1984. The YPG increasingly expect to be allowed to retain control of a fairly large area of Syria and they eventually hope that the prediction of US intelligence will prove to be correct: that, within less than ten years, there will be an internationally recognised Kurdistan. The YPG recognise that were it to come about, most of that territory will be carved out of Syria as the weakest element. Indeed, President Assad may well concede this in order to get international recognition for Syria, just as he might be persuaded, as discussed earlier, to make a leasing arrangement with Israel over the Golan Heights, and use the revenue for restoration of a war-ravaged country.

President Erdoğan, having achieved by a small margin the controversial vote to amend the constitution and having established an executive presidency, may be ready to re-engage in a discussion with the leader of the PKK in prison in Turkey, which at one stage appeared to be making some progress. But he has hitherto been resolutely opposed to any international recognition of an independent Kurdistan, even one confined to within the current boundaries of Syria. A report which emerged in 2012 from the US National Intelligence Council states that in the event 'of a more fragmented Iraq or Syria, a Kurdistan would not be inconceivable'. One of six scenarios presented in the report consisted of a rising Kurdistan which, in turn, affects Turkey's territorial unity by carrying a risk for them of separation which they will never concede. The report only says, however, that 'The predicted Kurdistan may include Kurdish regions in Iraq, Syria and Iran.'[24] The current aim of the PKK is the creation of an autonomous region in the south east of Turkey, rather than an independent state, and more cultural rights for ethnic Kurds who constitute the largest minority in Turkey. The PKK wants constitutional recognition for the Kurds, regional self-governance and Kurdish-language education in schools. Turkey refuses to recognise its Kurdish population as a distinct minority. It has, however, allowed some cultural rights, such as limited broadcasts in the Kurdish language and private Kurdish language courses with the prodding of the EU, but Kurdish politicians say the measures fall short of their expectations. The PKK is considered as a terrorist organisation by the Turkish government and also by the US government, and continues to be on the blacklist list in the EU, despite a court ruling which overturned a decision to place the PKK and its political wing on the EU's terror list.

The Kurds in Iran are quiet at present. The one thing that history seems to demonstrate is that Kurds spread across four countries are quietest when all four countries – Turkey, Iran, Iraq and Syria – are getting on well and are ready to act in a coordinated way to contain the Kurdish ambitions for an independent state. Inside Iraq, President Barzani is demonstrating his political power by demanding a referendum on Kurdish independence from Iraq and refusing to consider greater autonomy instead. The longstanding fight over oil revenues continues. As a Shi'ite, Prime Minister Haider al-Abadi of the Islamic

Darwa party knows that his highest priority particularly after the liberation of Mosul is to build up the confidence of the Sunnis in Iraq. There is no way that this can be done at present by conceding oil revenues being claimed by Barzani. At the very least there has to be a fair-minded Iraqi-wide formula as to the distribution of oil revenues and a means for checking it is fully abided by.

The complexity does not end with the Kurdish problem. Iran, on the ground in those parts of Syria that border Iran, also cannot be ignored. Saudi Arabia wants assurances from al-Abadi that he will not allow Iran to intrude in the governance of Iraq. If Iran and Iraq and Saudi Arabia can agree within OPEC oil quotas, that will be a big step forward. Lebanon presents special problems. Will Russia want to stay a regional player? It would be foolish to ignore this possibility, and Israel certainly is aware of the dangers and the possible benefits. Another player is Jordan, who wants an agreement with the Syrian government over refugees on both sides of their borders, and its voice could become more important.

In September 2014, the Global Coalition against Daesh was formed and its most recent conference was held in Washington in March 2017, where the new US Secretary of State, Rex Tillerson, took the opportunity to talk to fellow foreign ministers, and the Iraqi Prime Minister, al-Abadi, was able to bring them up to date what was happening in the fight to recover Mosul. There is no doubt that this grouping has done a lot to block ISIS's financing and reduce its funding as well as countering its propaganda and impeding the flow of foreign fighters. However, even if the ISIS caliphate in Syria and Iraq is destroyed in 2017, terrorist activity is likely to continue. Furthermore, the caliphate ideology, already dangerously evident in Libya, Nigeria and Somalia, will never lose sight of its main target – Saudi Arabia itself. Yemen is experiencing an al-Qaeda insurgency within the main conflict between the Houthis and al-Islah. The concerted efforts to deal with this threat will inevitably require the UK to devote significant resources in the Middle East, both diplomatic and military, for some time to come.

This challenge of how to deal with ISIS as it spreads out from

Iraq and Syria is a theme which runs through this book. It is an all-important challenge that faces governments throughout the world; words like 'war' or 'attack' on ISIS are commonplace. In Chapter Two, we quote from a US military seminar in 2016 on 'Deterrence of Violent Extremist Organizations' which asserted that these VEO's are not irrational and that 'we might need to lose something of ourselves' in order to defeat them. That is a profound thought and we have pondered it long and hard. The Manchester Arena attack on 22 May 2017, which killed twenty-two people, has still to be judged in the courts of law, but it appears that Libya was an essential part of the story. And Libya, as we have discussed elsewhere in this book, has played a major part in our foreign policy in recent years, and indeed in domestic terrorism for a longer period, including the shooting of PC Yvonne Fletcher outside the Libyan Embassy in 1984, and the downing of Pan Am flight 103 over Lockerbie in 1988. The Manchester attack is a reminder that domestic and foreign policies are not unrelated, and that there are deep underpinnings that extend into our own local communities.

We need to look at new ways and thinking in dealing with ISIS, wherever it is lodged. As we develop military strategies to counter ISIS, which is intent on physically capturing territory capable of providing a home for their caliphate, whose brutalities they do not hesitate to export, we must ask our military, in a sense, to 'lose something of themselves' and their traditional thinking as they approach their new campaigns. There are now many senior military commanders, particularly in the American forces as well as our own, who have experienced in the field the methods and motivations of these VEO's, and who are well placed to draw lessons from developments in the world since the Islamic Revolution in Iran in 1979. General Mattis, the US Secretary for Defense, is in a remarkably powerful position to try to bring new thinking and attitudes for dealing with ISIS, learning from the mistakes and achievements of the past thirty-eight years. There are many skilled State Department officials who could help too. UK military personnel and diplomats, along with those of other nations, can and should be offered to assist and President Trump should urge regional leaders to cooperate in full. We have all made many mistakes but this is no time for finger pointing: drawing on our combined experiences, we have to seek new approaches which enable us to improve our performance.

To date, the military strategy has been dominated by the US, though in Syria it appears there has been much more coordination with Russia than is often admitted. The time will come when this issue will be discussed, no doubt face to face between President Trump and President Putin, though domestic controversy over pre- and post-election links with Russia have set this back. Meanwhile, our own Prime Minister should meet Putin and our Foreign Secretary reinstate a meeting, perhaps at the same time, with Lavrov. There will also be more direct talks between Turkey, Saudi Arabia and Jordan, and we have already referred to the role of Israel. It is hard to escape the need for a regional organisation, of which this could form a basis, to pull together all parts of the Middle East and deal with the ongoing conflict with President Assad's forces in Syria, as well as dealing with the stability of Iraq. Even if it is judged necessary to keep these two separate, there will need to be institutional arrangements to deal with the overlapping problems between Iraq and Syria.

Another problem for the region came to a head in early June 2017, when Arab states led by Saudi Arabia broke off diplomatic relations with Qatar – recalling a similar move in 2014 – and announced the cutting of all transport links. This action was allegedly due to remarks by Sheikh Tamim al Thani, the Emir of Qatar, which suggests that Iran was a force for regional stability and might even go so far as to defend Hamas. Qatar denied the Emir had made the statement and claimed they had been victims of hacking.

This was coupled with allegations that Qatar's foreign minister, also a member of the al Thani family, had a secret meeting in Baghdad with the Iranian general Qassem Soleimani, commander of the al-Quds Force fighting on the ground in Syria. The underlying reason for the tensions is the concerns of Saudi Arabia and its regional allies of Qatari support for Iran and groups such as the Muslim Brotherhood.

The Saudi foreign minister, speaking in Paris on 6 June, said Qatar had to 'implement the promises it made a few years back with regard its support of extremist groups, regards its hostile media and interference in affairs of other countries'. He also claimed Qatar was undermining the Palestinian Authority and Egypt through its support for Hamas and the Muslim Brotherhood, and this had to end before diplomatic relations could be restored.[25]

Turkey has thrown its weight behind Qatar, with its Parliament adopting a law on 7 June to allow more Turkish troops to be stationed at a base in Qatar where Turkish troops have been stationed since 2015.

The US Secretary of State Rex Tillerson immediately offered to mediate, but the Emir of Kuwait made a whistle-stop tour of Saudi Arabia, the UAE and Qatar, and that was a welcome sign that the region may try and create a framework for a cooperative response. President Trump has encouraged a diplomatic solution, and, on 7 June, reiterated the US offer to help resolve the situation. Apart from having the largest regional US military airbase at al-Udeid in Qatar, America will be concerned that a prolonged dispute could open up their own domestic concerns relating to Wahhabism and the still-rumbling row about a continued cover up over Wahhabi links in Saudi Arabia to 9/11, which they hoped had been put to bed following Trump's visit. It is ironic that both the Saudi and Qatari ruling families adhere to the same Wahhabi version of Islam.

The disruption of air and sea transport is manageable in the short term, provided it is not escalated. However, the underlying differences cannot easily be papered over, and a genuine dialogue needs to take place to resolve them. The message from the UK to the region must be that its leaders have to commit to settling these issues regionally, and we must work with the US to achieve that goal.

The OSCE is an example of such a regional organisation, but it would be foolish to just reproduce that in the Middle East. The OSCE appoints missions for particular conflicts, as they have done for Ukraine, and a mission for dealing with Iraq and Syria together would make sense. It would need to be established in the region and consist of all the countries that abut Iraq and Syria with the addition of the Islamic Republic of Iran, Egypt and Palestine. Representation from the P5 should be built into such a mission. But they are not the key players, so they must not own the process. Relying on purely bilateral and multilateral negotiations with no overall coherence will be to reproduce what L. Carl Brown warned against:

> a continuation of Eastern Question politics from the late eighteenth century until just after the First World War during which the European powers slowly picked the Ottoman Empire to pieces, something which 'exacts a high cost from those involved' – significant economic resources are consumed on military requirements, persistent intergroup violence, penetration of Middle Eastern political life by outside influences, all of which curtail needed political and economic development.[26]

CHAPTER 7

CHINA AND ITS NEIGHBOURS

As argued in the first part of this book, in developing our relationship with China post-Brexit and, in particular, in the context of a global defence policy with a greater emphasis on 'blue water' diplomacy, there is a choice to be made which must not be evaded. We must recognise that our relationship with China has never mirrored that of the US, and we should not attempt for it to do so in 2017. In this regard it is different from our relationship with Russia. Ever since President Truman took office in 1945 our position towards the Soviet Union has been very similar to that of the US, in great part because of our joint membership of NATO. Over China, the UK has historical baggage which the US does not have, dating back to a century of humiliation at the start of the nineteenth century, when China suffered from the opium wars to the Communist revolution. On the positive side, unlike the US, we recognised the People's Republic of China in 1950, shortly after its establishment in 1949. The British decision in 1950 on early recognition was a carefully thought-out position, one of which Clement Attlee was proud. At the start of the twenty-first century China has become the world's second largest economy, and extended its influence across the globe, politically and economically. The Chinese Communist Party, ready to learn lessons from the collapse of the Soviet Union and having studied Russian history, took measures and adopted positions designed to avoid similar mistakes. It is a superpower and an authoritarian power. Its economic performance far surpasses that of Russia and it is accelerating away from Russia at a startling pace.

The UK must continue to build up our relationship in a considered and measured way. We clearly rule out the Royal Navy becoming militarily engaged against China in the South China Seas when we say in Chapter One that 'We should pursue the same selective policy post-Brexit today in not becoming a military protagonist.' The lesson from Vietnam, which is still worth reinforcing, is that if the UK is clear from the start on military matters with the US, we can resist very considerable pressure from the US to drag us with them into military commitment. Harold Wilson's first trip to Washington as Prime Minister was in December 1964, after winning a general election that October with a tiny majority of just four MPs in the House of Commons. He travelled with his Foreign Secretary, Gordon Walker, who served as Foreign Secretary for just a few months but was forced to step down from office, having lost his seat in the election and subsequently also losing a by-election. Walker told the US Secretary of State, Dean Rusk, that Britain already had troops in Malaysia, a former British colony under attack from Indonesia, that were comparable in number to the US presence in Vietnam, and 'he was emphatic that the United Kingdom could not have troops on the ground in Vietnam'.[1]

There must be no doubt in President Xi's mind or in President Trump's that the UK sees its relationship in the historic context of the peaceful withdrawal from Hong Kong in 1997; and we have no wish to return to garrisoning land in the Far East, nor any pretensions to wielding aggressive naval power. In enforcing the Law of the Sea, we should stand ready to help peaceful negotiations on these issues, not get sucked into military engagement.

We welcome the improvement of Sino-British relations. We see the post-Brexit situation as an opportunity to steadily improve our commercial relationships. We must be realistic in what we can achieve, and we must approach commercial opportunities in the wider context of seeing China as more and more a strategic partner on the Security Council. Not long after the first freight train arrived in the UK from China along the new Silk Road, Prime Minister May, speaking to the Republican Party conference on 26 January,[2] pointedly linked China with Russia, commenting that 'countries with little tradition of democracy, liberty and human rights – notably China and Russia – have grown more assertive in world affairs'. That direct linkage is inadvisable. There are very significant differences between the two countries and it is better to assess them separately and handle them differently. There are a range of areas in which the UK should be able to find common ground with China, not least in maintaining Chinese support for inclusive globalisation – which President Xi spoke of at the World Economic Forum in Davos in January 2017 – and continued engagement in bilateral trade and investment. However, the UK's approach to China cannot be limited primarily to developing economic ties. Important as they are, particularly post-Brexit, there needs to be continued and growing engagement in other areas.

The notion of acting as a bridge between the US and China is intrinsically attractive to the UK, yet talk of a global Britain should not lead us to exaggerate our power to swing the balance of forces this way or that. In the last forty years our ability to alter events in the Far East has weakened. Chinese power has grown immeasurably and Hong Kong has reverted to the mainland, and we should not pretend otherwise.

Our constraints were there pre-Brexit. Beijing is well aware of its economic leverage, and our post-Brexit reliance on expanding our trade with third countries, notably China, means the UK has to be cautious about crossing Xi Jinping. Signs of prudence are already there: the Prime Minister, on taking office, looked closely at the UK's stance on the security of Chinese nuclear investments in Britain and she decided, correctly, to continue the policy. On human rights there is no point in ignoring the need for a considered approach. The British government did its best over Hong Kong where the negotiations were conducted by Sir Geoffrey Howe and Sir Percy Craddock, with Margaret Thatcher fully involved. But faced by several refusals by the Chinese government to consider compromise arrangements, in December 1984 the Sino-British Joint Declaration was signed, agreeing to a complete handover of Hong Kong and its territories to China in 1997. China did, however, adopt the principle of 'one country, two systems' in which Hong Kong would be treated as a special economic zone continuing its capitalist system. In the years up to 1997 Chris Patten, then the last Governor of Hong Kong, introduced democratic and electoral reforms which pushed PRC–British relations almost beyond their limits, and the handover was less than smooth. Nevertheless, our moral obligations towards Hong Kong were fully discharged, even though it led to our losing ground commercially during and after this period.

China now governs Hong Kong and is hyper-sensitive about what they see as potential meddling by the ex-colonial power, and we must be mindful of this and the impact it can have on our relations. As China demonstrated during 2014's pro-democracy protests, its willingness to tolerate dissent is limited, as is its openness to the views of the international community on the subject. A Foreign Ministry spokesman made clear in November 2014 that 'Hong Kong affairs are China's domestic affairs; no foreign government or individual has the right to interfere in Hong Kong affairs in any way.'[3] As a Chatham House paper of February 2017[4] noted, this meant that:

> UK policymakers found themselves trying to balance domestic pressure to support a popular movement with the UK's historical legacy and commitments that set out a more gradual approach to democratic development, and wider considerations such as an increasingly important relationship with China, both politically and commercially.

It is for the ASEAN countries to settle their grievances with China's policies in the UN Security Council. We must work evermore closely with China on climate control where they are faced with pollution becoming a huge concern domestically. We must not appear to be a mere mirror of US policy in this region, where we are not in a formal alliance. Also, when it comes to China, the notion that cutting or curtailing our ties with the EU will make us a freer political agent is questionable. Unlike Russia, China is pro-EU, not least because of the attractions of selling to a large market of half a billion people, and as a destination for its investments. We must position ourselves to improve our attractiveness. But within the EU Germany has built a very good market position. Chancellor Angela Merkel, in particular, has done this aided and abetted by German engineering and technological skills, with exports of a volume and sophistication that it will take us in the UK time to even hope to match. But try to match it we must. In as much as we can, we should use our influence on President Trump to avoid clashes in WTO if at all possible, through proposing imaginative solutions of benefit to world trade.

Meanwhile, the Chinese can be relied on to exploit our post-Brexit need to build up exports and encourage investment to the full. George Osborne, as Chancellor, was right to give China a priority, to strive to give exports a push – and with some success. New opportunities are there and his successors must continue that approach. On trade Beijing is unsentimental. It drove an extraordinarily hard bargain on its mammoth 2014 gas deal with Beijing's friend President Putin. If they think we are too much of a *demandeur* in our post-Brexit trade relationship, they will exploit it. Business of mutual benefit can and should improve, but within limits which we should not be reluctant to admit.

Britain's handling of China's growing assertiveness and the development of our relations with China's neighbours is likely to become an increasingly challenging part of our foreign policy (which is already to some extent complicated by the relationship over Hong Kong). As indicated, there is also the potential to find ourselves at odds with key allies, notably the US, that are more directly involved in the region, but also regional players such as Japan. There appears to be a real risk that the high expectations of our relations with China could falter in the same way as the euphoria over the fall of communism in Europe and the ill-fated Arab Spring, unless we are well prepared to deal with the clouds on the horizon.

As many commentators have pointed out, the 'Asian Century' is seeing a shift in economic power from the West to the East, with China's growth, albeit now slowing, taking it to the second largest global economy behind the US, and India also continuing to grow.

This growing economic clout has also led to growing confidence in the international arena. Gideon Rachman states in his recent wide ranging study of geopolitical developments in Asia, *Easternisation*, 'Most senior analysts in Western governments are already operating on the assumption that the shift in economic power from West to East will continue and that economic change will translate into political power.'[5] This shift, and in particular China's resurgence, has given rise to tension in the region which threatens to intensify, with a real risk of military clashes, if not addressed in a diplomatic framework. In the closing sentences of his book, Rachman goes so far as to say that 'The great political challenge of the twenty-first century will be to manage the process of Easternisation in the common interest of mankind.'[6]

The immediate challenge is the complex and evolving situation in the South and East China Seas, where there have been a series of territorial disputes with claims of ownership based on arguments often drawn from far in the past. However, the last decade, and particularly the last few years, have seen a shift of intensity in the way China has been pursuing its claims over territory falling within the so-called 'nine dash line', which covers an extensive area stretching south and east from China's Hainan province. This line has demarcated Chinese claims since the 1940s and Chinese diplomats will show anyone interested the Chinese maps that prove this. The line encompasses the disputed island groups of the Spratlys and the Paracels; Brunei, Malaysia, the Philippines, Taiwan and Vietnam also have claims to parts of the sea. The area has significant fishing grounds and potentially significant mineral resources, in addition to being on major commercial shipping routes (seeing around $5 trillion of trade flows annually), which China is keen to exert control over.

China's burgeoning economy allowed it to increase its defence spending significantly, with 2017's slowdown to a growth of around 7 per cent, following 7.6 per cent in 2016. This is to be seen in the context of 'a nearly unbroken two-decade run of double-digit increases'.[7] This spending has had a particular focus on strengthening China's naval capabilities, including building outposts in the disputed area, and its ability to challenge the US military in the region. The growing threat to its aircraft carriers, which represent a key element in its regional strategy, has been identified as a particular concern for the US: 'More worrisome to US naval planners and their allies in the region are a range of new land-based ballistic missiles designed to sink naval ships or destroy airfields. One such missile, the DF-21D, is commonly known as the carrier killer.'[8]

The US's close defence ties with allies in the region have seen it take an increasingly high profile based on what it sees as protecting its own national interests, while officially not taking sides. At a regional conference in Hanoi in 2010, US Secretary of State Hillary Clinton set out the justification, stating that 'The United States has a national interest in freedom of navigation, open access to Asia's maritime commons and respect for international law in the South China Sea.'[9] The Trump administration also see this as a critical issue and are likely to pursue a similar agenda, though initial fears that the US would take a more aggressive stance were somewhat allayed in the early months of the administration. The April 2017 summit meeting between Presidents Xi and Trump went well, with Trump saying 'we have made tremendous progress in our relationship with China.'[10] The agreement reached between China and ASEAN countries in May 2017 on a framework for a code of conduct for the region is also a positive development. Nevertheless, the US Navy is likely to face a fairly long period of confrontation with China over their disputed claims in the South China Sea, and it would be wiser for the UK to stay out of this. In terms of our potential naval deployments in the Far East, as discussed in Chapter Two, we should be clear from the outset that the UK carrier force is neither configured nor conceived to be part of sustaining US policy in the region.

The East China Sea presents different foreign policy considerations for the UK than the South China Sea. We were party to the terms under which the war against Japan ended in 1945 and was later settled. We were also part of the UN force that fought in the Korean War which lasted from 25 June 1950 to 27 July 1953 and which ended in an armistice with the Demilitarized Zone (DMZ) being established between North and South Korea. Japan and South Korea are friends of the UK, and we have strong, and will build stronger, commercial and trading links with them. General Mattis, the new US Defense Secretary, wisely made his first trip abroad to South Korea and then to Japan where he found the country scrambling Japanese fighter jets at an increased rate to warn off Chinese military ships. A carefully calibrated diplomatic and military involvement for the UK will need to be developed, focused on finding solutions through the framework of international law and bearing in mind that our interests historically and in the present day are not the same as those of the US.

The interpretation and application of international law remains at the heart of the issue, both in the South China Sea and more broadly in the region. China drew a sharp reaction from the US and EU when it imposed an 'East China Sea Air Defence Identification Zone' in 2013. This action was criticised by the EU as a development which 'heightens the risk of escalation and contributes to raising tensions in the region.'[11] The EU statement also reiterated that 'the legitimate use of sea and airspace are rights enshrined in international law and are essential for security, stability and prosperity. Actions that bring or appear to bring these rights into question are not conducive to finding lasting solutions to the differences that exist in East Asia's maritime areas.'

China's attitude to the international legal system was tested when the Philippines took China to an arbitration tribunal under the auspices of the UN Convention on the Laws of the Sea. In 2016 the tribunal backed the Philippines' case,[12] although its judgment is not enforceable, stating that:

China had violated the Philippines' sovereign rights in its exclusive economic zone by (a) interfering with Philippine fishing and petroleum exploration, (b) constructing artificial islands and (c) failing to prevent Chinese fishermen from fishing in the zone. The Tribunal also held that fishermen from the Philippines (like those from China) had traditional fishing rights at Scarborough Shoal and that China had interfered with these rights in restricting access. The Tribunal further held that Chinese law enforcement vessels had unlawfully created a serious risk of collision when they physically obstructed Philippine vessels.

It went on to state that:

> China's recent large-scale land reclamation and construction of artificial islands was incompatible with the obligations on a State during dispute resolution proceedings, insofar as China has inflicted irreparable harm to the marine environment, built a large artificial island in the Philippines' exclusive economic zone, and destroyed evidence of the natural condition of features in the South China Sea that formed part of the Parties' dispute.

China boycotted the proceedings and rejected the ruling in a Foreign Ministry statement:[13]

> China's territorial sovereignty and maritime rights and interests in the South China Sea shall under no circumstances be affected by those awards. China opposes and will never accept any claim or action based on those awards.
>
> The Chinese government reiterates that, regarding territorial issues and maritime delimitation disputes, China does not accept any means of third party dispute settlement or any solution imposed on China. The Chinese government will continue to abide by international law and basic norms governing international relations as enshrined in the Charter of the United Nations, including the principles of respecting state sovereignty and territorial integrity and peaceful settlement of disputes, and continue to work with states directly concerned to resolve the relevant disputes in the South China Sea through negotiations and consultations on the basis of respecting historical facts and in accordance with international law, so as to maintain peace and stability in the South China Sea.

This approach of reiterating adherence to its obligations under international law, while rejecting criticism of its actions on the ground which others see as being in breach of those obligations, has been identified as a major contributor to instability in the region and more broadly. An article in *The Guardian* of February 2017[14] suggests that 'The breakdown of a legally defined international order is likewise being hastened by China's aggressive bullying of regional countries involved in South China Sea, its contempt for UN court rulings, its recent sabre-rattling over Taiwan, and its refusal to do anything meaningful to curb North Korea's nuclear weapons build-up.'

The Chinese approach has also led some to draw parallels between its attitude and that of Russia. In 2015, US Deputy Secretary of State, Antony Blinken, said: 'In both eastern Ukraine and the South China Sea, we're witnessing efforts to unilaterally and coercively change the status quo – transgressions that the United States and our allies stand united against.'[15]

As with the situation in Russia as described earlier, the risks of escalation, particularly as a result of a misunderstanding or an over-reaction, are dangerously high. There have been violent clashes in the past and, with the increased military activity, the stakes are ever higher. However, given the UK's interests as an island nation dependent on the free flow of international commerce and London's reputation as a centre of excellence in international law, this should be an area in which the UK has an honest broker role as an expert in international law.

That said, the Chinese reaction to the UK's view that the judgment of the Permanent Court of Arbitration should be binding demonstrates that a brokering role will be no easy task. The Chinese Foreign Ministry was quoted as saying that: 'The comments by Mr Swire [Foreign Office Minister of State] neglect the facts and are very discriminatory and one-sided and seriously go against Britain's promise not to take sides.' China critical reaction and cooling of relations following Prime Minister Cameron's meeting with the Dalai Lama in May 2012 also show how difficult it is to tread a broker's path, and UK public opinion is very sensitive in this area, with a strong sentiment in some quarters that economic interests are being put ahead of all others, including human rights. Hong Kong remains an important trading partner in its own right, and this too is an area which will have to be carefully managed, as indicated earlier.

The potential for straining relations with friends and allies is also high, if the UK is seen to be aligning itself too closely with China. The decision to become a founder member of the Chinese-sponsored Asian Infrastructure Investment Bank in 2015 was sharply criticised by the US. But we have weathered disapproval from the US over our policies in the region in the past. President Carter's administration was not happy with our decision to sell Harrier jump jets to China in 1978. They were never purchased, but as we expected at the time, they were testing the relationship and seeing if, in contrast to the Soviet Union, we would treat them differently in the area of defence. Such concrete examples of an independent approach, to which it is reasonable to add Hong Kong up until its return to China, should help the UK present itself as an honest broker.

Balancing the relationship with Japan, which was a major long term investor in the UK long before China, will be another factor. Under Prime Minister Abe, Japan has taken an increasingly nationalist line, which has had an impact on its dealings with China. Signs of this spilling over into the wider arena include allegations that Japan was paying a British think tank to produce anti-Chinese newspaper articles.[16] The UK will face attempts to get it to take sides in disputes in the region. We should resist, and focus, where we can, on encouraging constructive dialogue in an international framework in the search for long-lasting solutions.

The potential for further developing the commercial relationship with China looks distinctly more favourable than finding a near term resolution to the disputes over territorial waters. The importance of building this relationship, which remains a key element of the UK's foreign policy, was highlighted in the 2015 National Security Strategy and Strategic Defence and Security Review:[17]

Our engagement with China in recent years, following this model [strengthening our ties across the full range of government business, and developing our economic relationship through high-level Economic and Financial Dialogues], has led to direct financial benefits for the UK – and reflects our ambition for the UK to be China's leading partner in the West. The UK is now one of the most popular destinations for Chinese investment in Europe. Our goods and services exports to China increased by 84 per cent between 2010 and 2014, and up to £40 billion of trade and investment agreements were reached at the China State Visit in October 2015 alone.

Following the eighth session of the UK–China Economic and Financial Dialogue in November 2016, between Chancellor of the Exchequer Phillip Hammond and Chinese Vice Premier Ma Kai, the government made available a twenty-four page document setting out a 'Global Comprehensive Strategic Partnership For The 21st century'.[18] This sets out a very broad range of areas for cooperation including in boosting trade and investment; strengthening ties in financial services; 'recognising the UK as the world's leading offshore RMB centre'; developing infrastructure and energy projects, including the high profile Chinese investments in the UK's nuclear industry; tackling issues around IP protection; and collaborating in the health sector.

One of the striking features of the document is the number of references to the potential for collaboration internationally. This includes working together on global development issues, strengthening coordination in implementing the G20 Action Plan on the 2030 Agenda for Sustainable Development[19] and strengthening the roles of the multilateral development banks. In particular, it refers to both sides affirming 'their commitment to development in Africa' and 'note the importance of Foreign Direct Investment (FDI), particularly in manufacturing, to economic diversification and job creation in Africa, and the potential contribution of both Chinese and UK firms and investors to making this happen'.[20] Over recent years, China's investment in Africa, and support for major infrastructure and energy projects, has made a huge contribution to the development of a number of countries. However, it has not been without criticism, both external and from within the region. As the Council for Foreign Relations mentions in a background report on China in Africa,[21] China has faced 'growing international criticism over its controversial business practices, as well as its failure to promote good governance and human rights'. It goes on to say that:

> In addition to international observers, many Africans themselves have expressed frustration over China's role on the continent, having accused Chinese companies of underbidding local firms and not hiring Africans. At the same time, Chinese companies that do hire African workers have been criticised for failing to maintain fair labor relations.

That said, China's approach has also been evolving over time, with attempts made to address criticism. As Jessica Toale notes in her contribution to a Young Fabian report on the UK's relationship with China,[22] 'China has also consistently responded to criticisms of its approach by increasing its support for large social projects like schools, hospitals and malaria programmes.'

As the UK–China Global Comprehensive Strategic Partnership document highlights, collaboration in the infrastructure sector between British and Chinese companies could bring benefits to all parties involved, including helping to address at least some of the criticisms faced by the Chinese. To this end, the parties agreed to set up a hub in Beijing which would focus on facilitating this cooperation. In particular, partnerships between Chinese contractors and British design and engineering companies could provide a world class combination in executing major infrastructure projects in line with best practices. It would also provide a platform for UK companies to build their expertise in operating in new markets, where Chinese partners already have built up significant experience. Working more closely with Chinese companies and, in particular, with the large state owned enterprises, could also help the UK broaden and deepen its overall engagement with China. And such cooperation need by no means be restricted to African markets.

As the document also mentions, there is the potential for the UK and China to work together on China's 'Belt and Road Initiative', noting that 'China encourages enterprises to raise finance for Belt and Road Initiative projects in London'. This initiative could have profound benefits both for the UK's trading relationships with countries along the route, and as a basis for widening our broader relationships.

China's new focus on reviving the ancient silk routes from Asia to Europe was heralded during President Xi's visit to Kazakhstan in 2013. At a speech at Nazarbayev University he proposed that 'China and Central Asia join hands to build a Silk Road economic belt to boost cooperation'.[23] The concept was expanded further during a trip to Southeast Asia by President Xi in October 2013, when he proposed creating a new 'Maritime Silk Road' which would strengthen ties with ASEAN countries.[24] The two initiatives came to be referred to under the umbrella term of 'One Belt, One Road' or, more formally, the Belt and Road Initiative (BRI). The objective is to link China, and particularly its less developed western provinces, Xinjiang and Inner Mongolia, by land with the countries of central Asia and beyond into Europe, and by sea with the wider area of Asia and Africa.[25] The strategy is also very much linked to China's internal political dynamic, which requires a buoyant domestic economy to ensure stability. At a time when domestic growth is slowing, the Belt and Road Initiative will stimulate export industries. However, the project has been presented very much in terms of providing a platform which will boost development all along its routes, and boost trade through them. As an example, the opening of the rail route to Europe is estimated to save as many as twenty days compared with sea freight.[26]

At its heart is the objective of developing the infrastructure along the route, and in November 2014 President Xi announced that China would contribute $40 billion to establish a Silk Road Infrastructure Fund which would 'be used to provide investment and financing support to carry out infrastructure, resources, industrial cooperation, financial cooperation and other projects related to connectivity for countries along the "Belt and Road"'.[27] This came shortly after a memorandum of understanding had been signed on the establishment of the Asian Infrastructure Investment

Bank, which would also play a role in meeting the massive financing needs in the region; the bank opened in January 2016, with China holding 30 per cent of the shares. Without doubt, China sees its leadership in providing sources of finance for the infrastructure required as a key element of its foreign policy, reinforcing its influence with countries along the routes. In the Vision and Actions on Jointly Building Silk Road Economic Belt and 21st-century Maritime Silk Road issued in March 2015 by China's National Development and Reform Commission,[28] the project is described as one which will 'connect Asian, European and African countries more closely and promote mutually beneficial co-operation to a new high and in new forms'. President Xi has been at the forefront of driving the international efforts. Commenting on the release of what was described as the 'first authoritative report on 'Belt and Road' three-year progress'[29] China Daily has reported that:

> Between September 2013 and August 2016, President Xi visited thirty-seven countries (eighteen in Asia, nine in Europe, three in Africa, four in Latin America and three in Oceania), where he officially promoted the idea of building the 'Belt and Road' as a cooperation initiative and received warm response from concerned countries.[30]

It also reports that 'By the end of June 2016, China had issued joint proposals and statements with fifty-six countries and regional organizations on bilateral cooperation for implementing the BRI and signed the relevant MoUs or agreements accordingly'.

This is undoubtedly a hugely ambitious and long-term project, with many risks. However, as the report referred to above highlights, the implementation is already underway. By 30 June 2016, 'large state-owned enterprises such as China Railway Group Limited and China Communications Construction Company Limited signed construction contracts for thirty-eight large demonstration projects of transport infrastructure, covering twenty-six countries and focusing on key routes, port cooperation and the improvement of infrastructure in developing countries'.

China's energy security is also a key issue in terms of the development of the initiative, as it will help free China from dependence on choke points for tanker traffic, such as the Strait of Malacca. While some of the pipeline infrastructure, such as the Central Asia–China Gas Pipeline, pre-dates the Belt and Road Initiative, the plan involves significant additional capacity being added. Again, the report referred to above highlights the extent of the activity, noting that 'China's state-owned enterprises participated in the construction of forty overseas energy projects, including power plants, electricity transmission facilities and oil and gas pipelines, covering nineteen countries along the "Belt and Road"'.

Given the number and diverse nature of the countries involved in this initiative (with many of them being politically and/or economically fragile), there will undoubtedly be many challenges along the way. They include making a return on the heavy investment requirements, which China will need to manage carefully. That said, with dampened construction demand at home, this gives an opportunity to deploy excess capacity internationally. As well as its own funds, it will need to draw in funding from the local governments benefiting from the projects and the private sector if it is to avoid overstretching its own capabilities, and ensure an allocation of funds to viable projects. This offers opportunities for UK expertise in the construction sector.

Managing the relationships with countries along the route also risks encountering problems, in spite of China's pronouncements that this is a non-threatening and mutually beneficial endeavour. While the current relationship between China and Russia is relatively warm (including participation in joint manoeuvres in the South China Sea in 2016), by reaching out into Central Asia, China could be seen as posing a threat to Russian influence in the region. Given the issues it is facing on its western borders, Russia has been putting increasing importance on its relations with its Central Asian and Asian neighbours, including by building up the Eurasian Economic Union* – indeed, in May 2015 Russia and China signed an agreement on cooperation

---

* An economic union set up in May 2014 by Belarus, Kazakhstan and Russia, later joined by Armenia and Kyrgyzstan.

between the EEU and the BRI. There are also ties through the Shanghai Cooperation Organization,[31] an intergovernmental body set up in June 2001 in Shanghai by China, Kazakhstan, Kyrgyzstan, Russia, Tajikistan, and Uzbekistan. Nevertheless, over time, growing Chinese influence could lead to tensions, particularly if governments find themselves having to choose between one or the other. The important position of Pakistan on the route and the level of investment China is making there could raise issues with Pakistan's regional foe, India. During a visit in April 2015, President Xi announced investments of $46 billion[32] were focused on linking China's Xinjiang region to the Pakistani port of Gwadar with a network of roads, railways, which also helps Karachi, and pipelines, as well as much needed investment in Pakistan's electricity sector. The opening up of Chinese access to Gwadar on the Arabian Sea potentially gives China an alternative route for Gulf crude. On a more positive note, the route's potential contribution to the opening up and economic recovery of Afghanistan could provide a welcome boost to the prospects of stability in the region. The UK should urge China whenever the opportunity presents itself to develop more involvement in Afghanistan and influence Pakistan to stop supporting the Taliban inside and outside Afghanistan.

Navigating the development of the Maritime Silk Road will require even more careful handling, given the situation in the South China Sea referred to earlier, particularly as many of the countries involved are already competing with China in the commercial arena in the way that those on the land routes are not. Further afield, China's focus on developing its ties with Sri Lanka, including building up port facilities, has also drawn the attention of India.

The Belt and Road Initiative, as flagged earlier, opens up a wide range of opportunities for the UK, which the government has recognised. A joint China–Britain Business Council and FCO report[33] providing advice for UK businesses interested in the initiative notes:

One Belt One Road offers great potential opportunities for British business. Partnerships between UK and Chinese companies could support infrastructure development of this region and collaboration on projects and initiatives in third countries where UK and Chinese strengths are complementary. New markets will open and new supply chains will change the way goods move across the globe.

The report highlights infrastructure, financial and professional services, advanced manufacturing, and transport and logistics as major areas of opportunity, as well as a range of secondary areas, including energy, environment and healthcare. There are numerous ways in which UK companies can benefit, from raising finance or investing in projects; providing engineering and design advice; and supplying equipment and technology. Cooperation on joint initiatives will reinforce the UK's reputation in markets along the route where it already has a solid track record, such as Kazakhstan, allowing companies to expand into new areas as well as open up new markets. It should also be noted that while much focus has been given to the projects anticipated along the routes in Asia, Chinese companies are also involved in many related projects significantly closer to the UK, which should also provide opportunities for UK companies to engage. As noted in two recent papers from the European Union Institute for Security Studies[34,35] the Chinese are increasingly active in Southern and Eastern Europe, with projects including road, rail and port facilities.

Grasping these commercial opportunities and with the government playing a full role in supporting business – including by putting in place a comprehensive trade agreement – could provide the backbone for developing the broader relationship with China over the coming decades, and maintaining a shared commitment to global free trade, which President Xi spoke so strongly in favour of at the World Economic Forum in Davos in January 2017.[36] However, the UK should be alert for pitfalls along the way, particularly where the interests of our other key allies in Asia are involved, and remain conscious of the fact that there will be areas of potentially significant differences on subjects outside of our trading relationship.

CHAPTER 8

DEALING WITH EUROPE

With the UK outside the EU from March 2019, we believe British relations with Germany and France will improve, rather than decline. The reasons for this assertion, which some may find surprising, lie in the history of our three countries: in particular in the history of France's relations with the UK from 1940 to 2016, and the creation of the European Coal and Steel Community (ECSC) in 1951 to 2017. Having a sense of the history between Germany, France and Britain helps put the vote to leave the EU in the June 2016 referendum into context. Only a very small proportion of the electorate have a full understanding of this history but it percolates through to people.

It was the Franco-Prussian war of 1870–71 that led to France having to transfer almost all of Alsace and part of Lorraine to Germany. There were relatively few casualties but defeat left a burning resentment in France. Britain had no involvement. Russia, responding to the German refusal to renew their treaty, signed an agreement with France in 1891 that included a clause obliging France to give Russia diplomatic support in any colonial conflict with Great Britain. A Military Convention followed in 1894, covering the possibility of Russia and France being attacked by Germany. This Franco-Russian agreement with specific military clauses,[1] which George Kennan would later call the 'fateful alliance', started to fuel a German sense of encirclement. Up until the Entente Cordiale with France on 8 April 1904 we used to believe that Britain could stay out of continental Europe in splendid isolation. After the 1904 Entente, the agreement was extended to include Britain in the Triple Entente, and that feeling of encirclement, specifically denied by Germany at the time as one would expect, grew more intense. The British Foreign Secretary, Edward Grey, explains in his autobiography the theory of the encircling policy as having been encouraged by the Germans to hold their public to high levels of defence expenditure.[2] The Triple Entente never had the historic significance of its predecessor, the Entente Cordiale. Militarily Russia never lived up to the hopes vested in it by France in particular although it took heavy casualties in its share of the fighting from the onset of war in 1914 until its revolution in 1917.[3] Huge casualties were suffered on all sides in the First World War. The Second World War meant humiliation for France and devastation for Germany. Both wars left indelible marks on the continent.

Lasting peace between France and Germany has been a major British objective from 1945 onwards. There was no clamour from the US or from the USSR to bring the French into the four-power governance of Berlin and parts of Germany. It was a British influence, led by Anthony Eden, that made it possible. No British government from 1951 onwards was ever going to undermine, let alone try to break up, a growing friendship between Germany and France. As Robert Schuman, the French Foreign Minister, foresaw in May 1950 when he was the first to propose the concept of an ECSC, it 'materially' made war between these two countries impossible. It was the ECSC which set in motion a process whereby French and German officials from these two great coal and steel industries and their respective Finance Ministries developed friendships and familiarity which have deepened as the years have gone by, helping to bind the two countries together. In 1967, all the institutions of the ECSC were merged with those of the European Economic Community, but those initial steps had built up the political will in France and Germany for the Treaty of Rome in 1957, the Treaty of Maastricht in 1992, the Treaty of Lisbon in 2007, a European Union and European citizenship.

Britain stood aside in 1955 when the talks which culminated in the Treaty of Rome in 1957 began. There was no political figure of any weight in British politics at that time in either the Conservative or Labour Party who wanted the UK to be involved. The UK sent a relatively junior official as an observer to the talks between the six countries: France, Germany, Italy, Netherlands, Belgium and Luxembourg. In that sense, though it was a matter of regret for a small minority in the UK, it was not a lost opportunity, for no opportunity was seen to exist.

Attempts have been made by some to depict Churchill as being a closet believer in Britain always becoming part of a European Union and cite the 1940 offer of union. This union needs to be put in perspective. On 14 June the Germans entered Paris at dawn and on 15 June de Gaulle, a one-star general and deputy Defence Minister, left France. On 16 June he arrived early by train in London where he met with Corbin, the French Ambassador, and Jean Monnet, then a banker, to discuss the proposal circulating for a Franco-British Union. Some have chosen to depict this as an early sign of de Gaulle also favouring an eventual Union of Europe with Britain in it. In reality, both Churchill and de Gaulle were clutching at straws, trying to find a possible way of keeping France committed to the fight against Hitler.

That afternoon the Cabinet approved the Union Declaration and de Gaulle read it out over the telephone to Prime Minister Reynaud. Reynaud pledged to defend the proposal to his death. The French appeasers, however, within a matter of hours, denounced the Union; Pétain said it would tie France to a corpse! Some corpse. Without a vote, the union proposal was dropped by the French Cabinet and Reynaud resigned, having never even fought for it.[4]

President Lebrun asked Pétain to form a government and Pétain, in a national radio broadcast on 17 June, announced: 'It is with a heavy heart that I tell you today that the combat must be ended.'[5]

In truth, the proposed union was open to detailed criticism and inevitably so, given it was a spontaneous emotional response to the dire prospect of all resistance to the German advance collapsing in France.

The two nations under the Declaration of Union were to commit to 'declare that France and Great Britain shall no longer be two nations, but one Franco-British Union', a declaration of 'indissoluble union and unyielding resolution in their common defence of justice and freedom against subjection to a system which reduces mankind to a life of robots and slaves'. They were to have joint defence, foreign, financial and economic policy organs and, during the conflict, a single War Cabinet in charge of all their forces. Their parliaments would be associated. The British Cabinet excluded a proposal for a single currency. The declaration concluded with defiance: 'We shall conquer.'[6]

In the political battle over the EU some have selectively quoted various speeches Churchill made in 1946 in Zurich, in 1948 in The Hague and in London in 1949 at the founding of the European Movement and in 1949 at Strasbourg. In the 2016 referendum, his grandson, Conservative MP Christopher Soames, a committed believer in remaining in the EU, wisely said on BBC radio there was no way to predict how Churchill would have voted. The objective evidence points to him never really shifting from his three circles of power and influence: the US, the UK and the Commonwealth and continental Europe. The UK's role was ambiguous when he spoke of a European union, but he was very clear Germany must be part of a continental union along with France.

By 1944 relations between de Gaulle, and both Churchill and Roosevelt were stretched to breaking point. The problem Churchill and Roosevelt grappled with was how to keep France stable during the invasion and avoid chaos. For de Gaulle, who saw everything in terms of his battle with Vichy for legitimacy, he and his colleagues represented the continuation of the 1940 government and not the Vichy government. On 4 June 1944 in Portsmouth Churchill told de Gaulle he needed to go to Washington to see Roosevelt, who sooner or later would come round to recognising de Gaulle's Algiers government. De Gaulle exploded: 'Why do you seem to think that I am required to put myself up to Roosevelt as a candidate for power in France? The French government exists.' Churchill hit back. 'How do you expect us, the British, to adopt a position separated from that of the United States. We are going to liberate Europe, but it is because the Americans are with us to do so.' Then Churchill turned the verbal knife: 'Every time I have to decide between you and Roosevelt, I will always choose Roosevelt.'[7]

Churchill then took de Gaulle to see General Eisenhower on the eve of the expected D-Day. In a broadcast to the people of Western Europe, Eisenhower explained he would follow Roosevelt's policy and say that French people were required 'to carry out his orders'. French administrative officials could 'carry on in the exercise of their functions' until 'the French themselves should choose their representatives and their government'.[8]

This formulation was an anathema to de Gaulle and, in discussion with Churchill, he refused to make his own broadcast in support as planned or send French liaison missions with the invading forces. This reaction so infuriated Churchill that he said he would refuse to allow de Gaulle to cross the Channel. It was mainly Eden who both persuaded de Gaulle to continue with the broadcast and not call for a generalised insurrection, and encouraged Churchill to relent. In the end, de Gaulle did land in France on 14 June a little after midday. Virtually everywhere de Gaulle went, people made it clear that he, not Vichy, was seen as the future government and this eventually forced a change of mind. On 16 June de Gaulle returned to Algiers, where he was told on 30 June that Eden had made an agreement with the Americans that amounted to recognition of the provisional government. De Gaulle then met Roosevelt in America and it went well, but it was not until he arrived back in Algeria on 13 July that he heard the crucial news: 'The United States recognises that the French Committee of National Liberation is competent to ensure the administration of France.' On the afternoon of 25 August, de Gaulle headed the procession down the Champs-Elysees in Paris. Vichy France's day was over.

Again it was Eden's diplomatic skill and support for a French position of post-war influence which led, by the time of Yalta in 1945, to France being accepted as one of the four governing parties over Berlin, which was formalised in the Potsdam Agreement of 1945. Under Bevin and Attlee British post-war policy remained to first build up France and then Germany, and subsequently encourage their coming together.

In October 1950 the French Prime Minister René Pleven argued in the French National Assembly that though Germany was not a party to the Atlantic pact, it benefited from the security it provided and it was right that it should share in preparing for the defence of Europe. He stipulated three essential elements for the formation of a European army: the ratification of the Schuman Plan for coal and steel, the appointment of a European defence minister, and the establishment of a political body to supervise the defence minister's actions. The French Assembly voted for this Pleven Plan.

In 1953 Michel Debré, a prominent Gaullist in the Assembly, attacked the whole idea of European Defence. 'It is necessary to tell all the theologians of little Europe point blank: Europe is not a nation; it is an aggregate of nations. Europe is not a state; it is a grouping of states. To create Europe, this reality must be taken into account.'[9] On 5 June 1954 at a rare press conference de Gaulle denounced the European Defence Community (EDC). He had withdrawn from being head of government in 1946 and retired to write in 1952 to his house in Colombey-les-Deux-Églises, following the election in which his political movement had fallen short of becoming a majority government. On 30 August 1954, the Assembly refused to ratify the European Defence Community.

De Gaulle returned to power on 1 June 1958 as Prime Minister in the Fourth Republic, in the midst of the revolt in Algeria. He met the French Assembly that day, having not set foot in their building since 6 January 1946. Francois Mitterrand said: 'When the most illustrious Frenchman presents himself for our votes, I cannot forget that he is first and foremost presented and supported by an undisciplined army.'[10] When the crisis was over, de Gaulle asked Konrad Adenauer to his home in Colombey for two days of talks on 14 and 15 September. The two men already knew each other, but it was an honour that had been paid to no other foreign politician. It sealed the Franco-German rapprochement.

Yet even so on 17 September, de Gaulle wrote his famous Memorandum to President Eisenhower and Prime Minister Macmillan. Its second paragraph began:

France could, therefore, no longer consider that NATO in its present form meets the conditions of security of the free world and notably its own. It appears necessary to it that on the level of world policy and strategy there be set up an organization composed of: the United States, Great Britain and France.[11]

Having left out Germany, de Gaulle went on to say France would subordinate itself to this security organisation that it regarded as essential to any further development of its participation in NATO.

Eisenhower wrote back on 20 October reminding de Gaulle that, over the previous two years in NATO, consultation had gone beyond the limits of the European Zone, in the Far and Middle East and in developing a common policy with regard to the Soviet bloc, and that he did not think the US could allow itself to lose the good relations that were developing between the members of NATO or the bonds that were being forged between them. Wisely, Adenauer did not even bring the subject up when he met with de Gaulle on 26 November. He was quietly confident that his earlier meeting with de Gaulle was what really mattered and events were to prove him right.

Whatever doubts de Gaulle had about Monnet's federalism or the calls for an EDC, and the need he felt to assert the role of the French state, he had made up his mind. France and Germany were to be together the driving force in Europe. Adenauer recalled to his friends and the press and reasserted in his memoirs that de Gaulle's 'nationalism was much less virulent than is usually thought ... and [he was] aware of the great importance of Franco-German relations.'[12]

Macmillan had misjudged the importance and depth of the Colombey agreement between de Gaulle and Adenauer. He had also played a very bad hand in dealing with Adenauer over what was called the Berlin crisis that began on 10 November 1958. With no warning Khrushchev, the Soviet leader, suddenly demanded the withdrawal of all Allied troops from Berlin. Adenauer had sent Macmillan a personal message the next day imploring him to make representations to Moscow which Macmillan did. But Macmillan had long planned to go on a visit to Moscow and as a consequence, his response to the Soviet Union did not satisfy Adenauer, who suddenly invited himself to London on 7 December. According to Macmillan's biographer Alistair Horne, Macmillan noted, 'he of course wants to talk about Berlin. I shall talk to him about European trade.' Horne wrote that Adenauer was apparently 'fobbed off with *politesse*'. It was from this date that the crucial decline in their relations stems.[13]

On 4 December 1958 Sir Harold Caccia, the British Ambassador in Washington, reflecting Ministerial discussion, talked to the US Under Secretary of State, Douglas Dillon, about forming a free trade area with six other countries: Portugal, Norway, Sweden, Denmark, Austria and Switzerland (which became the EFTA of the Seven but then was called Uniscan). Dillon said he could do 'nothing', as America was too keen on Germany and France drawing together within the existing six to sponsor a rival European grouping.[14]

Macmillan went to Moscow on 21 February 1959, but this unilateral initiative carried a heavy price in terms of European unity. It 'infected Adenauer with a deep-seated, fundamental mistrust of Macmillan's intentions towards Germany'.[15] Meanwhile de Gaulle, who had become President of the 5th Republic on 21 December 1958, had not forgotten what Macmillan had told him six months before on 29 June. De Gaulle recorded Macmillan saying: 'The Common Market is the Continental System all over again. Britain cannot accept it. I beg you to give it up. Otherwise, we shall be embarking on a war which will doubtless be economic at first but which runs the risk of gradually spreading into other fields.'[16] The deeper question to ask is, had Macmillan already forgotten this? By February 1959, the then Chancellor of the Exchequer, Heathcoat-Amory, began to suspect that Macmillan 'was toying with the idea of applying for full membership of the EEC and was lukewarm about an EFTA of the Seven'. Maudling wrote a strong letter to Macmillan on 3 March 1959 in which he stated that France, with Adenauer's acquiescence the dominant force in the six member EEC, did not want Britain in Europe 'at all'. He went on to say that if Britain rejected 'the idea of forming some alternative association with our friends outside the Six we should be left without a friend in Europe...'[17] Rab Butler in his usual hesitant way supported the Uniscan project.

In May 1959 the British Cabinet backed negotiations with Sweden over a possible EFTA. On 21 July in Stockholm, ministers from all seven countries approved the convention and a schedule of tariff reductions to put the Seven on equal footing with the Six by 1 July 1960. These tariff reductions were accelerated at the end of November. In December 1959 Dillon, on a visit to London, told Macmillan the US wanted the UK to join the Six, but also to abandon its reliance on the special relationship.

Those who wish to understand the deeper reasons behind British politicians' views about whether to leave the EU in 2016 should focus attention on 1958 and 1959 far more than on what Macmillan actually said on 4 August 1961, when – buoyed up by his victory in the 1959 general election and increased authority within the Conservative Party – the government officially asked for Great Britain to be admitted to the Common Market. The EFTA Seven option could have been made very effective. It was a loss of nerve by Harold Macmillan on EFTA that shifted the direction of UK policy. Macmillan should have focused more on putting our own economic house in order as Margaret Thatcher did when she became Prime Minister. His period of vacillation started in 1959. On 19–20 December 1959, the heads of government of the United States, France, Germany and the UK met in Paris. The following day Macmillan recorded his assessment. 'Far the most important from our point of view (I mean the economic side) was the tripartite Rambouillet on Sunday and my talk with de Gaulle. I believe de Gaulle will play the game.' By this, Macmillan meant support British efforts for an agreement between the Six and the Seven. He, despite the close association he had had with de Gaulle in Algiers, was making a major misjudgement about de Gaulle's intentions, which culminated in the veto in 1963.

After his tripartite meeting with Eisenhower and de Gaulle, Macmillan believed that de Gaulle was tempted by the offer of equal access to US nuclear weapon secrets. He also thought that, on defence, de Gaulle would never want to integrate with Germany and would keep open NATO membership and other links to the US on nuclear deterrence. It was a major error of judgement. The US understood this German–French locking in and supported it. After two meetings with Dillon, Macmillan wrote to the Foreign Secretary a very revealing minute about his own personal anxiety.

> One of our basic reasons why we could not integrate with Europe was our desire to maintain a special relationship with the United States. Just what does that now mean? Is the pattern changing – will the Six replace us as the major ally of the United States? Why is it difficult to make the United States realise that the Six which they support for the sake of European political unity is in fact (because of the economic threat to the United Kingdom and others) a threat to European unity?[18]

Commentators frequently assess that France will never accept a federalist Europe and often quote de Gaulle and his heritage as the guardian of that concept. They are wrong. The truth is that at their meeting in Colombey in September 1958 Adenauer and de Gaulle built a meeting of minds which, as Lacouture argues, 'was to resist all reverses'.[19] Adenauer was certain of three things from thereon in his relationship with de Gaulle. Firstly, France was also wanting 'reconciliation over the Rhineland'; secondly 'they would be faithful to the West' because over Berlin France had shown far more firmness than the British or the Americans; and thirdly, they were 'good Europeans', not that they were integrationists but because the Treaty of Rome was the 'ideal framework for the economic development of France'. Initially, of course, France expected to take the lead in relation to Germany over all aspects of foreign and security policy.

The crucial moment that marked the consolidation of the Franco-German alliance was on 6 November 1958 in London. The French Foreign Minister, Couve de Murville, met with Selwyn Lloyd, the Foreign

Secretary, and Reginald Maudling, then Paymaster General. He made clear French opposition to the European Free Trade Association that was to come into existence in January 1960 with the UK as a member. He also made clear French support for the Common Market. Couve de Murville sensed that this was a dramatic moment and wrote, 'We are about to reach the most critical stage in Franco-British relations since June 1940.' This was no understatement since matters grew even worse on 15 December at a meeting in Brussels. The British, who had hoped to bring France around to their ideas, with German support, were amazed to see the Germans declare that they were against the 'Free Trade Area'.[20]

On 20 March 1960 Eisenhower and Adenauer issued a joint communique explicitly approving an acceleration of internal cuts in import tariffs in the EEC. This was seen as a negative step by EFTA. A painful process then began during which the Conservative Cabinet, while in the EFTA Seven, began to move towards leaving EFTA and joining the EEC Six, and in the process encouraged public opinion in Denmark and Austria to think about leaving for the EEC with the UK. Sir Frank Lee wrote an interdepartmental report which was presented to the government:

> The conclusion is inescapable that it cannot be compatible with either our political or our economic interests to let the situation drift on indefinitely on the basis of a divided Europe, with the United Kingdom linked to the weaker group. We must therefore seek a wider economic grouping which should at least comprise a single European market, assuming that any still wider grouping – e.g. an Atlantic Free Trade Area – is not a practicable objective – at any rate, at this time – and we must be prepared to examine what this is likely to mean in the way of positive 'contributions' on the part of the United Kingdom itself.[21]

A Cabinet meeting on 13 July still had a majority against applying to join the EEC Six. Macmillan was moving, however, towards applying because of business reasons like those presented by Lee.

On 27 July 1960 Macmillan made his first move. Heathcoat-Amory retired and he appointed Selwyn Lloyd as Chancellor. Edward Heath came in as deputy to Lord Home, who had replaced Reginald Maudling as Foreign Secretary, with responsibility for negotiations with Europe. This tilted the balance crucially from ministers who favoured staying with the Seven to those who wanted to go with the Six. A note came from our Ambassador to France, Sir Gladwyn Jebb, warning that the French would not join up the Six with the Seven. By 23 January 1961 the French Ambassador was warning Heath about French reluctance and the British Ambassador in Bonn was reporting that the German Finance Minister, Ludwig Erhard, had told him de Gaulle was not the 'key' but the 'lock' and had no intention of letting the UK into their private empire. On 31 July 1961 Macmillan, in spite of many warnings from UK Ambassadors about French attitudes and from Maudling as President of the Board of Trade, having got Cabinet approval, told the House of Commons the UK would apply to join the EEC. He had changed his mind over eighteen months.

Macmillan's belief that we might be able to join the EEC was shattered by President de Gaulle in 1963 and again in 1967. Only when President Pompidou replaced de Gaulle, after he lost a referendum on regional government in 1969, was the way cleared, but that was only because two British Prime Ministers had been ready to commit privately to monetary union. The first was Harold Wilson, who was drafting our application to join when Edward Heath's Conservative Party won the general election of 1970. Heath then quickly formally applied and after a cross-party struggle in Parliament, when the Conservative government needed the votes of Labour MPs ready to disregard three line whips, the legislation was passed and on 1 January 1973 Britain became a member of the EEC.

In retrospect, as viewed from 2017, perhaps de Gaulle was right in what he said explaining his first veto. On 14 January 1963 during a press conference at the Elysée Palace he commented:

England [sic] in effect is insular, she is maritime, she is linked through her exchanges, her markets, her supply lines to the most diverse and often the most distant countries; she pursues essential ly industrial and commercial activities, and only slight agricultural ones. She has in all her doings very marked and very original habits and traditions...

Yet it is possible that one day England might manage to transform herself sufficiently to become part of the European community, without restriction, without reserve and preference for anything whatsoever; and in this case the Six would open the door to her and France would raise no obstacle, although obviously England's simple participation in the community would considerably change its nature and its volume...

Lastly, it is very possible that Britain's own evolution, and the evolution of the universe, might bring the English little by little towards the Continent, whatever delays the achievement might demand, and for my part, that is what I readily believe, and that is why, in my opinion, it will in any case have been a great honour for the British Prime Minister, for my friend Harold Macmillan, and for his Government, to have discerned in good time, to have had enough political courage to have proclaimed it, and to have led their country the first steps down the path which one day, perhaps, will lead it to moor alongside the Continent.[22]

Had Macmillan never made his doomed application in 1961, it is unlikely we would have applied again in 1967. It was a premature application to the EEC from a panicked Macmillan, which went against his own earlier views as told to de Gaulle as recently as in 1958. It was not based on any real prospect of de Gaulle agreeing, as was Wilson's application in 1967.

British politicians of the left, right and centre have persistently denied the centrality of the underlying belief in federalism in Europe. It has waxed and waned for seventy years. Of course, the founding fathers of the European Economic Community, people like Jean Monnet and others, wanted federalism to be the end result. Hence their four founding principles which bedevil the EU still in 2017: the freedom of movement of goods, people, services and capital over borders. Whereas the principle of free movement of labour has little importance for a single market, it does have economic meaning for a single currency zone. The federalism of the founding fathers, scoffed at by some, is a religion for others, and a single currency is an inextricable part of that federalism. It is on the anvil of the single currency and its inherent federalism that the referendum to exit the EU was hammered out. President Macron's emergence in France demonstrates this. You do not campaign with Beethoven's 'Ode to Joy', the European Movement's anthem, along with 'La Marseillaise', or have the EU flag flying alongside the tricolour, without it sending a huge political message, a message which the French people have under their second vote system in part, if not in whole, embraced. All credit should be given to Macron for doing so. There is now going to be a very serious debate in France about reform of the Eurozone, and within that debate there lies the core issue of fiscal transfers amongst the Eurozone members. To do that, there needs to be a greater sense of European citizenship, and the German people must be readier than hitherto to be the largest contributors to the pool of funds which will finance such fiscal transfers. German resistance stems from the fact that their own politicians promised – and it is in the treaties – that there would be no fiscal transfers in the Eurozone. There are valid questions as to what constitutes a fiscal transfer, but they all have at their core the question of federalism. A separate Eurozone parliament to monitor a common budget for the Eurozone is not attractive to Germany unless accompanied by measures to reduce risk and tougher budget constraints, all difficult to make stick in France.

France began to lose its automatic leadership role in foreign affairs in 1989. Dominance on security issues began to seep away later when, for the first time, Germany agreed to deploy troops in UN blue helmets to Bosnia and Herzegovina after the Dayton Peace Agreement in 1995. They were not even equals when Chancellor Merkel and President Hollande negotiated with the Russian Federation in Minsk over

Ukraine. Unfortunately for France the economic gap between the two countries has widened, but even so it is possible that whatever party wins in the September 2017 elections, Germany will consider serious reforms in the EU.

Monnet, the great French federalist who had been with de Gaulle in London in 1940, as earlier mentioned, spent much time in America thereafter during the war and de Gaulle, who did not agree with Monnet on much, even began to see Monnet as an American agent. Monnet was fairly close to President Roosevelt and in the subsequent US Republican administrations was a friend of John Foster Dulles, Eisenhower's influential Secretary of State.

The State Department's longstanding support for a United States of Europe has been pretty obvious over the decades, never more so than when President Obama visited the UK during the actual referendum to support David Cameron's Remain campaign, and his visit provoked a step like increase in polls for the Leave campaign. This has been followed by Obama's endorsement – as a private citizen – of Macron to become the French President. State Department enthusiasm has often been checked by their political head the Secretary of State, by the Pentagon and most Presidents. Declassified memorandums from the State Department archives signed by General William J. Donovan, previously head of the wartime Office of Strategic Services (OSS), the precursor of the CIA, show that the US funded Monnet's European Movement. In 1949 Donovan, who was not officially in government, became the Chairman of the newly formed American Committee on United Europe (ACUE) promoting European Unity. Allen Dulles was then on its board. One memorandum from Donovan dated 26 July 1950 reveals a campaign to promote a full-fledged European Parliament. In 1958 ACUE provided 53.5 per cent of the European Movements Funds and the European Youth Campaign was 100 per cent funded by ACUE.[23] A memorandum released from the State Department written on 11 June 1965 appears to instruct the Vice President of the European Community to pursue monetary union by stealth, suppressing debate until the 'adoption of such proposals would become virtually inescapable'.[24]

The Labour leader Hugh Gaitskell decided on Labour's course of opposing European federalism linked to joining the Common Market between mid-July and mid-September 1962. He was heavily influenced by clashes with the powerful Dutch socialist and federalist Paul Henri Spaak, and reflected the content of another earlier meeting in April with Jean Monnet. Both had a strong federalist vision and disliked Gaitskell, concerned that nobody in Britain was advocating moves to early federation and by his refusal to go further than the exact wording of the Treaty of Rome.

On 21 September Gaitskell replied to Macmillan's broadcast the previous day, warning that federalism was a danger, but his most powerful intervention came at the Labour Party conference, when he spoke of what it would mean to enter a European federation:

> It means that powers are taken from national governments and handed over to federal governments and to federal parliaments. It means – I repeat it – that if we go into this we are no more than a state (as it were) in the United States of Europe, such as Texas and California. They are remarkably friendly examples, you do not find every state as rich or having such good weather as those two! But I could take others: it would be the same as in Australia, where you have Western Australia, for example, and New South Wales. We should be like them. This is what it means; it does mean the end of Britain as an independent nation state. It may be a good thing or a bad thing but we must recognise that this is so.[25]

Gaitskell's warning against a United States of Europe then and his stress on the need for vigilance about it emerging by default has remained as a guiding principle for many older Labour voters over all these years. It is that tradition which influenced the Leave vote in 2016, particularly amongst working class Labour supporters as evidenced by the voting pattern in the northern towns and cities of England, with the exception of Manchester and Liverpool.

The Labour Party differences in 1970 over Europe were intense.

So bad was this inter-party dissent that in 1972 the National Executive Committee, as well as the shadow Cabinet, decided that Labour
would support an amendment calling for a referendum before the UK
joined. That amendment was defeated because Roy Jenkins resigned
as Deputy Leader with some other shadow spokesmen, including
David Owen, though he had argued with Jenkins for accepting a referendum. But it was recognised that Labour should offer an In/Out
referendum in its 1974 general election manifesto. When Labour won
that election, the pledge was fulfilled in 1975 with the public voting
to stay in by a large majority. It was possible to believe because of
cross-party voting that there was then the 'whole hearted consent' that
Prime Minister Edward Heath had said initially would be necessary.
The referendum result was accepted publicly by virtually everyone in
the UK for a few years. In 1977, the Labour Cabinet met on a paper
from the then Foreign Secretary which was firmly anti-federalist and
it was endorsed overwhelmingly. But after losing the general election
in 1979, Britain's continuing membership of the EEC was again challenged by the Labour Party, with a manifesto commitment in the 1983
general election to come out of the European Community without
even a referendum. Labour lost that election very badly.

Prime Minister Margaret Thatcher supported the creation of the
Single European Act in 1986, despite two notes from her Chancellor
of the Exchequer, Nigel Lawson, warning perceptively that she should
not accept any mention of monetary union, for fear that it would be
built on. She very unwisely, given her opposition to a single European
currency, overrode his advice and the Single European Act of 1987 was
the precursor of the Maastricht Treaty in 1992. She won the general
election in 1987 but was ousted in 1990 by Conservative MPs, many in
favour of a single currency. With the successful military intervention
against Iraq's invasion of Kuwait in 1991 behind him, Prime Minister
John Major and the Conservatives again won the general election in
April 1992. On 16 September 1992, which became known as 'Black
Wednesday', sterling was forced out of the exchange rate mechanism
(ERM), a quite separate mechanism from the later introduction of the

euro. This humiliation made it even more difficult for Major to ratify the Treaty of Maastricht, despite the UK's decision to opt out from the single currency. Eventually ratification was very narrowly won with much bitterness inside the Conservative Party after the vote in July 1993 was made one of confidence in the government. The treaty came into force in November 1993, when all member states had ratified it. The 'bastards', as Prime Minister Major called some of his Eurosceptic colleagues, did not stop trying to disown the Maastricht Treaty right up until the 1997 general election which Labour won with a large majority. All three party leaders were forced by concerns over public opinion to pledge at that election that entry into the euro could only follow agreement through a referendum.

The incoming Prime Minister, Tony Blair, in 1997 was the most pro-European Union Prime Minister since Edward Heath but, despite a huge majority, he wisely did not seek an early referendum on joining the euro, which in his own time he was determined to do and the most likely moment would have been after what was referred to in No. 10 as a 'Baghdad bounce' in the opinion polls in 2003, which of course never materialised.

It has taken until 2017 for a European Defence Community (EDC), another federalist measure, to return to life. France agreed to join NATO in 1949 as part of the initial twelve countries: Belgium, Canada, Denmark, France, Iceland, Italy, Luxembourg, Netherlands, the US and the UK. In 1966 de Gaulle withdrew France from the integrated military and leadership structures and the HQ of NATO moved from Paris to Brussels. In 2009 under President Sarkozy France returned to NATO's integrated command but continued to pursue an EU defence role.

There have been two phases in the history of the European Community, EEC, or Common Market as it was more often called in the 1960s in the UK. The first started with the original six signing the Treaty of Rome in March 1957. This first phase was broadly successful and lasted over thirty years until the negotiations on the Treaty of Maastricht in 1992. The second phase was from 1992 to 2017, the central feature of which was the introduction of the euro currency and the initial failure of the single currency in a Eurozone consisting of a majority of member states. It was no accident that the failed phase of EU membership, the European Union of European citizens, involved the most deeply federalist measure – monetary union. Long discussed, it was embarked on with a flawed design. Never has a currency union been sustainable in the world's history without it becoming eventually, and often painfully as in the US, a single currency in a single country with a mechanism for fiscal transfers. The struggle over the Maastricht Treaty in the UK Parliament was between those who would have liked to have vetoed the whole euro concept and those who thought we could live comfortably alongside a Eurozone provided we were opted out and were retaining sterling. Had the Treaty legislation been presented to the House of Commons in early 1992 before the April general election, it would probably have been rejected. The whole project might have then stopped. In retrospect, this was the moment when the seeds were sown of a public resolve in the UK to leave the EU that took twenty-four years to emerge. The 2016 referendum was no 'flash in the pan' in terms of public opinion. It was common on the street to hear the word 'out', not 'leave', and said with a force and crispness that sounded as if their basic decision had been made years not months, let alone days, earlier.

The German Bundesbank, which had opposed the economic design for the euro in principle and had fought to retain the Deutschmark, was overridden by Chancellor Kohl. Some within the Bundesbank regret it to this day. In France, a referendum on the Maastricht Treaty was only very narrowly won, by fifty-one per cent to forty-nine per cent, by President Mitterrand in September 1992. Had that vote been lost, the whole project would have collapsed and the UK would not be leaving the EU.

Initially the early phase of the euro at the start of the twenty-first century gave some grounds for hope that the euro might succeed and that the EU was a sufficiently unique organisation that it could chart a new course for a single currency across many nations. Then, in the midst of the global economic turmoil of 2008, a crisis developed in the

Eurozone. That euro crisis is still with us in 2017 and was a key issue during the 2016 UK referendum debate. Some people asked in the referendum how long should Britain continue to be associated with a failed experiment that could lead to a euro collapse and profound collateral damage, even in countries that had opted out?

Today in 2017 the euro crisis is in its eighth year and mainly affects Greece and Italy, but that is now an issue for the EU on which the UK will have little influence in our remaining months as a member. We should not, however, attempt to block reform which has constantly been urged on EU finance ministers by US Treasury Secretaries and successive British Chancellors of the Exchequer. The analysis given by the former Governor of the Bank of England, Mervyn King, in his book with the thought provoking word 'Alchemy' in its title is both clear and simple.[26] The euro crisis will continue and a euro collapse will follow, unless in effect a country emerges inside Europe to run this currency with a fiscal union.

As already noted, the circumstances that led up to the Labour Party's manifesto commitment for a Remain/Leave choice over the UK's membership of the EU started within the Labour Party in 1972. The Conservatives' manifesto commitment of 2015 was influenced by the emergence of a grassroots movement that saw growing support for the UK Independence Party (UKIP). UKIP came first in the European Parliament elections of 2014 winning over 26 per cent of the vote and twenty-four out of seventy-three MEPs. UKIP had become a focus for disillusioned voters following the disbanding of the Referendum Party in 1997. By 2016, London was broadly speaking very supportive of the EU, as was Scotland, but elsewhere in England and Wales there was a deep sense of disillusionment, of being unfairly treated, of neglect and loss of control, which was hard to identify as it was spread across traditional Labour and Conservative voters.

When the Conservatives won outright in the 2015 general election the referendum course was set by Parliament and the Electoral Commission for an In/Out referendum before the end of 2017. The pledge had been announced before the Scottish referendum in 2014 when the Scottish people rejected independence. Prime Minister Cameron spent a lot of time negotiating with European heads of government a package deal and on 20 February 2016 announced the results to Parliament. However, it was viewed by a large number of MPs as insufficient, not just Conservatives, and many more of no formal party allegiances across the country. People will argue long and hard as to what were the key issues in the subsequent referendum campaign. Most say loss of control; others that immigration was a major aspect, due to the fact the UK could not control EU citizens having the right to move here to work whenever they wished. But one largely unspoken key issue, felt but not fully understood, within the framework of loss of control was a distrust, sometimes even fear, of what the cognoscenti call federalism but was for most voters referred to as 'Brussels'. It is denied by some, but the views stated on television by leading politicians on the Leave and Remain sides made it quite clear that it was recognised that Single Market membership available to all EU members was ruled out for the UK because there would be no shift in EU policy on free movement of labour, something David Cameron had also encountered.

It could not remotely be claimed that EU defence was a major vote-swinging issue in the referendum, but it was a swing-issue within the military, and they were well aware that all US governments, except to a limited extent that of President Obama, had opposed EU defence as distinct from NATO. All UK Prime Ministers too, except Blair to some degree, have been opposed to 'EU common defence'. Yet the words still appeared in EU Treaty texts culminating in the Treaty of Lisbon in 2007. This concept has been very damaging to NATO. When the UK, under Prime Minister Blair, agreed to 'autonomous defence' with President Chirac, it was claimed this would not lead to two autonomous planning centres for defence in Europe, one in the EU, one in NATO. Yet that is exactly what has happened. European financial contributions to NATO dropped precipitately after the Berlin Wall fell, and service personnel numbers were drastically reduced. Double-counting began to grow between NATO forces and the so-called EU forces. Every US Secretary of State for Defense warned against endorsing this illusion and giving credence to a vision of European defence that was all smoke and mirrors and little substance. The whole concept was held back during the UK referendum in 2016, but Germany went much further towards endorsing the concept immediately after the referendum, and a further step was taken at the sixtieth Anniversary of the Treaty of Rome in which the UK, correctly, did not participate.

There is another federalist development that gives ground for concern for those who are anti-federalist. In recent years the US State Department has also seemingly been content to watch the build up of the EU's Foreign Office or, as it is more blandly called, the European External Action Service (EEAS), which is replete with Embassies and Ambassadors around the world. The EEAS significantly increased its budget over the last five years from €488 million in 2012 to €614 billion in 2017.[27] During this time the mishandling of the EU–Ukraine Association Agreement blew up (see Chapter Five) and many independent commentators were critical of the diplomacy and lack of effectiveness of the EEAS. Europe came very close to a regional war; as it was, around 10,000 people have lost their lives. The one consolation is that by 2019 the UK will no longer be part of the EEAS, and the UK will be coordinating its own foreign and security policy internationally for this region within NATO and the UN Security Council. But in future years the UK is likely to miss the independence of French foreign policy. Europeanisation of French foreign policy will not happen overnight, but creep up. Some argue that after the Suez debacle, France chose Europe in foreign policy terms and the UK chose America. That is a little simplistic, but it was certainly the course that Adenauer advised the French and later de Gaulle, who inherited the mess, to follow. The challenge for the UK is to restore its independent voice in foreign policy which it has been losing within the EU since the Iraq debacle of 2003.

In 2016, the UK referendum vote allows the country to break out of both an EU Foreign and Security Policy and the longstanding incubus of federalism. No longer does the UK have to risk clambering into the single currency for fear of being in the second division in an EU which Germany firmly leads, with or without France as an equal partner. The UK, by leaving the EU, can define with far greater clarity desirable objectives in NATO about European defence, and through the 'Five Eyes' over intelligence and cyber security, and seek out the best policy framework for the UK through our own democratic debate. Clarity is perhaps the most important factor in developing coherent defence, foreign and security policies. If the UK develops coherence, it will help its development and relations with continental Europe. Britain will be free of the pretension that has been the besetting sin of the EU. The UK returning to self-government will have to build up the NSC, introduce its own laws and control its own borders, the essential prerequisites for an independent foreign policy.

It was never enough for a UK foreign policy just to be outside Schengen; 'Europe's porous borders allow terrorists to cross the continent with ease. Other European governments have lagged behind the United Kingdom in developing capabilities and legal frameworks for digital intelligence gathering and in cultivating effective cooperation between their many agencies', recently argued the UK's former Security and Intelligence Coordinator from 2002 to 2005, David Ormond.[28] Britain also needs its own system for immigration control. In broad terms, we have the same number entering the UK each year from the EU as the rest of the world. We can now have the same criteria for entry across both and be selective in how we reduce numbers of entry from both. Apart from genuine asylum seekers, we should take people in who can best help our economic recovery. A certain ruthlessness in the application of general admission rates will be necessary within and between these two categories if post-Brexit expectations of a significant drop in the numbers over the years ahead are to be met.

President Macron may well be a critical influence over the next five years. In French politics, he once said, 'is the absent figure of the King, whom I fundamentally believe the French people never wished dead'. This void, he has argued, is one France is doomed to seek forever – 'with Napoleonic and Gaullist moments'.[29] He has gone so far to create his own Party, En Marche. We will see how he evolves. He was well regarded by the late Michel Rocard, the Prime Minister and Social Democrat in European terms, a strong federalist and a good judge of character.

If the EU creates something more resembling a typical sovereign country, the UK has nothing to fear or regret in that development. It is true that UK opposition to federalism has held it back in part, but only in part, because federalism as yet does not carry public opinion in most EU countries, and in particular there will be resistance in France. A federal Eurozone will probably grow faster than at present with President Macron, but not fly under its true colours EU wide for some years. If successful, it could have a global economic stabilising effect, and it is likely to be popular with the young, though there is a danger of thinking the opinion of the young is unified. It too reflects nationally divided opinions. Macron may not succeed in his fight. He has watered down the economic reforms championed by the Republican presidential candidate François Fillon. He will face strong resistance from the unions and there are many deep-seated obstacles to his reforms. Nevertheless, those reforms are not against British interests and as we argue repeatedly in this book, Franco-German unity has been and remains an overriding British interest since 1945.

In reality a smaller Eurozone and more integrated grouping would deserve to be called a Union, but its emergence will depend on the financial discipline of its participating countries. The non-Eurozone members and ex-Eurozone members would then be more realistically called a Community, but that is unlikely. The EU will almost certainly remain a Single Market aiming for a single currency for all. Ambitious? Yes. Unrealistic? Who knows.

There is now a special responsibility for the UK as an integral part of our leaving the EU to devote much effort and even more resources to NATO. All our savings from the EU CFSP budget should go into the NSC budget and that gradually must increase our contribution to 2.5 per cent of GDP before 2022, as argued in Chapter Two. This includes, where it can be justified bearing in mind international accounting guidelines, using aid budget funds on direct and indirect security related measures, given the importance of the present poorest states becoming stable and contributing to global peace and development.

NATO must be retained as the most effective international defence organisation in the world. The UK is vital in keeping the US onboard for NATO and the Canadians are important too. The Americans have the right to demand Europeans contribute more of the total budget. We only have to think of the US coming in late to the defence of Europe in 1918, then again only in December 1941, having been attacked by Japan, to realise why President Truman's decision to stay in Europe and not withdraw US forces as he was beginning to do in 1946 was of such huge historic significance. The Atlantic Alliance has been very good for Europe. Maintaining the US as fully committed to Europe must be the UK's main task in the next few years when détente looks like it is lagging behind defence threats. But since détente is part of the equation, it cannot be relegated to a second-level priority. The UK leaving the EU is the best hope of keeping NATO and building it up. There is a viable prospect of a real peace returning to Europe in the foreseeable future, enabling its armies to be reduced and aiding its economic growth. We saw a glimpse of what might have been during the early Yeltsin period in office. It was not just Moscow that lost that opportunity, but Washington, London, Paris and Berlin. Differences over President Assad must not block a dialogue starting between President Trump and President Putin. President Xi showed the way in his meeting with Trump in April 2017 in Florida.

While these major issues of foreign and security policy have been given prominence in this book, it cannot be denied that how the UK handles its own economy and the transition out of the EU after March 2019 will determine how much our independent voice carries real weight and influence. The former head of the Bank of England for ten years, Lord Mervyn King, said in March 2017 on the BBC Radio Four *Today* programme: 'I don't think it makes sense for us to pretend we should remain in the single market and I think there are real question marks about whether it makes sense to stay in the customs union.' The EEA Agreement is a serious option for the implementation period after we leave the EU and before we have an EU–UK trade agreement. It is discussed in David Owen's foreword as it is outside the scope of this book, which is not about the Article 50 negotiations. King had previously said before the referendum that warnings of economic doom outside the EU were overstated. After the referendum, he welcomed the fall in the value of the pound and said he believed Britain could be better off alone. On the BBC he said: 'I think the challenges we face mean it's not a bed of roses – no one should pretend that – but equally it is not the end of the world and there are some real opportunities that arise from the fact of Brexit we might take.' This is a vital point. We must leave the EU with the medium to long term fully in our sights. This is a historic shift we are embracing.

As to the fall of the pound, the Bank of England's Deputy Governor is reported in the *Financial Times* on 24 March to have said that the pound dropped 'for a reason' to take account of more difficult trading relations once the UK leaves the EU. Lord King has been less forthright arguing that Britain had 'until the Brexit referendum, an over-valued exchange rate'. The most likely guess is that both explanations played a part in the necessary revaluation.

As far as the City of London goes, in the same edition of the *Financial Times* quoted above, there was a letter from Professor David Blake of the Cass Business School in London, author of *Brexit and the City*, which argued:

> the UK financial services industry is in situ and it is hard if not impossible to move it in whole or in part. Financial services companies benefit from huge agglomeration economies from being physically located near each other in a whole range of ways, from recruiting workers from a highly skilled talent-pool of bankers, lawyers, accountants and so on to having a more effective lobbying voice. While this is possible in Paris or Frankfurt, the scale isn't there. Banks have spent the thirty or so years since the Big Bang in 1986

investing in the infrastructure of the financial services industry in London. Not only does that include the buildings and the millions of miles of electronic cables, it also includes a conducive operating environment that comes from thirty years of political lobbying. All this would need to be replicated in a different European city.

It is as ridiculous to believe that the City of London will move to Paris or Frankfurt after Brexit as it is to believe that the French wine industry or the German car industry will move to the UK after Brexit. The City should stop whining and refuse to move business out of London.

On 17 October 2016, Open Europe issued a report entitled 'How the UK's financial sector can continue thriving after Brexit'. It argued that 'if banks, for instance, were still unclear about what the future holds one year before the UK formally exits the EU, they would be forced to start making decisions – including over whether to shift part of their business elsewhere'. It is not just British banks that would be affected if, by the end of March 2018, it is not becoming fairly clear when and how the issues affecting the City of London are going to be resolved. For this reason, the UK announcing that it might have to accept an implementation period was sensible. But implementation is different from transition; it carries a commitment to at least a prior heads of agreement as to what you are negotiating to implement in detail. Businesses in all EU member states need to know the direction of travel, and that can only be set in early 2018 when a new German government will be up and running. But progress does need to be made in the first quarter of 2018.

There is another dimension to the City of London, and that is the extent to which EU countries' own companies are invested and intend to continue to invest in the City. For example, 19 per cent of Deutsche Bank's total net revenues come from the UK. The Bank announced on 23 March 2017 that they were moving into a new HQ in London with a 25-year lease. The CEO of the Bank told their employees: 'The move underlies the Bank's commitment to the City of London.' This demonstrates that London is not just a UK asset but a benefit to the whole of the EU and the EEA, as well as the wider Europe and beyond. Finding a collaborative way to ensure most of the present cross-border financial activity continues is a doable deal which traders, left to do their own negotiations, would soon achieve.

The worry is that the EU in 2017 looks dysfunctional. It appears no longer able to make decisions in any acceptable timescale. The saga surrounding the Transatlantic Trade and Investment Partnership (TTIP) – negotiations had little flexibility, the package was disowned, rightly, in Europe in relation to healthcare – demonstrates this. The EU–Canadian agreement, CETA, was more flexible and eventually was ratified, though not without its own drama involving a divided Belgium. Whether TTIP will be revived and negotiations restarted with President Trump's administration is still uncertain, and it will in any case take a long time.

Following Brexit the UK will become a member of WTO in its own right. On the positive side *The Times* had the headline on 23 February 2017: 'World Trade deal "is £1bn chance" for UK.' This was the result of 110 nations ratifying WTO's trade facilitation agreement (TFA) the first multilateral agreement by WTO since it was created. The agreement aims to slash red tape and waiting times at borders, with measures such as fast lanes for food and allowing pre-arrival processing of documentation. To trade seamlessly means shortening the queuing time for lorries, which currently adds to wage costs and risks missing delivery times. It is claimed that these measures could cut trade costs by 14 per cent on average and would add 2.7 per cent to global trade by 2030. The question is, how much of these WTO reforms will automatically apply in the EU single market by 2019 when the UK might leave without agreement? There is no rational reason why not only these but also other mechanisms developed for seamless trade in, and with, the EU should not automatically apply to the UK, because the trade traffic literally goes both ways. Such mechanisms include Mutual Recognition Agreements, by which trading partners recognise each other's conformity assessment in relation to areas such as quality control standards. It is mutually beneficial that the mechanisms operate on both sides of the Channel and it would be easier if there was a nil-tariff regime. In practical terms, the electronically based system in the single market currently allows thousands of British lorries a day to enter the rest of the EU with no delays (and vice versa). Michel Barnier, the EU negotiator and former French minister, just prior to the triggering of Article 50 commented how the UK, in the event of a no deal situation, would be faced with 'the reintroduction of burdensome customs checks, inevitably slowing down trade and lengthening lorry queues in Dover'.[30] But the idea that Britain would simply accept this is absurd. We can trade with the Continent through many different ports, some of them currently underused. Dover–Calais is not the only route with potential, and its enlargement as currently planned may need to be reassessed. No sensible person puts all their eggs in one basket; nor should a country. To prevent such spats arising, it is not necessary to make the resolution of this issue await a detailed EU–UK trading agreement. We are all in Europe under WTO rules but, regardless of that, there is a need to progress sensible and technical ways of overcoming trade blockages which, on a much smaller scale, and in different circumstances, we are going to have to resolve in relation to the Northern Ireland border.

There is, however, a worrying side to WTO that is building up: namely, it appears that the Trump administration is readying to ignore rulings by WTO relating in particular to China. Hopefully meetings between Trump and Xi will reach an accommodation but even after the seemingly successful initial meeting in Florida it is possible Trump might use the US Trade Act of 1974, which allows the US to impose punitive tariffs. The Trump administration is very favourable to the UK in words about a new trading agreement, but the question is whether it will materialise. One way to translate words into action might be if the Trump administration started soon to introduce reform around the North American Free Trade Area (NAFTA) and find ways of extending that to the UK, in which case we might not need to be involved in a follow on to TTIP.

Roberto Azevedo, the head of WTO, has made it crystal clear that there will not be a trade 'vacuum or a disruption'[31] when we exit from the EU. This represents a big change from what the WTO said before the referendum. It is now clear what many have always believed – there will be no discontinuity in membership and as Azevedo has said he and the WTO Secretariat will make the transition as smooth as possible. WTO tariffs, at present levels, are comparatively low, in the single digits. Outside the EU and outside the Single Market non-EU trade for the UK is growing fast. We had a £30 billion annual surplus in 2015, and non-EU trade accounts for the majority of our exports as our exports to the EU have contracted – from 55 per cent of exports in 2000 to 44 per cent in 2015 – and showed a massive £60 billion deficit.[32] We can make accommodations with the EU under WTO rules. EU specific deals will be mutually advantageous and the UK under Article 50 has not challenged EU founding principles. What will matter, above all, is that Britain is a trading nation, has been for centuries, and will remain so. The City of London has proven its capacity to adapt over the centuries and it will do so again if the spirit is right. That national spirit in the UK must be the hallmark of how we proceed. We have had a general election, and especially the unelected House of Lords must work with, not against, the government of the day. Partisan party politics have no place in the international treaty negotiations we now face.

The EU, as the months have gone by since the UK voted to leave, has been less inclined to dismiss Brexit as an event of little significance or a matter just for the British. The Eurozone is more likely now, after the French election, to start to face long overdue reform, but Britain has to reform to make a success of Brexit.

Germany's reaction to President Macron, whether under a Christian Democrat or Social Democrat Chancellor after their elections, will depend on the level of public support not only in Germany but also in France, and on whether Macron has demonstrated that he can carry the necessary financial disciplines through the French Assembly. He has said that he will use Article 49 (3) of the Fifth Republic constitution introduced by Michel Debré, which allows the Prime Minister to commit the government on financial matters and social security finance in a way that can only be blocked by a motion of censure. A wise former Ambassador to Germany has written in *Berlin Rules*: 'If Germany is disinclined to introduce Eurobonds or other measures of debt communitisation, then they will not be introduced. And if Germany chooses not to stimulate imports of consumer expenditure, no one can force it to do so.'[33] That is the reality of which President Macron is well aware from his time as Minister of Economy. He has 'no choice but to adjust to German priorities.'[34]

It seems out of the question that German public opinion will accept any system of large automatic money transfers to Italy. They may not need to, for public opinion is building up in Italy on the need to come out of the Eurozone of their own volition. What has this got to do with British foreign policy post-Brexit? The answer is that we in the UK will find our economy hit by the French and Italian economies weakening within the Eurozone, let alone by Eurozone collapse. To some extent this would happen in or out of the EU, but out of the EU the impact fortunately should be far less.

The as yet unanswered question is whether the German people are ready, if they vote in Martin Schultz the new SPD leader as Chancellor in the autumn of 2017, to also commit to a form of fiscal transfer union. If they did it would raise expectations that, with President Macron, it would be possible to start to save the Eurozone from collapse. Both men, in principle in opposition, have been favourable to developing a Fiscal Union, where financial resources would move through independent decision-making from the Eurozone's richer areas to its poorer regions. It would probably require the appointment of an economic head of the Eurozone to work with the ECB. The reluctance of the French people to accept even European Commission disciplines within the present framework hitherto also needs to be faced up to in France by its new President Macron. He is attempting to build his movement into a major political party to support him in a period of weeks and months in the French Assembly and in the country. The tests will come from militant unions to reforms that are necessary but will be resisted. But it will be more than that. Marine le Pen has enlarged her constituency against top down reform which protects the well off. Her support does not just come from old French nationalism.

For the UK, the challenge is different as a result of Brexit – how to persuade Macron in particular that the City of London, which he knows well, is ready to demonstrate that its skills and assets can serve all EU countries. The Financial Stability Board (FSB) currently chaired by Mark Carney, was established in 2009 as the successor to the Financial Stability Forum, and is not an EU body. It serves the G20, its decisions are not legally binding, and it operates by moral persuasion and peer pressure. It is useful and could influence a post-Brexit Europe by bringing some sense to the debate about the continuing role of London. In its present form it would not be the organisation to help develop Eurozone relations with the UK; but it might be able to adapt.

In negotiating the UK's exit, the one path we must avoid at almost any cost is to embark on a deliberate course of undermining, politically or economically, the EU and any of its twenty-seven countries; and, with that consideration in mind, we must eschew 'beggar our neighbour' economic policies. This in particular applies to their Eurozone. The Eurozone is certainly flawed but it could prosper with greater federalism. It may be doomed to fail, but let that be because of its own contradictions, not UK actions. In the midst of the 2010 general election, the then Chancellor of the Exchequer, Alistair Darling, approached the then shadow Chancellor of the Exchequer, George Osborne, to agree on a specific policy at the request of the EU to ease the economic crisis in Greece to avoid collateral damage to the Eurozone. They mutually agreed that it should be undertaken and it should be known that there was no principled opposition to the Eurozone across party lines in the UK. Ever since the Conservative–Liberal Democrat coalition and the subsequent majority Conservative government, the UK has urged reforms of the Eurozone but has forsworn any policies to destabilise the Eurozone. That must remain our UK position post-Brexit and it will help people who voted remain to live more easily with the result. There is no room for a spirit of vindictiveness. As mentioned earlier in the book, it is Article 8, as distinct from Article 50, which offers hope that we can all be good neighbours. Whatever the temptation in the rough and tough of exit negotiations, the UK must not cross the line of becoming a bad neighbour.

This approach is fully in line with the spirit of Article 8 on good neighbourliness that should, but may not, run in parallel with Article 50. It is, however, much more than just good neighbourliness; it is the expression of a national interest – the City of London has thrived on belonging to European countries as well as the UK. To make that feeling a widespread reality in the EU, amongst EEA member states and the wider Europe of Switzerland, Turkey, Ukraine, Georgia, Belarus, Moldova and Russia is an essential task for the UK. Carney, the Canadian head of the Bank of England, has shown himself over Brexit to be independent – in the true sense of the word – of the British government and is, therefore, carrying more conviction in the EU of twenty-seven states and the wider Europe when he argues that London serves their interests as well as the British.

Any new cooperative machinery designed in the spirit of Article 8 should take its cue from long-established and efficiently functioning collaborative structures like the OECD, the Bank for International Settlements, and the European Bank for Reconstruction and Development, which, without begging questions of national sovereignty, get on with the practical job of oiling the wheels of international exchange.

British good faith could be demonstrated and new credibility injected into such proposals by offering to internationalise or 'Europeanise' some of our London institutions. While currencies and monetary policies would remain national responsibilities and, in the UK's case, the post-1997 architecture of an independent central bank, targeting a low inflation number set by government, would continue. The regulation of London as a financial centre might be delegated to a new Financial Regulation Authority governed by directors from participating countries.

This should not be achieved by somehow offering key roles in the governance of the Bank of England to such representatives of other nations. But this, apart from the unduly provocative nature of implying that Europe's financial markets should be regulated by something called the Bank of England, would compromise the Bank of England's own integrity as the body established by the British Parliament to conduct British monetary policy according to the government's inflation target. It would be thoroughly retrograde to jeopardise the Bank's independence in monetary policy by giving it a governance structure that blurred the clear responsibilities of the Monetary Policy Committee and the Governors. However, if independent national monetary policies are to be reconciled with international regional regulation and supervision of, for example, banking, we might face again the problem which proved so intractable in 2007–08, namely how to manage macro-prudential crises if the central bank is not also the banks' supervisor.

A lot has been learnt since 2007–08 about this tangle of issues; and Mervyn King's *The End of Alchemy* shines a bright light upon it, separating causes from symptoms. What is clear is that there is no general reason why in a global economy with free exchange and nationally based currencies and exchange rate cooperation between national authorities, nations cannot usefully address over time the imbalances and misperceptions which were the root causes of the 2008 crisis. This needs to be really understood and taken into practical policies for the City and the continent of Europe. By the middle of 2018, let us hope a working model of such a City of London is emerging.

By championing the practical economic case for the gradual restoration of internationally minded cooperation amongst nation states, Britain can more credibly build up the City of London and also foreign and security policies worthy of its historic outward-looking consciousness, and consistent with its own interests in inhabiting both a wider Europe and a world characterised by free exchange, multilateral cooperation and collective security. But this will take time, and is why the suggested implementation period of three years could be worthwhile.

What of France and, more specifically, Paris, for whom the British have both a deep ambivalence and affection? There is a view, with growing evidence to support it, that a three-way relationship between France, Germany and the UK will never work. Such became the consistent view of one of our wisest diplomats. Sir Ewen Fergusson, who died in April 2017, served as Ambassador to France from 1987 to 1992, his final Diplomatic Service posting. He lived in France after retirement from his role as Chairman of Coutts bank. He knew much about French wine. He loved France and its people. In his obituary in the *Daily Telegraph*, it was recorded that he had been

described in one newspaper as a 'latter-day Prospero', he excelled in bringing together under his spell politicians and diplomats from across political and national divides. Even Edith Cresson (French Prime Minister, 1991–92), notorious for her claim that one in four British men were homosexual, threw caution to the wind and graced the ambassador's table.

Yet, as it emerged after his retirement, Fergusson's time in Paris had transformed him from a self-described 'convinced European' to something of a Eurosceptic, and in 1999 he emerged as a prominent member of New Europe, a group established by the former foreign secretary, David Owen, to campaign against Britain joining the euro.

In an interview in 1998 for the British Diplomatic Oral History Project, Fergusson explained that the years in Paris had made him much more sensitive to the difficulties of Britain's role in an EU whose key members, France and Germany, place far more importance on their relationship with each other than on that with their troublesome offshore neighbour.

He was particularly alarmed by the 'forced speed' with which continental Europe was rushing towards a single currency, a process he saw as 'inherently very dangerous'. In 2000 he admitted to *The Times* that he had found his job, in the run-up to the Maastricht Treaty in 1992, 'very uncomfortable', adding that if he were still ambassador he would find it 'almost impossible'.

'Being in the Foreign Office is like being a eunuch,' he explained. 'You cannot say what you think. The Foreign Office is always painted as a bunch of Europhiles but I don't think that is quite so.'[35]

In a wider Europe, there is every reason to believe – not just to hope – that, as we argued at the start of this chapter and have tried to demonstrate throughout this book, post-1945 British, French and German relations are too deep to die away by the mere act of the UK leaving the EU. Rather they will improve as a result of the clarity Brexit will bring to all three countries. It will give France and Germany, if they wish, an unfettered opportunity in both the EU and the Eurozone to build a much closer relationship or it may result in this but also with a measure of separation between their two countries as their people wish. For the UK, Brexit is an unfettered opportunity to re-establish a country that our people wish to live in, to work for its prosperity, and to defend its people and interests worldwide.

NOTES

INTRODUCTION

1   David Owen, *Europe Restructured: The Eurozone crisis and its Aftermath*, Methuen, 2012.
2   Gill Bennett, *Six Moments of Crisis*, Oxford University Press, 2013, p. 175.
3   Vienna Convention on the Law of Treaties 'Part V: Invalidity, Termination and Suspension of the Operation of Treaties', Article 42 – Article 72, pp. 342–9.
4   Vienna Convention on Succession of States in respect of Treaties. Vienna, 23 August 1978. Relevant extracts available on www.lorddavidowen.co.uk

A FOUNDATION FOR GLOBAL DIPLOMACY

1   https://www.gov.uk/government/speeches/prime-ministers-speech-to-the-republican-party-conference-2017
2   Isaiah Berlin, *Four Essays on Liberty*, Oxford University Press, 1969, p. 129.
3   Kirsten Sellars, *The Rise and Rise of Human Rights*, Sutton Publishing, 2002, pp. 134–7.
4   Kirsten Sellars, ibid., p. 152.
5   House of Commons Foreign Affairs Committee, 'The United Kingdom's relations with Russia', https://www.publications.parliament.uk/pa/cm201617/cmselect/cmfaff/120/120.pdf
6   Stein Ringen, *The Perfect Dictatorship: China in the 21st Century*, Hong Kong University Press, 2016, p. 4.
7   Mark Landler, *Alter Egos: Hillary Clinton, Barack Obama, and the Twilight Struggle over American Power*, WH Allen, 2016, pp. 154–7.
8   Kori Schake, 'Will Washington Abandon the Order? The False Logic of Retreat', *Foreign Affairs*, January/February 2017, pp. 41–6.
9   Peter Hain, *The Guardian*, 6 April 2017.
10 David Owen, *In Sickness and In Power: Illness in Heads of Government, Military and Business Leaders since 1900*, Methuen, 2016, pp. 161–210.
11 https://www.un.org/disarmament/publications/occasionalpapers/no-28/
12 Warren Zimmerman, *The Origins of a Catastrophe: Yugoslavia and its Destroyers. America's last Ambassador to Yugoslavia*, Three Rivers Press, 1996, pp. 222–3.
13 Elizabeth Drew, *On the Edge: The Clinton Presidency*, Simon & Schuster, 1994, pp. 657–8.
14 https://www.rand.org/MRI365.ch3.pdf
15 Scott R. Feil, 'Preventing Genocide: How the early use of force might have succeeded in Rwanda. A Report to the Carnegie Commission on Preventing Deadly Conflict', Carnegie Corporation of New York, April 1998. Membership of the Commission was David Hamburg, Cyrus Vance, Gro Harlem Brundtland, Virendra Dayal, Gareth Evans, Alexander George, Flora MacDonald, Donald McHenry, Olara Otunnu, David Owen, Shridath Ramphal,

Ronald Sagdeev, John Steinbruner, Brian Urquhart, John Whitehead, Sahabzada Yaqub-Khan, Carnegie Corporation of New York, April 1998.

16 Ibid., p. 66.

17 Richard Lloyd Parry, 'France seeks defence pact with Commonwealth over Brexit fears', *The Times*, 5 June 2017.

18 'Manipulation of the Oil-for-Food Programme by the Iraqi Regime', Report by the Independent Inquiry Committee into the United Nations Oil-for-Food Programme, 27 October 2005, http://www.iic-offp.org/story27oct05.htm

19 Christopher Meyer, *DC Confidential: The Controversial Memoirs of Britain's Ambassador to the US at the Time of 9/11 and the Iraq War*, Weidenfeld & Nicolson, 2006, pp. 8, 223–4.

20 Quoted in Andrew Pierce and Thomas Harding, 'Top aide's damning attack on Blair's Iraq war', *Daily Telegraph*, 22 February 2007.

21 George Packer, *The Assassin's Gate: America in Iraq*, Farrar, Straus & Giroux, 2005, p. 114–15.

22 Damien McElroy, 'Pakistani takes reins of "Muslim Nato"', *Sunday Times*, 2 April 2017.

23 https://www.publications.parliament.uk/pa/ld201617/ldselect/ldeucom/78/7802.htm

24 https://www.newscientist.com/article/mg21528744-100-geoengineering-with-iron-might-work-after-all/

THE UK'S ROLE IN GLOBAL SECURITY

1 Christopher Hill, 'Powers of a kind: the anomalous position of France and the United Kingdom in world politics', *International Affairs*, March 2016, vol. 92, no. 2, p. 399.

2 https://www.gov.uk/government/news/uk-takes-lead-in-policing-skies

3 Kenneth O. Morgan, *Callaghan*, Oxford University Press, 1997, pp. 431–4.

4 Letter to *The Guardian*, 5 March 2015, https://www.theguardian.com/world/2015/mar/05/nato-expansion-and-the-ukraine-conflict

5 Letter to *The Guardian*, 8 March 2015, https://www.theguardian.com/world/2015/mar/08/nato-is-misquoting-mikhail-gorbachev

6 John Simpson, 'Russia's shell game', *New Statesman*, 27 March–9 April 2015.

7 Joshua Partlow, *A Kingdom of Their Own: The Family Karzai and the Afghan Disaster*, Knopf Publishing Group, 2016.

8 'Defence of the Realm. A drastic cutback in British troop numbers would send out a message of decline', *The Times*, 3 June 2017.

9 Sam Jones, 'Spiralling cost of UK defence projects signals hard choices', *Financial Times*, 6 February 2017.

10 Mark Hookham & Tim Ripley, 'Killer sub delayed as costs soar by £191m', *Sunday Times*, 12 February 2017.

11 Charles Moore, *Margaret Thatcher. The Authorised Biography Volume I: Not For Turning*, Allen Lane, 2013, pp. 572–3.

12 Kristan Stoddart, *Facing Down the Soviet Union: Britain, the USA, NATO and Nuclear Weapons 1976–83*, Palgrave Macmillan, 2015.

13 David Owen, *Nuclear Papers*, Liverpool University Press, 2009.

14 Michael Quinlan, *Thinking about Nuclear Weapons: Principles, Problems, Prospects*, Oxford University Press, 2009.

15 Ibid., p. 124.

16 Peter Hennessy & James Jinks, *The Silent Deep*, Allen Lane, 2015.

17 David Owen, *Nuclear Papers*, Liverpool University Press, 2009, p. 8.

18 Tony Blair, *A Journey*, Hutchinson, 2010, p. 636.

19 Des Browne MP, King's College London, 25 January 2007.

20 https://www.youtube.com/user/stratcompa

21 Kristan Stoddart, ibid.

22 Mark Urban, Saudi nuclear weapons 'on order' from Pakistan, *BBC*, 6 November 2013, http://www.bbc.co.uk/news/world-middle-east-24823846

23 Quoted from speech by President Rouhani, 21 May 2017, http://www.irna.ir/en/News/82539048/

24 Quoted in the *New York Times*, 2 May 2017, https://www.nytimes.com/2017/05/02/world/middleeast/saudi-arabia-iran-defense-minister.html?_r=0

25 David Albright, *North Korea's Nuclear Capabilities: A Fresh Look*, Institute for Science and International Security, 28 April 2017, http://isis-online.org/isis-reports/detail/north-koreas-nuclear-capabilities-a-fresh-look

26 David Owen, *In Sickness and In Power: Illness in Heads of Government during the Last 100 Years*, Methuen, 2008, pp. 181–6.

27 http://www.nato.int/docu/pr/1996/p96-165e.htm

28 Aaron Donaghy, *The British Government and the Falkland Islands, 1974–79*, Palgrave Macmillan, 2014, pp. 170–72.

29 CAB 292/25 Falkland Islands Review Committee (chaired by Lord Franks): transcript of oral evidence by Sir Frank Cooper and Sir Terence Lewin, 4 October 1982, National Archives.

30 Peter Hennessy & James Jinks, *The Silent Deep*, Allen Lane, 2015, pp. 598–604.

31 John Sweeney, Jens Holsoe, Ed Vulliamy, 'Nato bombed Chinese Deliberately', *The Observer*, 17 October 1999, https://www.theguardian.com/world/1999/oct/17/balkans

32 https://en.wikipedia.org/wiki/Astute-class_submarine

33 Mark Hookham & Tim Ripley, 'Killer sub delayed as costs soar by £191m', *Sunday Times*, 12 February 2017.

34 Peter Hennessey & James Jinks, ibid., p. 616.

35 David Willetts, 'Royal Navy's Entire fleet of attack submarines is out of action', *The Sun*, 10 February 2017.

36 Mark Hookham, 'Misfire as new navy ships lack missiles', *Sunday Times*, 26 February 2017.

37 https://www.gov.uk/government/news/uk-strengthens-defence-partnership-with-france

38 Nick Childs, *The Age of Invincible: The ship that defined the modern Royal Navy*, Pen & Sword Maritime, 2009.

39 Air Chief Marshall Sir Stephen Hillier speaking at the Royal Aeronautical Society's Air Power Conference, RAF Museum Hendon, 29 September 2016.

40 Nick Childs, *Britain's Future Navy*, Pen & Sword Maritime, 2012, p. 76.

41 General David Richards, *Taking Command*, Headline Publishing, 2014, pp. 299–300.

42 https://www.gov.uk/government/speeches/f-35-great-for-britain

43 HM government press release, 30 March 2016, https://www.gov.uk/government/news/multi-million-pound-joint-venture-announced-between-britain-and-oman

44 Cleo Paskal, 'France dives back into the Pacific', *The World Today*, February & March 2017, pp. 28–32.

45 Roger Bootle, 'Why the Government should be spending more on defence', *Sunday Telegraph*, 9 April 2017.

46 http://www.nato.int/nato_static_fl2014/assets/pdf/pdf_2017_03/20170313_170313-pr2017-045.pdf

47 Charles Moore, 'Field Marshal Lord Guthrie: Why I now back the Leave campaign', *The Telegraph*, 17 June 2016, http://www.telegraph.co.uk/news/2016/06/17/field-marshal-lord-guthrie-why-i-now-back-the-leave-campaign/

BUILDING A PROSPEROUS FUTURE

1 Commerce Secretary Wilbur Ross quoted on Bloomberg 1 March 2017, https://www.bloomberg.com/politics/articles/2017-03-01/ross-pledges-to-fix-nafta-get-tough-with-china-on-trade-rules

2 https://www.gov.uk/government/speeches/liam-foxs-free-trade-speech

3 https://www.planforbritain.gov.uk/a-global-britain/

4 National Security Strategy and Strategic Defence and Security Review 2015, p. 69, https://

www.gov.uk/government/uploads/system/uploads/attachment_data/file/478933/52309_
Cm_9161_NSS_SD_Review_web_only.pdf

5   http://www.parliament.uk/business/publications/written-questions-answers-statements/
written-statement/Commons/2016-07-18/HCWS94

6   FCO Annual Report 2015–16, p. 8, https://www.gov.uk/government/uploads/system/uploads/
attachment_data/file/539413/FCO_Annual_Report_2016_ONLINE.pdf

7   https://www.gov.uk/government/uploads/system/uploads/attachment_data/file/587374/
DFID-Economic-Development-Strategy-2017.pdf

8   https://www.gov.uk/government/speeches/the-governments-negotiating-objectives-for-
exiting-the-eu-pm-speech

9   HMRC, Overseas Trade Statistics.

10 https://www.publications.parliament.uk/pa/cm201617/cmselect/cmintrade/817/817.pdf,   pp.
52–3 and pp. 58–9.

11 http://www.bexa.co.uk/wp-content/uploads/BExA-Manifesto-for-Exporters-Aug-2016.pdf

12 http://greatbritaincampaign.com/#!/about

13 https://www.gov.uk/government/news/international-trade-secretary-2017-must-be-year-of-
exporting

14 A fuller history of DFID can be found at http://www.DFID.gov.uk/About-us/History

15 See 'Eliminating World Poverty: A Challenge for the 21st Century', White Paper on
International Development, 1997, http://webarchive.nationalarchives.gov.uk/+/http://www.
DFID.gov.uk/policieandpriorities/files/whitepaper1997.pdf

16 Ashraf Ghani & Clare Lockhart, *Fixing Failed States: A Framework for Rebuilding a Fractured
World*, Oxford University Press, 2009.

17 The Conservative Green Paper on International Development states: 'Poverty breeds
extremism, incubates disease and drives migration and conflict. Instability around the world
threatens us all'. Source: One World Conservatism: A Conservative Agenda for International
Development.

18 https://www.gov.uk/government/uploads/system/uploads/attachment_data/file/587374/
DFID-Economic-Development-Strategy-2017.pdf, p. 23.

19 David Cameron, 'Even in an age of austerity, aid works. We have to keep giving', *The
Guardian*, 2 March 2017, https://www.theguardian.com/commentisfree/2017/mar/02/
david-cameron-age-of-austerity-aid-works

20 https://sustainabledevelopment.un.org/?menu=1300

21 https://www.gov.uk/government/news/pm-dedicates-1bn-in-aid-money-for-syrian-
refugees-and-host-countries

22 https://data.oecd.org/oda/net-oda.htm

23 https://stats.oecd.org/Index.aspx?DataSetCode=TABLE1

24 https://www.nao.org.uk/wp-content/uploads/2016/01/Responding-to-crises.pdf

25 HM Treasury, Government Responses on the Thirty Fourth to the Thirty Sixth; the
Thirty Eighth; and the Fortieth to the Forty Second reports from the Committee of
Public Accounts: Session 2015–16, July 2016, Cm 9323, pp. 6–7, http://www.parliament.
uk/business/committees/committees-a-z/commons-select/public-accounts-committee/
publications/?type=&session=28&sort=false&inquiry=all

26 See commitments made by the UK and other donors at the 2005 G8 Summit in Gleneagles,
http://researchbriefings.files.parliament.uk/documents/RP07-51/RP07-51.pdf

27 http://www.legislation.gov.uk/ukpga/2015/12/pdfs/ukpga_20150012_en.pdf

28 http://www.parliament.uk/business/committees/committees-a-z/commons-select/
public-accounts-committee/news-parliament-2015/st-helena-airport-report-published-16-17/

29 Larisa Brown & Jason Groves, 'Britain scraps £9 million foreign aid for Ethiopia's Spice Girls', *Daily
Mail*, 6 January 2017, http://www.dailymail.co.uk/news/article-4095882/Britain-scraps-5million-
foreign-aid-Ethiopia-s-Spice-Girls-Mail-revealed-blood-boiling-waste-taxpayers-money.html

30 Report of the House of Commons International Development Committee on UK Aid:
Conclusions and Recommendations, para. 9, 27 March 2017, https://www.publications.
parliament.uk/pa/cm201617/cmselect/cmintdev/100/10008.htm#_idTextAnchor091

31 2017 Report On The DAC Untying Recommendation, OECD, Paris, 3 April 2017, p.16, http://www.oecd.org/dac/financing-sustainable-development/development-finance-standards/2017-Report-DAC-Untying.pdf

32 http://www.bexa.co.uk/wp-content/uploads/BExA-2016-UKEF-ECA-Comparison-Paper-Final.pdf

33 http://www.bexa.co.uk/wp-content/uploads/BExA-Manifesto-for-Exporters-Aug-2016.pdf

34 'UK aid: tackling global challenges in the national interest', HM Treasury and DFID, Cm 9131, 23 November 2015, p. 17.

35 http://www.oecd.org/dac/aft/Aid4Trade-SustainableDevAgenda.pdf

36 Izabella Kaminska, 'As goes correspondent banking, so goes globalisation', *Financial Times*, 26 July 2016.

37 'The Withdrawal of Correspondent Banking Relationships: A Case for Policy Action', IMF Staff Discussion Note SDN/16/06, June 2016, https://www.imf.org/external/pubs/ft/sdn/2016/sdn1606.pdf

38 https://www.gov.uk/government/publications/doing-business-with-iran/frequently-asked-questions-on-doing-business-with-iran

39 Jon Lunn & Lorna Booth, 'The 0.7% aid target: June 2016 update', House of Commons Briefing Paper Number 3714, 20 June 2016.

40 http://www.oecd.org/dac/stats/documentupload/DAC%20List%20of%20ODA%20Recipients%202014%20final.pdf

41 www.icai.independent.gov.uk

42 Cabinet Office, Infrastructure and Projects Authority, Project Validation Review 2228 Prosperity Fund, March 2016 and Cross Whitehall Prosperity Fund Gateway Report VI.0, September 2016. Not available online.

43 http://icai.independent.gov.uk/new-report-prosperity-fund/

44 https://www.gov.uk/government/uploads/system/uploads/attachment_data/file/602044/HMG_response_to_ICAI_review.pdf

COORDINATING AND IMPLEMENTING POLICY

1   David Owen, *Cabinet's Finest Hour: The Hidden Agenda of May 1940*, Haus Publishing, 2016.

2   General Sir David Richards, *Taking Command*, Headline Publishing, 2014, p. 308.

3   Ibid, p. 309.

4   Jon Lunn, Louisa Brooke-Holland & Claire Mills, 'The UK National Security Council', House of Commons Library Briefing Paper Number 7456, 11 January 2016.

5   Ibid., p. 43.

6   Ibid., p. 43.

7   National Security Strategy and Strategic Defence Review 2015. A Secure and Prosperous United Kingdom, Cm 9161, 23 November 2015, pp. 81–4.

8   Building Stability Overseas Strategy.

9   HC Deb 16 July 2015 c688. In the same source, the government said that there are no plans currently to update the BSOS.

10 'The Scale-up of DFID's Support to Fragile States', 12 February 2015.

11 PQ 224151, 23 February 2015. Note that these figures cover both bilateral and multilateral aid from all sources.

12 Lord Mayor's Banquet 2015: Prime Minister's speech, 16 November 2015.

13 HM Treasury and DFID, 'UK aid: tackling global challenges in the national interest', Cm 9131, 23 November 2015, p. 13.

14 PQ 9455, 11 September 2015.

15 'Conflict, Stability and Security Fund', Joint Committee on National Security Strategy Second Report of Session 2016–17, published 7 February 2017, p. 8.

16 http://www.oecd.org/dac/stats/officialdevelopmentassistancedefinitionandcoverage.htm

17 The Conservative and Unionist Party Manifesto 2017, https://www.conservatives.com/manifesto

18 Ibid., p. 13.
19 The FCO and the 2015 spending review, HC 467, 23 October 2015, p. 11.
20 DFID, Main Estimate 2015/16: Memorandum to the International Development Committee.
21 'Conflict, Stability and Security Fund', Joint Committee on National Security Strategy Second Report of Session 2016–17, 7 February 2017, p. 35.
22 National Security Strategy and Strategic Defence and Security Review 2015, HL Paper 18, HC 153.
23 Mark Landler, ibid., p. 169.
24 Anthony Seldon & Peter Snowdon, *Cameron at 10: The Inside Story 2010–2015*, William Collins, 2015, p. 62.
25 Ibid., p. 103.
26 Ian Black, 'Qatar admits sending hundreds of troops to support Libya rebels', *The Guardian*, 26 October 2011, https://www.theguardian.com/world/2011/oct/26/qatar-troops-libya-rebels-support
27 Anthony Seldon & Peter Snowdon, ibid., pp. 110–11.
28 Ibid., p. 113.
29 General Sir David Richards, *Taking Command*, Headline Publishing, 2014, p. 317.
30 Ibid., p. 321.
31 David Owen, articles in Huffington Post, 11 September 2015; *World Post*, 22 February 2016; Huffington Post, 27 September 2016.
32 Joe Watts, 'Former UK Ambassador to Syria accuses Foreign Office of lying about the country's civil war', *Independent*, 23 December 2016.
33 http://www.msf.org/en/article/syria-thousands-suffering-neurotoxic-symptoms-treated-hospitals-supported-msf
34 S. A. Goodman, *The Imperial Premiership*, Manchester University Press, 2016, Prologue, pp. 5–18.
35 David Owen, 'Why Syria crisis must be taken seriously by its allies in Russia', *Daily Mirror*, 27 August 2013.
36 Lakhdar Brahimi, 'Did the UN fail Syria?', UNA-UK Journal, Vol. 1, 2017.
37 David Smith, 'John Kerry links Britain to derailing of Obama's plan for intervention in Syria', *Guardian*, 5 January 2017.
38 The Report of the Iraq Inquiry Executive Summary. HC 264, 6 July 2016.

RUSSIA AND STABILITY IN WIDER EUROPE

1 Henry Kissinger, *Diplomacy*, Simon & Schuster, 1994, p. 109.
2 Tony Judt, *Postwar: A History of Europe Since 1945*, Pimlico, 2007, p. 443.
3 http://data.parliament.uk/writtenevidence/committeeevidence.svc/evidencedocument/foreign-affairs-committee/the-uks-relations-with-russia/written/44709.html
4 http://www.presidency.ucsb.edu/ws/?pid=20035
5 https://www.socialeurope.eu/2017/01/reset-wests-relations-russia/
6 Edmund Burke, 'Remarks on the Policy of the Allies', *The Works of the Right Honorable Edmund Burke*, Vol. 4, F & C Rivington, 1802, p. 134.
7 Thomas L. Friedman, 'Foreign Affairs; Now a Word From X', *New York Times*, 2 May 1998, http://www.nytimes.com/1998/05/02/opinion/foreign-affairs-now-a-word-from-x.html
8 https://www.publications.parliament.uk/pa/ld201415/ldselect/ldeucom/115/11510.htm
9 http://www.osce.org/mc/39516?download=true
10 Matthias Schepp & Britta Sandberg, 'Gorbachev Interview', *Der Spiegel*, 16 January 2017, http://www.spiegel.de/international/world/gorbachev-warns-of-decline-in-russian-western-ties-over-ukraine-a-1012992.html
11 http://www.un.org/en/ga/search/view_doc.asp?symbol=A/49/765
12 http://www.nato.int/cps/en/natolive/official_texts_25468.htm
13 http://www.nato.int/docu/pr/1997/p97-081e.htm
14 http://www.nato.int/cps/en/natolive/official_texts_25457.htm
15 http://www.nato.int/nrc-website/en/about/index.html

16 http://en.kremlin.ru/events/president/transcripts/21611
17 http://news.bbc.co.uk/1/shared/bsp/hi/pdfs/30_09_09_iiffmgc_report.pdf
18 http://en.kremlin.ru/events/president/transcripts/320
19 http://www.russianmission.eu/userfiles/file/foreign_policy_concept_english.pdf
20 http://en.kremlin.ru/events/president/news/20113
21 https://eeas.europa.eu/sites/eeas/files/association_agreement_ukraine_2014_en.pdf
22 http://en.kremlin.ru/events/president/news/20603
23 Richard Sakwa, 'The death of Europe? Continental fates after Ukraine', *International Affairs*, May 2015.
24 Foreign Affairs Select Committee, Report on the United Kingdom's relations with Russia, Conclusions, para. 28, https://www.publications.parliament.uk/pa/cm201617/cmselect/cmfaff/120/12010.htm#_idTextAnchor081
25 http://data.parliament.uk/writtenevidence/committeeevidence.svc/evidencedocument/foreign-affairs-committee/the-uks-relations-with-russia/written/45481.html
26 http://en.kremlin.ru/events/president/transcripts/speeches/50385
27 'How the EU lost Russia over Ukraine', *Der Spiegel*, 24 November 2014, http://www.spiegel.de/international/europe/war-in-ukraine-a-result-of-misunderstandings-between-europe-and-russia-a-1004706-2.html
28 http://www.skidelskyr.com/print/russia-under-medvedev-a-window-of-opportunity
29 http://www.rusemb.org.uk/osce/
30 https://www.gov.uk/government/speeches/prime-ministers-speech-to-the-republican-party-conference-2017
31 House of Commons Foreign Affairs Committee, Report on The United Kingdom's Relations with Russia, March 2017, Conclusions, para. 16.

THE CHALLENGES OF THE MIDDLE EAST

1   L. Carl Brown, *International Politics and the Middle East: Old Rules, Dangerous Games*, I. B. Tauris, 1984, pp. 16–18.
2   http://www.balfourproject.org
3   http://www.balfourproject.org/film-of-britain-in-palestine-1917-1948
4   http://www.balfourproject.org/the-companion-guide-to-britain-in-palestine-1917-1948/
5   Imperial Conference 1926: Inter-Imperial Relations Committee – Report, Proceedings And Memoranda, E (I.R./26) Series, http://www.foundingdocs.gov.au/resources/transcripts/cth11_doc_1926.pdf
6   R. J. Q. Adams, *Balfour: The Last Grandee*, John Murray, 2007, pp. 331–3.
7   Jonathan Schneer, *The Balfour Declaration: The Origins of the Arab-Israeli Conflict*, Bloomsbury, 2010, pp. 337–40.
8   Schneer, ibid., pp. 342–3.
9   Schneer, ibid., pp. xxviii-xxix.
10 Alan Bullock, *Ernest Bevin: Foreign Secretary 1945–1957*, Heinemann, 1983, p. 90.
11 Ibid., p. 165.
12 Ibid., p. 564.
13 David McCullough, *Truman*, Simon Schuster, 1992, p. 616.
14 HC Hansard, 20 December 1956, vol. 562, col. 1518.
15 David Owen, *In Sickness and In Power: Illness in Heads of Government during the last 100 years*, Methuen, 2008, pp. 123–35. Revised 2016 edition, *In Sickness and In Power: Illness in Heads of Government, Military and Business leaders since 1900*, pp. 142–55.
16 Ibid,. 2016 edition, p. 124.
17 Philip Ziegler, *Edward Heath*, Harper Press, 2010, pp. 385–6.
18 Moshe Dayan, *Break-Through*, Weidenfeld & Nicholson, 1984, p. 308.
19 Peter Beaumont and Martin Chulov, 'Israeli fighter jets fired upon during Syria mission in clash with pro-Assad forces', *The Guardian*, 17 March 2017.

20 Will Worley, 'Britain refuses to back outcome of Paris peace negotiations on Israeli-Palestinian conflict', *The Independent*, 15 January 2017, http://www.independent.co.uk/news/world/europe/paris-peace-talks-israel-palestine-britain-refuses-back-benjamin-netanyahu-john-kerry-a7528846.html

21 John Kerry, Remarks on Middle East Peace, Dean Acheson Auditorium, 28 December 2016.

22 http://www.europeanleadershipnetwork.org/president-trump-europe-and-the-iran-deal_4309.html

23 http://www.europeanleadershipnetwork.org/trumping-proliferation-from-a-one-off-deal-to-a-global-standard_4301.html

24 Report by National Intelligence Council's Office of the Director of National Intelligence, 'Global Trends 2030: Alternative Worlds', *Ekurd Daily*, 11 December 2012.

25 John Irish, 'Saudi minister says Qatar must end support for Hamas, Muslim Brotherhood', Reuters, 6 June 2017, http://www.reuters.com/article/us-gulf-qatar-saudi-fm-idUSKBN18X2CR

26 L. Carl Brown, ibid., p. 269.

CHINA AND ITS NEIGHBOURS

1 Rhiannon Vickers, 'Harold Wilson, the British Labour Party and the War in Vietnam', *Journal of Cold War Studies*, Vol. 10, No. 2, Spring 2008, p. 47.

2 https://www.gov.uk/government/speeches/prime-ministers-speech-to-the-republican-party-conference-2017

3 '"Times have changed" China tells Chris Patten, Hong Kong's last British governor', *Straits Times*, 5 November 2014, http://www.straitstimes.com/asia/east-asia/times-have-changed-china-tells-chris-patten-hong-kongs-last-british-governor

4 Roderic Wye et al., 'The Critical Transition: China's Priorities for 2021', Chatham House, 2 February 2017, https://www.chathamhouse.org/publication/critical-transition-chinas-priorities-2021

5 Gideon Rachman, *Easternisation: War & Peace in the Asian Century*, Bodley Head, 2016.

6 Ibid., p. 255.

7 Michael Martina & Philip Wen, 'China's 2017 defence budget rise to slow again', *Reuters*, 4 March 2017, http://uk.reuters.com/article/uk-china-parliament-defence-idUKKBN16B03R

8 Clay Dillow, 'How China's military buildup threatens the US', CNBC.com, 13 October 2015, http://www.cnbc.com/2015/10/12/chinas-military-and-naval-buildup-in-south-china-sea-threatens-the-us.html

9 Mark Landler, 'Offering to Aid Talks, U.S. Challenges China on Disputed Islands', *New York Times*, 23 July 2010, http://www.nytimes.com/2010/07/24/world/asia/24diplo.html

10 http://www.reuters.com/article/us-usa-china-idUSKBN1792KA

11 EU declaration on 'East China Sea Air Defence Identification Zone', https://www.gov.uk/government/world-location-news/eu-declaration-on-east-china-sea-air-defence-identification-zone

12 Press release on the South China Sea Arbitration, Permanent Court of Arbitration, 12 July 2016, http://www.pcacases.com/web/sendAttach/1801

13 Full text of statement of China's Foreign Ministry on award of South China Sea arbitration initiated by Philippines, 12 July 2016, http://news.xinhuanet.com/english/2016-07/12/c_135507744.htm)

14 Simon Tisdall, 'Munich conference: three dangerous superpowers – and we're stuck in the middle', *The Guardian*, 19 February 2017, https://www.theguardian.com/commentisfree/2017/feb/19/munich-security-conference-nato-trump-russia-china-superpowers-europe-pig-in-middle?CMP=twt_gu

15 'U.S. compares China's South China Sea moves to Russia's in Ukraine', Reuters, 26 June 2015, http://www.reuters.com/article/us-usa-china-blinken-idUSKBN0P62O120150627

16 Richard Kerbaj & Michael Sheridan, 'Rifkind a stooge in secret PR war on China', *Sunday*

Times, 29 January 2017, http://www.thetimes.co.uk/article/rifkind-a-stooge-in-secret-pr-war-on-china-xfq2qp2br

17 https://www.gov.uk/government/uploads/system/uploads/attachment_data/file/478933/52309_Cm_9161_NSS_SD_Review_web_only.pdf – para. 6.22

18 https://www.gov.uk/government/uploads/system/uploads/attachment_data/file/567521/UK-China_8th_EFD_policy_outcomes_paper.pdf

19 https://www.g20.org/Content/DE/_Anlagen/G7_G20/2016-09-08-g20-agenda-action-plan.pdf?__blob=publicationFile&v=4

20 Cooperation in Africa is also referenced in the 2015 National Security Strategy, para. 5.74.

21 Christopher Alessi & Beina Xu, 'China in Africa', Council on Foreign Relations, updated 27 April 2015, http://www.cfr.org/china/china-africa/p9557

22 Jessica Toale, 'Fear & Delight: Engaging with China on Development Cooperation', in Joel Mullan & Adam Tyndall (eds), *China-Ready: Equipping Britain for an Asian Future*, Young Fabians, February 2015, pp. 35–9, https://d3n8a8pro7vhmx.cloudfront.net/youngfabians/pages/501/attachments/original/1428561065/China_Ready_WEB.pdf?1428561065

23 'Xi suggests China, C. Asia build Silk Road economic belt', *Xinhua*, 7 September 2013, http://news.xinhuanet.com/english/china/2013-09/07/c_132700695.htm

24 Wu Jiao & Zhang Yunbi, 'Xi in call for building of new "maritime silk road"', *China Daily*, 4 October 2013, http://usa.chinadaily.com.cn/china/2013-10/04/content_17008940.htm

25 For map see Xinhua Finance Agency, http://en.xfafinance.com/html/OBAOR/

26 Sun Hui, 'Chongqing-Xinjiang-Europe railway sees maiden journey', *China Daily*, 25 October 2016, http://www.chinadaily.com.cn/regional/chongqing/liangjiang/2016-10/25/content_27170173.htm

27 'China pledges 40 bln USD for Silk Road Fund', *Xinhua*, 8 November 2014, http://news.xinhuanet.com/english/china/2014-11/08/c_133774993.htm

28 http://en.ndrc.gov.cn/newsrelease/201503/t20150330_669367.html

29 'Adhering to the Planning, Orderly and Pragmatically Build the "Belt and Road"' prepared by a research team at Chongyang Institute for Financial Studies of Renmin University of China.

30 'The first authoritative report on "Belt and Road" three-year progress released', Yang Yuntao, *China Daily*, 26 September 2016, http://www.chinadaily.com.cn/opinion/2016-09/26/content_26901304_2.htm

31 http://eng.sectsco.org/about_sco/

32 'China's Xi Jinping agrees $46bn superhighway to Pakistan', BBC News, 20 April 2015, http://www.bbc.co.uk/news/world-asia-32377088

33 http://www.cbbc.org/cbbc/media/cbbc_media/One-Belt-One-Road-main-body.pdf

34 Michal Makocki, 'China's Road: into Eastern Europe' European Union Institute for Security Studies, 15 February 2017, http://www.iss.europa.eu/publications/detail/article/chinas-road-into-eastern-europe/

35 Plamen Tonchev, 'China's Road: into the Western Balkans', European Union Institute for Security Studies, 15 February 2017, http://www.iss.europa.eu/publications/detail/article/chinas-road-into-the-western-balkans/

36 President Xi Jinping, 'Jointly Shoulder Responsibility of Our Times, Promote Global Growth', Keynote speech at the opening session of the World Economic Forum Annual Meeting, Davos, 17 January 2017, http://news.xinhuanet.com/english/2017-01/18/c_135991184.htm

DEALING WITH EUROPE

1 Henry Kissinger, ibid., p. 181.

2 Edward Grey of Fallodon, *Twenty-Five Years, 1892–1916, vol. 1*, Hodder & Stoughton, 1925, p. 203.

3 David Owen, *The Hidden Perspective: The Military Conversations 1904–1914*, Haus Publishing, 2014, p. 6.

4   Jonathan Fenby, *The General: Charles De Gaulle and the France he Saved*, Simon & Schuster, 2010, pp. 26–7.
5   http://www.charles-de-gaulle.org/pages/l-homme/dossiers-thematiques/1940-1944-la-seconde-guerre-mondiale/l-appel-du-18-juin/documents/discours-du-17-juin-1940-du-marechal-petain.php
6   *Parliamentary Debates*, Fifth Series, Volume 365. *House of Commons Official Report Eleventh Volume of Session 1939–40*, London, His Majesty's Stationery Office, 1940, columns 701–702, http://www.ibiblio.org/pha/policy/1940/400616a.html
7   Jean Lacouture, *De Gaulle: The Rebel 1890–1944*, Collins Harvill English, 1990, pp. 520–21.
8   Ibid., p. 522.
9   Quoted in David Owen, *The Politics of Defence*, Jonathan Cape, 1972, p. 195.
10   Jean Lacouture, *De Gaulle: The Ruler 1945–1970*, trans. Alan Sheridan, Harvill Harper Collins, 1991, p. 178.
11   https://history.state.gov/historicaldocuments/frus1958-60v07p2/d45
12   Jean Lacouture, *De Gaulle: The Ruler 1945–1970*, trans. Alan Sheridan, Harvill Harper Collins, 1991, p. 216.
13   Alistair Horne, *Macmillan 1957–1986, Vol II of the Official Biography*, Macmillan, 1989, pp. 117–20.
14   Richard Lamb, *The Macmillan Years 1957–1963: The Emerging Truth*, John Murray, 1995, p. 128.
15   Alistair Horne, ibid., p. 120.
16   De Gaulle, *Memoirs of Hope*, trans. Terence Kilmartin, Weidenfeld & Nicolson, 1971, p. 188.
17   Richard Lamb, *The Macmillan Years 1957–1963: The Emerging Truth*, John Murray, 1995, p. 129.
18   Richard Lamb, ibid., p. 132–3.
19   Jean Lacouture, ibid., p. 336.
20   Jean Lacouture, ibid., pp. 49 & 219.
21   Memorandum by Economic Steering (Europe) Committee: 'The Six and the Seven: Long Term Arrangements', CAB 134/1852, London, 25 May 1960, para. 8, http://dfat.gov.au/about-us/publications/historical-documents/volume-27/Pages/121-memorandum-by-economic-steering-europe-committee.aspx
22   http://www.cvce.eu/obj/press_conference_held_by_general_de_gaulle_14_january_1963-en-5b5d0d35-4266-49bc-b770-b24826858e1f.html
23   Ambrose Evans-Pritchard, 'Eurofederalism financed by US Spy Chiefs', *Daily Telegraph*, 19 September 2000.
24   Ambrose Evans-Pritchard, 'The European Union always was a CIA project, as Brexiteers discover', *Daily Telegraph*, 27 April 2016.
25   Hugh Gaitskell, speech made at the 1962 Labour Party Conference, 3 October 1962, http://www.cvce.eu/content/publication/1999/1/1/05f2996b-000b-4576-8b42-8069033a16f9/publishable_en.pdf
26   Mervyn King, *The End of Alchemy: Money, Banking and the Future of the Global Economy*, Little, Brown, 2016.
27   http://eur-lex.europa.eu/budget/data/DB/2017/en/SEC10.pdf
28   David Ormond, 'Keeping Europe Safe. Counterterrorism for the Continent', *Foreign Affairs*, September/October 2016, p. 83.
29   Ben Judah, 'Monsieur le president?', *Sunday Times Magazine*, 2 April 2017.
30   Speech to European Committee of the Regions, Brussels, 22 March 2017, http://europa.eu/rapid/press-release_SPEECH-17-723_en.htm
31   Interview with Sky News, 26 October 2016, http://news.sky.com/story/brexit-will-not-cause-uk-trade-disruption-wto-boss-10632803
32   http://visual.ons.gov.uk/uk-trade-partners/
33   Paul Lever, *Berlin Rules: Europe and the German Way*, I.B. Tauris, 2017, pp. 138–9.
34   Ibid.
35   Obituary of Sir Ewen Fergusson, *Daily Telegraph*, 25 April 2017.

INDEX

Caccia, Sir Harold
  British Ambassador to Washington
    DC 250
Caetano, Marcello 55
Cairo Conference (1921) 193
Callaghan, James
  defence policy of 64
  foreign policy of 55, 199
Cambodia
  Genocide (1975–9) 39
Cameron, David 7, 13, 119, 125, 144, 257
  foreign policy of 89, 136–8, 148–9, 263
  international development policies of
    100–101, 117–18, 130
  meeting with Dalai Lama (2012)
    234–5
Camp David Agreement (1978) 199
Campaign Against Arms Trade (CAAT)
  40
Canada vii, 7, 47–8, 84, 131, 168, 260
  Ottawa 87
Carnegie Commission on Preventing
  Deadly Conflict 28–9
Carney, Mark
  Chairman of FSB 274
Carrington, Lord 24
Carter, Jimmy 6–7
  foreign policy of 198–9, 235
Cass Business School 268
Central Asia–China Gas Pipeline 240
CH-47 Chinook (helicopter) 83
Chamberlain, Neville 119
Charter 77 7, 20
Chechnya 183
Chernomyrdin, Viktor 27
Chilcot Report (2016) 34, 157
Childs, Nick
  Age of Invincible, The 80
Chile 113
China, People's Republic of 9, 11–12, 15,
    18–19, 38, 40, 42, 46, 76, 81, 91, 96, 99,
    113, 136–7, 198, 204, 216, 225–8, 237,
    240–41
  Beijing 18, 237
  Belt and Road Initiative (BRI) 238–41
  Communist Revolution (1945–50)
    225
  East China Sea Air Defence
    Identification Zone 232–4

economic investments of 227, 229,
    236–8, 241
economy of 230
energy security of 240
Hainan Province 230
Handover of Hong Kong (1997) 226–7
Hong Kong 226–9, 235
National Development and Reform
    Commission 239
navy of 230–31
nuclear programme of 69–70
People's Liberation Army (PLA) 11
pro-democracy protests (2014) 228
Shanghai 241
Silk Road Infrastructure Fund 239
Summer Olympics (2008) 19
Xinjiang Province 241
China Communications Construction
    Company Limited 239
China Railway Group Limited 239
Chinese Communist Party 225
Chirac, Jacques 263
Christian Democratic Union of Germany
    (CDU) 272
Christianity 5, 199, 213
Christopher, Warren
  US Secretary of State 25
Churchill, Winston 194, 246–7
  Colonial Secretary 193
  electoral victory of (1945) 194
  visit to Palestine (1921) 193
Citigroup ix
Clapper Jr, James R.
  US National Intelligence Director 154
Clarke, Ken
  Minister for Justice 122
Clegg, Nick 148
  Deputy Prime Minister 122
climate change 8–9
  marine environment 46–7
Clinton, Bill 42
  foreign policy of 24–5, 154, 201
Clinton, Hillary 14, 136–7, 203
  US Secretary of State 14, 231
Coats Viyella ix
Cohen, William
  US Defense Secretary 77
Cold War 16, 19, 22, 57, 161, 163, 169, 173
  end of 20, 53, 58, 68